*Edward L. Hendrickson*
*Marilyn Strauss Schmal*
*Sharon C. Ekleberry*

# Treating Co-Occurring Disorders
## *A Handbook for Mental Health and Substance Abuse Professionals*

*Pre-publication*
*REVIEWS,*
*COMMENTARIES,*
*EVALUATIONS . . .*

"This is a comprehensive review of the state of the art in the treatment of patients with co-occurring disorders. It can serve as the primary reference work for treatment professionals, case managers, and program administrators, as well as students. The succinct review of Axis I and II disorders is excellent. The authors have focused on the nuts and bolts of treatment and program management, and family interventions address difficult issues with practical solutions. When questions arise in the treatment of patients with co-occurring disorders, *Treating Co-Occurring Disorders* provides clear and useful answers."

**Jacob I. Melamed, PhD**
*Consulting Clinical Psychologist,*
*Arlington County, Virginia,*
*Substance Abuse Services*

"This book provides a brief and useful overview of a number of essential areas related to the knowledge and skills needed in working with persons having both substance use and mental disorders. The authors, who have years of real practice experience, understand the real-life demands on therapists and counselors who practice in mental health and substance treatment settings. They provide practical methods of helping clinicians and supervisors 'think on their feet' in managing caseloads comprised of persons with differing diagnostic combinations, functional capacities, and treatment readiness. Of particular merit is their chapter on recovery movements, including strategies for working collaboratively, in partnership with service users and their families, to promote personal recovery."

**Taylor B. Anderson, MSW, LSW, CPRP**
*Associate Director, Division of Behavioral Healthcare Education,*
*Department of Psychiatry,*
*Drexel University College of Medicine*

# Treating Co-Occurring Disorders

## *A Handbook for Mental Health and Substance Abuse Professionals*

# HAWORTH Addictions Treatment
## F. Bruce Carruth, PhD
## Senior Editor

# Treating Co-Occurring Disorders
## *A Handbook for Mental Health and Substance Abuse Professionals*

Edward L. Hendrickson, MS, LMFT, LSATP
Marilyn Strauss Schmal, MA, LPC, LSATP
Sharon C. Ekleberry, MSW, LCSW, LSATP

The Haworth Press®
New York • London • Oxford

The Haworth Press, Inc., 10 Alice Street, Binghamton, NY 13904-1580.

PUBLISHER'S NOTE
Identities and circumstances of individuals discussed in this book have been changed to protect confidentiality. Any resemblance to actual persons, living or dead, is entirely coincidental.

Cover design by Brooke Stiles.

**Library of Congress Cataloging-in-Publication Data**

Hendrickson, Edward L.
   Treating co-occurring disorders : handbook for mental health and substance abuse professionals / Edward L. Hendrickson, Marilyn Strauss Schmal, Sharon C. Ekleberry.
      p. ; cm.
   Includes bibliographical references and index.
   ISBN 0-7890-1801-2 (hard : alk. paper)—ISBN 0-7890-1802-0 (soft : alk. paper)
   1. Dual diagnosis—Handbooks, manuals, etc. [DNLM: 1. Mental Disorders—therapy. 2. Diagnosis, Dual (Psychiatry) 3. Mental Disorders—diagnosis. 4. Mental Disorders—psychology. 5. Substance-Related Disorders—diagnosis. 6. Substance-Related Disorders—psychology. 7. Substance-Related Disorders—therapy. WM 140 H498t 2004] I. Schmal, Marilyn Strauss. II. Ekleberry, Sharon C. III. Title.

RC564.68.H46 2004
616.89—dc21

2003012416

# CONTENTS

# ABOUT THE AUTHORS

**Edward L. Hendrickson, MS, LMFT, LSATP,** is retired as a clinical supervisor with the Arlington County, Virginia, Alcohol and Drug Treatment Program. Mr. Hendrickson has provided treatment, supervision, training, and consultation in the area of substance abuse since 1971, and has specialized in co-occurring disorders since 1982. He has authored numerous articles and reports in these areas. Mr. Hendrickson currently is a private practitioner and consultant, and teaches at Northern Virginia Community College and Virginia Polytechnic Institute.

**Marilyn S. Schmal, MA, LPC, LSATP,** is program manager of Dual Diagnosis Services for Arlington County, Virginia, Division of Behavioral Healthcare. She has provided treatment, training, and consultation for the seriously mentally ill since 1974 and for individuals with co-occurring disorders since 1988. She has co-authored a number of articles and reports on co-occurring disorders.

Ed and Marilyn have served as co-editors of the Dual Diagnosis Page of *TIE-Lines* and are founders of the Metropolitan Washington Council of Governments' Co-Occurring Disorders Committee. They are recipients of an achievement award from the National Association of Counties for their work with clients with co-occurring disorders.

**Sharon C. Ekleberry, MSW, LCSW, LSATP,** is Division Director of the Adult Community Services Division of Fairfax County Mental Health Services in Virginia. Ms. Ekleberry is experienced in providing treatment for individuals with co-occurring disorders. She has specialized in consultation and training in the treatment of individuals with co-occurring personality disorders and addiction; she also addresses ethical issues specific to this population. Ms. Ekleberry serves on the Licensure Board for Social Work in Virginia. She has authored articles on dual diagnosis issues and served on the Consensus Panel for the revision of the Treatment Improvement Protocol (TIP) #9 for the Center for Substance Abuse Treatment.

# Preface

By the early 1980s it had become apparent that the mental health and substance abuse treatment systems had numerous clients with disorders they were neither mandated nor equipped to treat. This situation created several dilemmas for these treatment systems. First, how many of these clients were there? Second, which of the clients truly had co-occurring substance use and mental disorders and which had substance-induced disorders? Third, when clients truly had co-occurring disorders, how should they be treated similarly or differently than other clients? Finally, should clients with co-occurring disorders be treated at either or both of these agencies? The purpose of this book is to examine how these dilemmas have been addressed, the treatment approaches that appear to be most effective for clients with multiple disorders, and how best to manage multifarious caseloads composed of individuals with and without co-occurring disorders.

Initially most treatment systems attempted to avoid developing services for individuals with co-occurring disorders by taking the position that they represented just a very small portion of their total client population. However, by the early 1990s research had clearly answered the first question (how many) by finding that individuals with co-occurring disorders existed in significant numbers in both the substance abuse and mental health treatment systems. Chapters 1 through 4 discuss the prevalence of co-occurring disorders in the general population and in the treatment population; and the prevalence associated with substance use and specific psychiatric disorders.

Because of the high co-occurrence of many psychiatric disorders with substance use disorders, the final dilemma (who should treat these clients) is easily answered: both systems, because neither can treat its mandated population without encountering many clients with co-occurring disorders. Chapter 5 addresses the second dilemma (is it a substance-induced disorder or co-occurring disorders). Although an accurate diagnosis is always very difficult to obtain while alcohol and drug use continues, this chapter provides guidance in beginning to differentiate substance-induced disorders from true co-occurring disorders. The chapter also makes recommendations concerning what information is needed during the assessment phase in order to develop comprehensive treatment plans. Chapters 6 through 10 address the third dilemma (how to treat individuals in a heterogeneous caseload similarly and differently) when providing individual, case management, group, relapse prevention, and family treatment.

Additional important issues that mental health and substance abuse treatment systems and therapists must address in their work with multifarious caseloads are covered in the last three chapters of this book. Chapter 11 presents an overview of the substance abuse and mental health recovery movements and suggests how therapists can most effectively interact with them. Chapter 12 examines the common issues that clinical supervisors encounter when supervising staff working with multifarious caseloads and suggests how to best address them. Finally, Chapter 13 presents treatment outcome measures and performance standards that can be used to assess change and program performance with this population and provides reasonable benchmarks for determining treatment success and program effectiveness.

Since the early 1980s a great deal of effort has gone into developing effective treatment services for individuals with co-occurring disorders. In fact, many mental health and substance abuse professionals are now trained to treat these individuals, effective treatment models have been designed, and it is now rare that an individual would be denied treatment services for having a co-occurring disorder. Many of the initial attempts at providing services for these individuals involved the interagency models of sequential (treating one disorder at a time) or parallel (each system treating specific disorders) treatment. Both models were soon found to be ineffective because they lacked comprehensiveness. Today the general consensus, documented by initial research, is that the intra-agency model, in which all disorders are treated concurrently in a single treatment setting, is the most effective method for treating individuals with co-occurring disorders.

Intra-agency models in use today include stand-alone treatment programs designed specifically for individuals with co-occurring disorders and inclusion of specialized services in existing mental health and substance abuse programs. These programs and services have been found to be effective and have been successfully incorporated into all components of the mental health and substance abuse continuums of care. However, individuals with co-occurring disorders are a very diverse population. Some have severe substance use symptoms and mild psychiatric symptoms, some have severe psychiatric symptoms and mild substance use symptoms, others have both mild psychiatric and substance use symptoms, and still others have severe substance use and psychiatric symptoms. Because of the heterogeneity of this population and the lack of dollars to fully fund all the needed mental health and substance abuse treatment services, it is highly unlikely that a separate continuum of care for this population will ever be practical. Thus the question we face today is how to best fit individuals with co-occurring substance use and mental health disorders into our existing mental health and substance abuse treatment systems.

With minor modifications (such as adding medication services for clients) individuals with severe substance use symptoms and less severe psychiatric symptoms can normally be treated effectively in existing substance abuse treatment systems. Also with minor modifications (such as offering a substance abuse psychoeducation group) individuals with mild or severe psychiatric symptoms and less severe substance use symptoms can be effectively treated in existing mental health treatment systems. However, individuals with severe mental health and substance use symptoms do find their way into either treatment system and major modifications are required for effective treatment. Ultimately our treatment systems must be capable of serving all of these individuals while at the same time providing services to individuals who have a single disorder. We hope that this book builds on the significant efforts of many who have been working to build comprehensive substance abuse and mental health treatment services for individuals with co-occurring disorders. The infrastructure has been laid, a core of expertise has been forged, but it now falls upon all therapists working in the substance abuse and mental health field to expand their knowledge and skills so that they can be effective with a multifarious caseload.

The concepts and ideas presented in this book have evolved over time from our many interactions with clients and other substance abuse and mental health professionals working with individuals with and without co-occurring disorders. The number of treatment professionals to whom we are indebted is far too numerous to mention. Each professional who has written or trained on this subject or who has asked us a question during a training or consultation for which we had to find an answer has played a significant role in the development of this book. By far the greatest contributors to this book have been our clients. Their willingness to share their life experiences and their daily struggles with these disorders has provided and validated the material in this book. Most important, it has been their courage to continue to struggle in the face of seemingly overwhelming obstacles and their willingness to do whatever is necessary to maintain their stability and sobriety that have given us the energy to continue in this profession and daily confirm that treatment does work.

# Chapter 1

# The New Reality: Multifarious Caseloads

The substance abuse therapist and the mental health therapist both have a similar problem. The substance abuse therapist has clients who, in addition to having a substance use disorder, also have symptoms of other mental health disorders. The mental health therapist, likewise, has clients with substance use problems as well as other mental health disorders. However, neither type of therapist is trained to treat both types of disorders, and they tend to work in agencies that are mandated to treat just one type of disorder. The purpose of this chapter is to describe the composition of multifarious caseloads and present treatment methods and intervention strategies that can be used with clients who have multiple disorders.

## *PREVALENCE OF CO-OCCURRING DISORDERS*

Numerous studies of substance abuse and mental health treatment populations and two major studies of the general population document significant rates of co-occurrence of substance use with certain other mental disorders. Studies of substance abuse treatment populations have found 60 percent or greater co-occurrence rates when personality disorders are included (Nace, 1989; Powell et al., 1982; Ross, Glaser, and Germanson, 1988; Westerman, Myers, and Harding, 1980); studies of mental health treatment populations have found co-occurrence rates of 40 to 50 percent (Ananth, 1989; Caton et al., 1989; Drake and Wallach, 1989; Ridgely, Goldman, and Talbott, 1986). Regier et al. (1990) presented the first major study of co-occurrence of substance use and mental disorders in the general population. They examined the National Institute of Mental Health's Epidemiologic Catchment Area (ECA) study and found that: 29 percent of individuals with a mental disorder also had a substance use disorder; 37 percent of individuals with an alcohol disorder also had a mental disorder; and 53 percent of individuals with a drug disorder other than alcohol also had a mental disorder. They also found that individuals with co-occurring disorders were twice as likely to be in treatment for at least one of their disorders. The National Longitudinal Alcohol Epidemiologic Survey (NLAES), sponsored by the National Institute of Alcohol Abuse and Alcoholism (NIAAA), also found that individuals with alcohol and co-occurring mental disorders were much more likely to be in treatment than individuals with just alcohol disorders (Onken et al., 1997). The results of the National Comorbidity Survey reported by Kessler et al. (1994) found that 51 percent of individuals with a mental disorder also experienced a substance use disorder during their lifetime, while 41 to 66 percent of individuals with a substance use disorder experienced a mental disorder sometime in their lives. Those with alcohol abuse disorders had the lowest level of co-occurrence, and individuals with drug dependency disorders experienced the greatest co-occurrence. This study also found that individuals with dependency and co-occurring mental disorders were much more likely to be in treatment than individuals with just one disorder.

## TYPES OF CLIENTS FOUND
## IN A MULTIFARIOUS CASELOAD

Although the substance abuse therapist's caseload normally consists of individuals with mental disorders that only somewhat impact their ability to function independently in the community (such as dysthymia, social anxiety, or antisocial personality disorder), an occasional case will present with a major mood or psychotic disorder. The mental health therapist, on the other hand, normally works with individuals with major mental illnesses who *abuse* substances, but she too will treat a client with a serious substance *dependence* disorder. Hence the first task for both the mental health therapist and the substance abuse therapist is to take a larger view of their varied caseloads for the purpose of developing similar treatment strategies for similar clients. Multifarious caseloads for substance abuse and mental health therapists can be divided into five broad categories:

1. Individuals with mental health (MH) disorders only
2. Individuals with substance abuse (SA) disorders only
3. Individuals with a substance abuse disorder and a mental disorder
4. Individuals with a substance use disorder and a personality disorder
5. Individuals with a substance use disorder, a mental disorder, and a personality disorder

## ESSENTIAL PHILOSOPHICAL VIEW

Once therapists identify the types of clients in their caseloads, they need to develop a philosophical base that allows them to work effectively with clients who have many needs. Their philosophy needs to be based on optimism and treatment flexibility. The TAUT-SOAR Model (see Figure 1.1) is useful in working with such diverse caseloads. It is based on the philosophy that the more difficult the issues that the client presents, the more growth opportunities for the therapist.

TAUT stands for Thoughts of incompetence; Apprehension; Unclear what and how to treat; and Treatment avoidance. These are thoughts, feelings, and behaviors that therapists may experience or demonstrate when encountering problems that they believe they are unequipped to treat effectively. For example, the substance abuse therapist might have these reactions to a young adult male client who

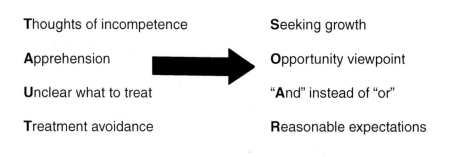

**T**houghts of incompetence          **S**eeking growth

**A**pprehension          **O**pportunity viewpoint

**U**nclear what to treat          "**A**nd" instead of "or"

**T**reatment avoidance          **R**easonable expectations

FIGURE 1.1. TAUT-SOAR Model

presents with a history of alcohol and cocaine dependence but also reports hearing voices occasionally and believes that the FBI is following him with helicopters and has bugged his home and car. The mental health therapist might react with TAUT in treating a young female with a history of bipolar disorder who reports drinking excessively and smoking marijuana on a daily basis. When therapists' anxious thoughts and feelings combine with their confusion concerning a treatment approach, there is a temptation to avoid treating the client. They may either refer the client to another agency based on the excuse that the client has a principle diagnosis that they are not mandated to treat, or make treatment demands that a client cannot achieve. The first method, if successful, simply results in either the mental health therapist treating the substance abuse therapist's client or the substance abuse therapist treating the mental health therapist's client, leaving both therapists still feeling only capable of treating part of the client's problem. The second method—such as the mental health therapist requiring her client to stop all alcohol and drug use before offering medication or other services, or the substance abuse therapist requiring his very paranoid client to attend ninety Alcoholics Anonymous meetings in ninety days—inevitably leads to clients dropping out of treatment. Though the therapist has achieved his or her goal not to treat the individual, the client remains untreated.

To engage and maintain such clients in treatment, both the substance abuse and the mental health therapist must approach treatment from a different perspective. The second part of our model, SOAR, stands for Seeking growth, Opportunity viewpoint, "And" instead of "or," and Reasonable expectations. This approach allows therapists to view their clients with less anxiety, more optimism, and more flexibility. Treating these clients becomes an opportunity for the therapists to expand their knowledge about mental disorders and treatment techniques. The client often comes with a history of many treatment failures, so the therapist can feel free to try various techniques with hopes of finding one that works. Each client becomes a research project with an opportunity for that client to obtain something that they had not yet achieved: a treatment success. Furthermore, therapists never have to forget what they already know; however, they now have the opportunity to expand that knowledge and integrate the new and old knowledge into a broader paradigm, which ultimately makes them more effective.

Finally, once a therapist decides to treat a dual diagnosis case, he can establish more reasonable expectations. For example, the mental health therapist can help her client attend an alcohol and drug education class as a first step in addressing the substance abuse disorders; the substance abuse therapist may introduce the concept of schizophrenia to the client, and slowly move him toward a medication evaluation while probing to understand how the psychiatric symptoms impact the client's substance use. Approaching treatment from a SOAR viewpoint increases the chances that the client will remain in treatment and helps therapists gain confidence in their ability to promote change in clients who have complex problems.

## *ESSENTIAL KNOWLEDGE AND SKILLS*

In addition to having a philosophy that supports working with a multifarious caseload, therapists also need to expand their knowledge and skill bases. Table 1.1 outlines the additional knowledge and skills that both mental health and substance abuse therapists need to work effectively with their diverse caseloads.

The mental health therapist needs to learn about the different types of drugs that her clients may be using and what short- and long-term effects the drugs may have on her clients. She also needs to learn how to monitor urine screens or administer breath tests in a manner that does not interfere with her therapeutic relationship with clients. In addition, she must come to understand the power and the nature of addiction and not be surprised or offended when clients say they want to abstain but then give in to cravings and compulsions. The substance abuse therapist, on the other hand, needs to learn how to identify the various mental disorders that cluster frequently with substance use, and gain an appreciation of how these disorders affect a person's social skills and ability to function independently in the community.

The substance abuse therapist also needs to understand the different types of medications used to treat these disorders and be able to identify their side effects. He also must learn how to promote medication compliance and deal with any negative values or attitudes that his clients, members of their families, self-help groups, or other substance abuse professionals may have concerning the use of medications. The mental health therapist will have to gain the understanding

TABLE 1.1. Additional Knowledge and Skill Needs

| Mental Health Therapists | Substance Abuse Therapists |
|---|---|
| Nature and effects of psychoactive drugs and the importance of drug testing | Nature and effects of mental disorders |
| Nature of addiction | Importance of functioning level |
| Importance of abstinence | Importance of medication |
| Importance of self-help involvement | Long-term view of self-help involvement |
| Working with court-referred clients | Engaging self-referred clients |
| Being more concrete, directive, and confrontive | Being less directive, more flexible, and confronting more gently |
| Use of self-disclosure | Maintaining clear boundaries |

that abstinence is necessary for individuals with substance dependency disorders or major mental illnesses if they are to achieve and maintain stability. She will need to learn about the purpose, culture, and traditions of twelve-step self-help groups, such as Alcoholics Anonymous and Narcotics Anonymous, and become comfortable promoting clients' participation in these groups. The substance abuse therapist who is used to requiring his clients to go to these meetings will have to learn that for some individuals, such as those who have social phobias or paranoid thoughts, attendance at these meetings may have to be a long-term goal. He will first need to help them manage their fears about attending such meetings, teach them what to talk about and what not to talk about, and help them understand that some meetings may be open to discussing psychiatric symptoms and others may not. With so many different types of self-help recovery groups now available for both substance use and mental health disorders, both types of therapists need to understand the principles of each in order to help clients select the type of group that is most effective for them.

The substance abuse therapist who is used to having court-ordered clients must learn how to engage self-referred clients, or individuals with whom the court has little leverage. The mental health therapist, on the other hand, must learn to work with clients whose only perceived problem is getting the court system off their backs. Thus the substance abuse therapist will have to learn to be less directive, more flexible, and gentler during confrontations in an effort to engage and keep clients who are not court ordered. The mental health therapist, meanwhile, must learn to be more concrete and directive in setting treatment contracts. She needs to learn to use psychoeducation and confrontational feedback techniques to motivate some clients to address their substance use; such techniques also may help these clients in controlling some of their psychiatric symptoms.

The mental health therapist whose professional training may have taught her never to self-disclose, must learn that some clients need self-disclosure to help them differentiate normal feelings and behaviors from those generated by their mental health or substance use disorders. Take the case of a client whose mother has recently died and is experiencing significantly more depressive symptoms but attributes it all to her medication no longer working. The mental health therapist can assure the client by telling her that's exactly how she or her friends felt when a parent died and that such feelings are normal and will pass with time. The substance abuse therapist, on the other hand, must learn that maintaining clear boundaries is essential when interacting with some clients. The recovering substance abuse therapist is used to sharing with clients his history of dependency and may in fact encounter clients when he attends his own self-help meetings. However, for clients with certain psychotic, anxiety, and personality disorders, too much self-disclosure or even a simple touch of a shoulder can trigger confusion concerning what is intended or really meant. Thus the substance abuse therapist must learn to be much more withholding with certain clients than he has been in the past.

Finally, both mental health and substance abuse therapists must learn that words they use in their everyday work may have very different meanings for professionals in another field. For example, when the mental health therapist uses the term "defense mechanisms," she means a psychological process that protects individuals from pain and thus helps them function effectively in the community. The substance abuse therapist, of course, sees defense mechanisms as a negative process that prevents clients from recognizing and acknowledging the fact that they have a substance use disorder. When the substance abuse therapist uses the term "enabling," he is referring to a behavior that protects individuals from the consequences of their substance use and thus contributes to continued use. The mental health therapist sees enabling as a positive process that is often used in behavioral training or case management services to promote effective community functioning, such as helping a client learn how to ride the bus. Similarly, to a mental health therapist, "residential" refers to a facility that provides housing and support for individuals but to a substance abuse counselor, the term refers to an intensive substance abuse treatment. Both therapists need to learn the multiple definitions for many commonly used psychological terms in order to communicate effectively with each other and avoid misunderstandings.

## INTEGRATED TREATMENT

In addition to expanding their philosophical, knowledge, and skill bases, both mental health and substance abuse therapists also need to ensure that their treatment repertoire includes the ability to provide integrated and competency-based treatment for clients who have multiple treatment needs and/or failures. Integrated treatment differs from sequential or parallel treatment. Sequential treatment involves treating one disorder at a time; parallel treatment involves treating both disorders concurrently but by different therapists or agencies. Integrated treatment means treating both the substance use and mental health disorders concurrently. The report of the National Consensus Conference, *Improving Treatment for Individuals with Co-Occurring Substance Abuse and Mental Health Disorders,* held by the federal government's Substance Abuse and Mental Health Services Administration (SAMHSA) (1998a), recommended integrated treatment as most effective for individuals with co-occurring disorders. The federal government's Center for Mental Health Services (CMHS) 1998 report on standards of care for individuals with co-occurring disorders recommended that, "Whenever possible, dual primary treatment is integrated into a single setting and interventions. Ideally, individuals receive treatments for both disorders in the setting which they are treated for the most serious disorder" (p. 37).

Four major principles are involved in providing effective integrated treatment. The first is observing and giving feedback to clients concerning how each disorder affects them and how each disorder can affect the symptoms of the other. For example, the substance abuse therapist points out to a client that his cocaine dependence disorder is causing work, financial, and relationship problems, and his dysthymic disorder is causing similar difficulties. He also points out to his client that while the cocaine he uses initially reduces his symptoms of depression, these symptoms get worse than before when the stimulating effects of the drug wear off. The second principle of integrated treatment uses the Gestalt concept of foreground and background: although the therapist is aware of how each disorder affects a client, he will not necessarily intervene with the same intensity with each disorder at a particular time.

A mental health therapist has a client who reports serious suicidal thoughts and has a fairly detailed suicide plan. The mental health therapist knows that this client has been drinking for several days and that she always gets much more depressed when she drinks.

At this point, the mental health therapist focuses on the suicide risk (foreground) to ensure her client's safety. She will wait until the client is stabilized to address the drinking issue (background).

The third principle of integrated treatment is to develop a treatment plan that has goals and objectives for both the substance use and mental health disorders. If the substance abuse therapist has a client who is diagnosed with alcohol dependence and co-occurring bipolar disorder, the treatment plan needs to include goals and measurable objectives for both disorders to help him assess his client's progress. Minimally, his treatment goals for this client would include abstinence from alcohol and psychiatric stability. His objectives might include the client acknowledging the existence of both disorders, stating his desire to manage these disorders more effectively, achieving and maintaining abstinence, medication compliance, and so forth. A treatment plan that addresses both disorders not only requires the substance abuse therapist to be constantly aware that he is dealing with multiple treatment issues, but also gives him a framework to help chart his client's progress toward resolving those issues.

The final principle of integrated treatment is that all therapeutic interventions impact the symptoms of each of the client's disorders to some degree; thus, the intervention should be designed to promote all the goals of a treatment plan and they should be monitored for both positive and negative effects. In working with a client with borderline personality and co-occurring alcohol abuse disorders, the mental health therapist may first have to help her client learn how to abstain from alcohol before accomplishing the treatment plan's objective of eliminating self-harm, because drinking almost always precedes such an episode. On the other hand, a similar client who had only minimal alcohol involvement, might significantly increase her drinking once the episodes of self-harm are less frequent or eliminated. Thus the mental health therapist must always ask herself whether this intervention effectively addresses both disorders, and then monitor the effect this intervention has on the symptoms of all disorders.

## *A COMPETENCY-BASED FOCUS*

Another treatment skill that substance abuse and mental health therapists must have is focusing their feedback on clients' strengths and competencies instead of their problems. Many clients with and without co-occurring disorders have life histories full of failures and often view themselves as incompetent to manage their lives effectively. When new members join our treatment group for individuals with co-occurring disorders, they are asked to introduce themselves and identify a personal strength. It is not uncommon for a new group member to be unable to identify a strength. If clients are to learn to manage their disorders effectively, they must come to see themselves as having the necessary skills and abilities to do so. A competency-based focus promotes that viewpoint and has five important components.

1. The first component of this model involves helping clients identify their strengths and skills.

A substance abuse therapist has, for example, a client with both a cannabis dependence disorder and a co-occurring generalized anxiety disorder and occasional panic attacks. He is currently unemployed, living in a shelter, and has not had a significant relationship for more than ten years. When asked to identify a personal strength during his introduction to the treatment group, he states, "I have none." The substance abuse therapist counters that by saying, "You're here and that wasn't easy for you to do."

The substance abuse therapist, instead of focusing on what was wrong, focused on what was right.

2. These interventions, though often initially rejected by the client as inaccurate and naïve, eventually lead to the second essential component of this model: a sense of optimism.

> A mental health therapist has a client with major depressive disorder and a co-occurring alcohol dependence disorder that have been in remission for three years. This client makes a decision unknown to the mental health therapist to discontinue her medication and quickly experiences major depressive symptoms and returns to drinking. The result is hospitalization.

If the mental health therapist were to first focus on medication noncompliance and relapse when the client returns, it would only reinforce the client's sense of failure. However, if she simply asks the client, "What did you learn from this experience?" and "How might you apply that new knowledge to prevent such an occurrence in the future?" the event becomes a learning opportunity instead of a failure. Such interventions help promote a sense of optimism that one can learn to manage these disorders effectively.

3 and 4. The third and fourth components of this model are to integrate these strengths into treatment plans and make the goals both realistic and achievable.

> A substance abuse therapist has a client with a long history of treatment noncompliance with alcohol and cocaine dependence disorders and a co-occurring paranoid personality disorder. The client is now getting older and has few work or housing options left if the drug use continues. He now appears more willing than in the past to participate in treatment. The client's strength, even though it is out of desperation, is that he might now be willing to stay in treatment because homelessness is too frightening to him.

Using a competency-based focus, the goals of the treatment plan are to help the client remain in treatment, explore how he might learn to effectively manage his personality disorder, and to achieve and maintain abstinence. If the goals of the treatment plan were to require the client to attend all scheduled treatment sessions, attend self-help groups regularly, and immediately achieve abstinence, achievement would be beyond the reach of this client because the goals require skills that he does not yet possess. However, if he remains in treatment, the likelihood that he will begin to develop the skills needed to achieve these longer-term goals are much greater.

5. The final component of this model is that any positive change equals success.

A mental health therapist has a client with borderline personality disorder and co-occurring alcohol dependence disorder. The mental health therapist has worked with this client for a long time to help her extinguish her self-harm and drinking behaviors. Every time the client drinks she engages in self-harm behaviors. During a session she reveals that she drank the night before but had not harmed herself.

The mental health therapist immediately praises her strongly for not harming herself and asks the client to clarify how she accomplished it. The mental health therapist also reinforces this positive change by getting the client to acknowledge that this indeed was a positive change. It is important that the client sees the actions of the previous evening in a positive light because, in fact, change had occurred. The mental health therapist will not ignore the fact that her client also drank, but by focusing on what had changed, a new skill is identified that ultimately can be used to help achieve abstinence. Using a competency-based focus for clients with few life successes greatly increases the chances of ultimately achieving treatment goals.

## TREATMENT GOALS

The next step in providing effective clinical services is establishing treatment goals for an extremely diverse group of clients. Table 1.2 presents treatment goals for each of the five categories of clients originally described under Types of Clients. We believe that any alcohol or drug use will, to some extent, increase psychiatric symptoms or reduce the ability to manage them effectively. Thus one of our treatment goals for clients with co-occurring disorders is abstinence, whether they have a dependence disorder or not. In addition, for many clients, the previous goals will be long term as they develop the concepts and the skills necessary to achieve and maintain them. Another goal we also have for all clients—except those with only a substance abuse disorder or mental health disorder with mild symptoms—is involvement in long-term community supports such as Alcoholics Anonymous (AA), Narcotics Anonymous (NA), Dual Recovery Anonymous, Emotions Anonymous, and other self-help or support groups. Dealing with these disorders is often a lifetime task and requires more support than is normally available through private practitioners and community agencies. These goals provide the sub-

TABLE 1.2. Treatment Goals

| Disorder Type | Treatment Goals |
| --- | --- |
| MH disorders only | Psychiatric stability |
| SA disorders only | Abstinence (dependency disorders) Nonproblematic substance use (abuse disorders) |
| SA and MH disorders | Abstinence and psychiatric stability |
| SA and personality disorders | Abstinence and interpersonal stability |
| SA, MH, and personality disorders | Abstinence, psychiatric stability, and interpersonal stability |

stance abuse therapist and the mental health therapist with a direction for their work.

## STANDARD INTERVENTIONS FOR ALL CLIENTS WITH CO-OCCURRING DISORDERS

Finally, even though the mental health and the substance abuse therapists' caseloads may be extremely diverse, twelve standard interventions can be used with all clients who have co-occurring disorders, regardless of their diagnosis, functioning level, or interest in treatment. These standard interventions are presented in Box 1.1 and are described in the remaining portion of this chapter.

### Use Leverage to Promote Treatment

Many clients with co-occurring disorders acknowledge that they have some level of psychological distress, however, they do not as readily acknowledge the extent of their alcohol and other drug involvement. The reasons for this are varied, but often have to do with the fact that they experience some relief from their psychological symptoms by using these substances. To acknowledge the use of these substances or the problems they cause would require them to potentially eliminate a source of relief and comfort. Thus clients are

---

### BOX 1.1. Standard Interventions

1. Use leverage to promote treatment.

2. Match treatment demands with what is possible.

3. Set clear treatment goals and expectations early for clients mandated to treatment.

4. Provide information for self-diagnosis.

5. Identify and discuss the positive benefits of substance use and psychiatric symptoms.

6. Connect alcohol and drug use and behaviors resulting from psychiatric symptoms with negative life consequences.

7. Connect how psychiatric symptoms affect alcohol and drug use and how this usage affects psychiatric symptoms.

8. Require clients to be abstinent during treatment sessions.

9. Promote medication compliance.

10. Promote skills needed to achieve treatment goals.

11. Use group treatment as much as possible.

12. Promote self-help involvement.

---

often much more resistant to addressing their substance use than their psychiatric symptoms. As most substance abuse professionals are aware, few individuals voluntarily enter substance abuse treatment. The mental health therapist and the substance abuse therapist need to be willing to develop relationships with outside sources, such as the family, social services, and the criminal justice system, that have some leverage over the client to help ensure that such clients will attend and participate in treatment. The role of the substance abuse and the mental health therapist is not to enforce the consequences that these other individuals or agencies might place on a client for not entering or staying in treatment, but they should in no way attempt to protect the client from pressures that promote treatment. Research concerning treatment outcomes for both individuals with and without co-occurring disorders all point to the fact that retention in treatment is the most important variable that predicts long-term treatment success (see Chapter 13). Thus to promote treatment participation is to promote long-term psychiatric stability and abstinence.

### *Match Treatment Demands with What Is Possible*

Since retention is so important to treatment outcome, treatment requirements and placements should be based on a compromise between what is needed, what is available, what the client is willing to do, and what leverage or influence is available to the therapist. For example, after a thorough clinical assessment, it becomes obvious that the best clinical course for one of the substance abuse therapist's clients, who is diagnosed with schizophrenia and alcohol and cocaine dependence disorders, would be placement in a substance abuse residential treatment setting. However, the local substance abuse residential treatment program will not accept individuals with schizophrenia. In addition, the client has absolutely no interest in being placed in a residential treatment setting, and even if a facility were available, there is no real leverage for the substance abuse therapist to use to promote admission. Hence what is possible in this instance is outpatient treatment (which the client states he is willing to do). Although the substance abuse therapist is aware that both abstinence and psychiatric stability are highly unlikely in outpatient treatment and that ultimately a residential setting will be needed, by offering outpatient treatment, the therapist begins to engage the client in a therapeutic system that will increase his knowledge and awareness of his co-occurring disorders. This potentially increases the client's willingness to accept treatment. At the same time, the substance abuse therapist can work on identifying a residential program that would accept such a client, and possibly work with other systems, such as the family, social services, or the criminal justice system, to identify potential points of leverage or influence that could be used to promote residential treatment in the future. By matching his treatment demands with what is possible, the client becomes involved in treatment; thus the chances are increased that the client will ultimately receive the level of care needed.

### Set Clear Treatment Goals and Expectations Early for Clients Mandated to Treatment

A significant number of clients with co-occurring disorders are mandated to treatment from other agencies or their families. Thus it is important to clearly establish at the beginning of treatment what the purpose of treatment will be, and what will be expected of them.

A mental health therapist has a client with schizoaffective disorder and anti-social personality traits and co-occurring alcohol and cannabis abuse disorders, who has been referred to treatment by her probation officer. This client does not see her substance use as a problem and has a history of medication noncompliance.

To ensure that the client knows what she must do to comply with her probation officer's treatment requirement, the mental health therapist informs her at their initial session that the goals of treatment are medication compliance and abstinence. The mental health therapist also clearly spells out what she expects from her client during treatment, specifically what services the client will be required to use, for how long, acceptable attendance patterns, medication compliance, providing urines, etc. The mental health therapist's mandated client does not want to be in treatment, but she can choose treatment over other alternatives (such as jail). To make that choice, she needs to know exactly what treatment entails. When everything is clear up front, the mental health therapist's client can choose treatment or other options. This choice begins to give the client some sense of power over her life. It also begins to establish one of the essentials of a therapeutic relationship: the ability to trust that the mental health therapist is being honest. One of the worst actions the mental health therapist could take with such a client is to change what is required of her in the middle of treatment, because that would destroy all the trust that had been established.

### Provide Information for Self-Diagnosis

Many clients entering treatment are still minimizing or denying the existence of either one or all of their disorders. In addition, substance use and many mental disorders can have significant impact on cognitive functioning, and thus reduce a client's ability to connect negative experiences with the symptoms of their disorders. Clients therefore need appropriate information and feedback in a variety of formats to help them recognize their disorders themselves.

A substance abuse therapist has a client with cannabis dependence disorder and co-occurring generalized anxiety disorder, who acknowledges neither, and attributes his employment and relationship problems to excessively demanding bosses and girlfriends.

The substance abuse therapist ensures that his client participates in a psychoeducation series that will provide information about substance dependence, abuse disorders, and mental disorders that often co-occur with them. He also provides his client with information to read about marijuana and anxiety disorders. In addition, he gives the client direct feedback during treatment sessions that connects his life problems with these disorders. The substance abuse therapist also might review with his client the criteria for diagnosis in the DSM-IV to point out that mental health experts recognize these disorders and to give the client what information he needs to make a self-diagnosis. Until the substance abuse therapist's client acknowledges to himself that he has these disorders, he will have no motivation to address them.

### *Identify and Discuss the Positive Benefits of Substance Use and Psychiatric Symptoms*

It is important to acknowledge that clients may seem to benefit to some extent from the substances they use—something clients already believe. When the mental health therapist tells her client with bipolar disorder, for example, that his alcohol use helps reduce some of his manic symptoms or that he finds relief from his never completely controlled depressive symptoms by going off of his mood-controlling medication to experience some level of mania, she is acknowledging the client's reality. Such interventions strengthen the therapeutic relationship by allowing the client to be more truthful about his behaviors and motivations; they also increase the effectiveness of the mental health therapist's input by specifically targeting those issues which are most hindering the achievement of the treatment goals.

## Connect Alcohol and Drug Use and Behaviors Resulting from Psychiatric Symptoms with Negative Life Consequences

Negative life consequences are the other part of the reality for individuals having these disorders. When therapists present a comprehensive and balanced (positive and negative) picture of how these disorders are affecting a client, the client can then compare the benefits of pursuing no treatment with the benefits of having them effectively treated. However, as previously discussed, because of minimization, denial, and cognitive impairment, therapists often need to point out the negative consequences of these disorders time and time again. Thus, though the mental health therapist acknowledges to her client with bipolar disorder that the alcohol and mania have some benefits, she also points out that the alcohol usually makes the client more depressed and unstable the next day. By going off of his medication he inevitably ends up in the hospital. We have not yet seen a case where the positive effects of these disorders ultimately outweigh the negative effects.

## Connect the Effects of Psychiatric Symptoms on Alcohol and Drug Use, and Alcohol and Drug Use on Psychiatric Symptoms

Co-occurring disorders always have a reciprocal relationship. Part of the mental health therapist's work with her client with bipolar disorder involves showing her client how his alcohol use relates to his bipolar disorder. The client must understand how his substance use and psychiatric symptoms are connected, because such insight helps him conceptualize that, while his substance use may initially help reduce psychiatric symptoms, in the long run, it usually makes them worse. Without this knowledge, he will continue to have only half the picture and continue believing that his substance use helps manage his psychiatric symptoms; he also will reject the mental health therapist's goal of abstinence, because it makes no sense to him.

## Require Clients to Be Abstinent During Treatment Sessions

When working with clients who use alcohol and other drugs, it is necessary to refuse treatment whenever a client is under the influence of these substances. Allowing a client with major depressive disorder to be under the influence of alcohol during a treatment session with a substance abuse therapist undermines the clinician's stance that abstinence is a treatment goal. In addition, the effects of the alcohol impair the cognitive processes necessary for fully utilizing the treatment session. The substance abuse therapist can simply remind the client that she needs to be drug free during a treatment session and ask her to return for her next scheduled appointment. The purpose of this intervention is not to catch a client using, but to set appropriate therapeutic boundaries.

### Promote Medication Compliance

Most individuals with co-occurring disorders will need to be on medication at some time during their treatment. Medication compliance promotes psychiatric stability and reduces psychiatric symptoms that can increase the desire to use alcohol and other drugs.

A mental health therapist has a client with dysthymia who has co-occurring alcohol and cocaine abuse disorders and a history of medication noncompliance. The mental health therapist is aware that, when depressive symptoms are present, the client is more likely to drink or use cocaine, which results in the worsening of the symptoms of depression.

The mental health therapist must determine why her client decides to go off her medication and focus some of her interventions toward preventing that. If the client fails to comply with her medication regimen, the long-term goals of psychiatric stability and abstinence are unlikely.

### Promote Skills Needed to Achieve Treatment Goals

Few individuals with co-occurring disorders enter treatment with all the skills needed to achieve and maintain psychiatric stability and abstinence. These skills vary from controlling emotional impulses and refusing drugs when offered to managing anger and tolerating being alone.

A substance abuse therapist has a client who has alcohol, narcotics, and cocaine dependence disorders and co-occurring cyclothymic disorder. Although he acknowledges these issues as problems, he enters treatment with little ability to tolerate emotional discomfort, is quick to anger and violence, and has not gone more than five days without drugs in the last four years. He also has been psychiatrically unstable and a regular alcohol and drug user since he was thirteen years old.

Before this client can achieve either abstinence or psychiatric stability, he needs to develop a set of new skills. The substance abuse therapist, in addition to promoting detoxification, must help his client learn to manage: emotional discomfort and drug cravings; anger; refusing drugs when offered; socially interacting with others without the assistance of drugs; and learning to follow someone else's (the doctor's) directions about taking drugs (medications). The substance abuse therapist's initial treatment with this client should focus on developing these building block skills that are necessary to achieve the longer-term goals.

### *Use Group Treatment As Much As Possible*

For several reasons, group treatment should be the treatment of choice whenever possible. Not only is it the most time efficient, cost effective, and most inclusive of peer input, but therapeutically, group treatment is preferable as well. Individuals with serious mental illness are usually isolated and have few friends. Because groups for seriously mentally ill individuals are made up of members with similar problems and functioning levels, members often feel more understood and comfortable than being out in the "real world." Attending group often is a valuable support. The group is also a venue to improve socialization skills and even to make friends who (we hope) will support one another in recovery activities such as going together to self-help meetings. Furthermore, substance abusers can recognize in others the same unhelpful defenses that they themselves use. They confront those defenses in others and learn to identify them in themselves. Members support one another in every positive step they take toward recovery and identify negative behaviors in others that they themselves have experienced. Finally, members act as role models for one another. It is inspiring for members to interact with individuals who cope with the same disorders they have, yet have moved farther along the ladder of recovery, learning and using the skills needed to achieve and maintain sobriety and stability.

Many individuals with co-occurring disorders may not initially be ready to participate in a group, and many others will need additional individual, case management, and family services to supplement their group treatment. The strengths and limitations of each of these four modalities for this population are discussed in detail in Chapters 7 through 9. The vast majority of our clients have been able to participate in group sessions at some point in their treatment.

### Promote Self-Help Involvement

Managing co-occurring disorders is a twenty-four-hour, seven-days-a-week, 365-days-a-year process. Treatment agencies and families quite frankly have neither the resources nor the emotional energy to provide all the support that such individuals need for long-term recovery. Furthermore, peer feedback is often more valuable to these individuals than professional input. The mental health therapist and the substance abuse therapist must promote their clients' involvement in mental health and substance abuse self-help recovery groups. Doing this ensures that they will receive all the support and varying viewpoints they need for long-term recovery. A description of these support groups is found in Chapter 11.

## CONCLUSION

Although the substance abuse therapist and the mental health therapist may find that they have multifarious caseloads, all of their clients can be placed in one of five categories. By doing so, decisions concerning treatment planning, who can be treated in the same group, what advice to give families, and how much case management should be offered, become much more manageable. Having specific treatment goals for each subgroup helps to narrow the focus of potential treatment interventions.

# Chapter 2

# Then and Now: Concepts and Treatment of Co-Occurring Disorders

Much has changed in the mental health and substance abuse professions during the last forty years. In 1960, few people used drugs other than alcohol or nicotine, and most persons with major mental disorders spent long periods in state institutions. The general public viewed addictions and other mental disorders as character flaws. Public programs for addictions were primarily hospital-based and focused on detoxification, not long-term recovery issues. Alcoholics Anonymous was the only community-based recovery program available to most individuals with alcohol dependence. Few psychiatric medications were available and most public mental health services were provided only at large state hospitals, with few services available to individuals living in the community. Both addiction and mental health services were primarily delivered using the medical and psychoanalytic models. These models involved little, if any, input into treatment decisions by the individuals affected by the disorders, and looked for underlying and unresolved issues from an individual's childhood that would explain the symptoms.

However, by 1970, much was evolving both in our society and in the fields of mental health and addictions. Beginning in the mid-1960s, the use of drugs other than alcohol and nicotine exploded. A much broader spectrum of society started using drugs such as marijuana, LSD, amphetamines, and barbiturates. New and much more effective medications to treat serious mental disorders were introduced. With the ability to better manage psychiatric symptoms through medication, many individuals were released from state hospitals and returned to the community. In addition, the gender, racial, and other consciousness-raising and empowerment movements sparked an increase in the desire for self-growth and awareness. Therapies that focused on personal growth and involved the client equally in the change process flourished. All these forces exerted pressure on the limited existing mental health and substance abuse treatment resources and created the political will for the federal and state governments to begin to expand their systems of care.

Federal and state governments responded by enacting community mental health centers legislation which provided funds for community-based mental health and substance abuse treatment programs. The federal government also created the National Institute of Mental Health, the National Institute on Drug Abuse, and the National Institute on Alcohol Abuse and Alcoholism to provide funding, research, and national guidance concerning these issues. Most states soon followed and developed similar organizations. New funding supported academic and paraprofessional training programs designed to equip staff with the knowledge and skills needed to provide these new services. New professional titles such as "substance abuse counselor," "mental health worker," and "rehabilitation counselor" evolved. In addition, the functions of professions such as social work changed and came to focus more on providing therapy than monitoring parent/child behaviors or linking individuals with community services. All this activity also spurred the creation of disability-specific treatment programs that were supported by separate funding streams. Thus the new substance abuse and mental health systems evolved separately, each providing treatment for only one type of condition. At this point the concept of co-occurring disorders was still on the distant horizon.

During the 1970s, the movement of treatment from the state hospitals to the community meant that younger adults received most of their treatment in outpatient settings rather than in hospitals. It also meant that these young adults would no longer be isolated from their peers and thus they would practice the same behaviors as others in their age group. Hence, individuals with major mental disorders began to use alcohol and drugs in unprecedented proportions. As the youth of America grew alienated from mainstream society, many never entered treatment but instead traveled around the nation or lived on communes. Many were only partially treatment compliant and mixed alcohol and drugs with their medications. Neither treatment system was adequately equipped to treat the multiple needs of these individuals.

Furthermore, in most areas, the substance abuse treatment system was broken into separate alcohol and drug treatment programs in the early 1970s. The alcohol treatment programs tended to have older clients who used only alcohol, while drug treatment programs had younger clients who used a variety of drugs that usually included alcohol. Primarily, those who viewed drug use as the result of some underlying psychological problem ran outpatient drug treatment programs, while individuals who believed that alcoholism had a genetic and biological origin worked in alcohol treatment programs. Although some alcohol and drug abuse programs merged into a single treatment system for substance use disorders by the mid-1970s, some systems did not combine until the 1990s. Mental health programs, on the other hand, seldom assessed their clients for either alcohol or drug use, believing that abuse of these substances would terminate once the mental health condition was resolved. Throughout most of the 1970s the mental health and substance abuse treatment systems operated very separately from each other, were ill-equipped to treat multiple disorders, and in many instances, had opposing philosophical views of etiology and intervention strategies.

## GENESIS AND EARLY CONCEPTS

The publication of the American Psychiatric Association's *Diagnostic and Statistical Manual of Mental Disorders,* Third Edition (DSM-III) in 1980 created the framework for the development of services for individuals with co-occurring disorders. Unlike the previous editions of this manual, the DSM-III allowed for individuals to have multiple diagnoses. Hence, an individual now could be diagnosed with a disorder such as major depression and, concurrently, could also be diagnosed with personality and substance use disorders. This meant that individuals receiving treatment in either the mental health or substance abuse treatment system could also have a disorder that would normally be treated by the other system. The DSM-III laid the groundwork necessary to begin the process of developing conceptual models for co-occurring disorders.

The first step of this process involved identifying a term to describe this subgroup of individuals in an agency's treatment population. The term dual diagnosis or the dually diagnosed, borrowed from the mental retardation field, was the first term to gain wide acceptance. However, that term never satisfactorily described the complexity of this population and other terms quickly evolved, such as dually disordered, mentally ill chemical abusers (MICA), substance abusing mentally ill (SAMI), mentally ill substance abusers (MISA), mentally ill chemical abusers and addicted (MICAA). These terms tended to describe only a segment of the population who had substance use and mental disorders. Federal government agencies initially used the term co-morbid disorders, but later changed the term to co-occurring disorders, which has currently gained the widest acceptance. All of these terms continue to be used by professionals in the mental health and substance abuse treatment fields, often interchangeably. Although many terms are used, they all denote the fact that a client has both a substance use and a mental disorder in need of treatment.

Though the DSM-III gave credibility to the concept that individuals could have multiple disorders, the primary illness model that states that one disorder is the cause of all other observed symptoms still dominated professional thinking into the early 1980s. Many alcoholism experts stated that the alcoholic population had no more psychopathology than the general population, and attributed most of the depression and anxiety that they observed to extended withdrawal symptoms. Khantzian (1985) proposed a self-medication theory that he believed explained the origin of substance use by persons with mental illnesses; and Bean-Bayog (1988) theorized that some mental illness was caused by brain trauma resulting from excessive substance use. Even those professionals who accepted the existence of co-occurring disorders generally agreed that their number was probably small. These philosophical differences, combined with a lack of staff capable of treating multiple disorders and exclusion criteria that prevented individuals with certain disorders from being treated in a particular program, resulted in widespread unavailable or ineffective treatment for individuals with co-occurring disorders. In fact, McLellan et al. found in 1983 that individuals with co-occurring disorders did not benefit from treatment.

To gain a better understanding of the dually diagnosed population, the National Institute of Mental Health (NIMH) sponsored a review by Ridgely, Goldman, and Talbott (1986) of all existing research concerning these individuals. The review found three important facts: first, the dually diagnosed are in the substance abuse and the mental health treatment systems in numbers greater than had been thought; second, untreated co-occurring disorders have significant conse- quences for both the individuals and the community; and third, no proposed treatment models were based on research outcomes.

In response, NIMH sponsored a second report by Ridgely, Osher, and Talbott (1987) that was based on NIMH-sponsored site visits to programs across the country which had begun to provide treatment services for individuals with co-occurring disorders. The report rec- ommended that the co-occurring disorders be treated concurrently with either hybrid treatment programs using substance abuse and mental health staff or cooperative treatment arrangements made be- tween substance abuse and mental health treatment programs. Both of these reports sparked an increase in research concerning this popu- lation in both the substance abuse and the mental health fields. Ross, Glaser, and Germanson (1988) published an extensive study of indi- viduals with mental disorders receiving treatment in substance abuse treatment programs, and Drake and Wallach (1989) published a study of substance abuse disorders among individuals with serious mental disorders.

## *EARLY TREATMENT ACTIVITIES AND NATIONAL ACCEPTANCE*

As the concurrent conditions model began to gain a foothold in the treatment professions, treatment systems began to initiate services for individuals with co-occurring disorders. These initial services used either a sequential, parallel, or integrated model for their treat- ment. The sequential services model advocated that one treatment system initiate treatment, and when that disorder was stabilized, the client would be referred to the other system to complete treatment for the other disorder. For example, an individual with major depression is treated in the mental health system, and when his depression sub- sides, he is referred to the substance abuse system to treat his alcohol dependence. The parallel services model advocated using the mental health system to treat the mental health disorder and the substance abuse system to treat the substance use disorder at the same time, rather than sequentially. A few programs initiated the integrated services model that designated certain staff to treat both disorders concurrently at a single treatment site.

Sequential treatment was quickly found to be ineffective because it was very difficult to stabilize one disorder without stabilizing the other. Parallel treatment was also fairly ineffective because it was difficult for an individual to participate in two different treatment programs in different locations that focused on different and sometimes conflicting treatment agendas. By the late 1980s several integrated treatment models had been proposed (Hendrickson, 1988; Minkoff, 1989; Osher and Kofoed, 1989; Pepper and Ryglewicz, 1984), and by the mid-1990s it was generally accepted that integrated treatment was the most effective treatment model for this population. The report of a consensus conference convened by the federal government's Substance Abuse and Mental Health Services Administration (SAMHSA, 1998a) concluded that integrated treatment was the treatment of choice for individuals with co-occurring disorders.

By the very early 1990s, most community mental health and substance abuse treatment systems accepted that individuals with co-occurring disorders, in need of specialized services, were prevalent in their programs. Furthermore, a growing number of professionals were specializing in this type of treatment and more and more conferences and articles focused on the treatment of this population. Also by the mid-1990s two major studies of the general population, the NIMH's Epidemiological Catchment Area (ECA) Study (Regier et al., 1990) and the National Comorbidity Survey (NCS) (Kessler et al., 1994), had documented that significant numbers of Americans had co-occurring disorders. A national awareness concerning the extent of co-occurring disorders and what was needed to treat them effectively had finally taken root.

However, although the integrated treatment model was generally accepted as the most effective treatment approach for this substantial population, few programs had staff qualified to provide it. A study conducted by the Inspector General of Health and Human Services (1995) found that few staff felt that they were adequately trained to effectively treat individuals with co-occurring disorders. Identifying the most effective treatment model also did not determine who should provide this integrated treatment and whether it should be offered in separate programs or be part of the existing substance abuse and mental health treatment systems.

# FACTORS AFFECTING THE DEVELOPMENT
# OF SERVICES FOR INDIVIDUALS
# WITH CO-OCCURRING DISORDERS

Although the U.S. economy experienced unprecedented growth during most of the 1990s, the cost of health services was daunting to society. Also, health insurance companies and others believed in limiting how much mental health and substance abuse treatment could be offered in the effort to prevent health care costs from spiraling out of control. As a result, not enough funding was available to realistically develop a new treatment system for individuals with co-occurring disorders. Thus, with a few exceptions, treatment services for this population had to be developed in the context of existing substance abuse and mental health treatment and funding systems.

Another trend in the 1990s, in the hope of saving money, was to contract out mental health and substance abuse treatment services to private providers. This had mixed results. Private programs were often less bureaucratic and less entrenched in the historical separateness of mental health and substance abuse services, which made the development of integrated services easier. Because they were beginning anew, the staff they hired would be expected to work with individuals with co-occurring disorders. However, in their effort to get the services contract, program developers often submitted bids that ensured that staff salaries would be so low that they had to hire less qualified or less experienced individuals than those who had been providing the services through governmental agencies. In addition, because governmental agencies had historically provided these services, administrators had few private entities from which to choose. Thus they often had a dilemma: if they terminated a contract because a private agency was not providing effective services, they would have no other qualified agency available to provide the service.

Also in the 1990s many mental health and substance abuse treatment services came under the umbrella of some form of managed care system, whose goal was to save money by insuring only "necessary services." As with privatization, the results of managed care initiatives have been mixed. Because managed care, as suggested by Mee-Lee (1994), theoretically has no historical reasons for keeping mental health and substance abuse services separate and hates inefficiencies, it has contributed in some instances to more integrated treatment being available. Managed care also has the ability to require an agency to provide integrated treatment for individuals with co-occurring disorders. However, the availability of services under a managed care system is totally based on what is authorized in the contract, and how well employees authorizing treatment services understand the specific treatment needs of an individual. Thus many contracts were developed that did not adequately provide for the full scope of treatment needed by individuals with co-occurring disorders, and few managed care companies had experts in the treatment needs of these individuals. In addition, because of the innate tug-of-war in a managed care system between cost savings and treatment need, the services authorized for an individual were not always based on the treatment need.

Finally, two other important factors affected the development of services for individuals with co-occurring disorders. First, more and more of these individuals were appearing in the criminal justice system. Regier et al. (1990) reported that 90 percent of individuals in a prison setting with a major mental disorder had a co-occurring substance use disorder. Pepper and Massaro (1992) reported that a trans-institutionalization was occurring; that is, individuals with mental disorders were placed in jails or prisons instead of state hospitals. This was the direct result of implementing deinstitutionalization without adequate treatment and support services available in the community, few thoughtful laws that both protected individuals' rights but still required participation in appropriate treatment, and the widespread use of alcohol and other drugs by this population. Pepper (1995) later proposed a community and client protection system model that advocated cooperative activities between the treatment and criminal justice systems. Its purpose was to create a cooperative treatment team composed of treatment and criminal justice professionals who were to ensure both the safety of the individual with co-occurring disorders and the community. By the mid-1990s professionals in the criminal justice system had become important partners with professionals in the treatment systems in providing services to individuals with co-occurring disorders.

The final factor that impacted the development of services for this population was identifying individuals with co-occurring disorders in the homeless population (Drake, Osher, and Wallach, 1991; Herman, Galanter, and Lifshultz, 1991; Fischer, 1991; Tessler and Dennis,

1989). Unaffordable housing, lack of independent living support services, alcohol and drug use, and medication noncompliance all contribute to homelessness. Professionals working with homeless populations now needed to know how to screen for substance use and mental disorders, and they needed either the skills to provide integrated treatment for individuals with co-occurring disorders, or to be able to link them to these services. This contributed to the development of the phases of treatment model proposed by Osher and Kofoed (1989), which includes preengagement and engagement phases of treatment that are particularly useful with the homeless population. These factors, combined with the national acceptance that specialized services had to be implemented for individuals with co-occurring disorders, all played a part in beginning to build a system of care for this population.

## BUILDING THE INFRASTRUCTURE FOR A SYSTEM OF CARE FOR INDIVIDUALS WITH CO-OCCURRING DISORDERS

In addition to the initiation of many new services in the 1990s designed specifically for individuals with co-occurring disorders, the infrastructure needed to provide effective treatment services for these individuals was beginning to form. This included developing and identifying assessment instruments for this specific population; training activities to increase the number of skilled therapists; identifying subgroups of this population; conducting research to document effective treatments; and publishing specific standards and best practices that agencies could use to evaluate their services for individuals with co-occurring disorders.

The first assessment tool specifically designed for individuals with co-occurring disorders was introduced in 1992, and since that time several other instruments have been developed. In addition, research shed light on how effective other commonly used substance abuse assessment instruments were for assessing substance use with individuals with co-occurring mental disorders. The creation of these new instruments and research on existing ones gave professionals working with this population effective and standardized tools for identifying co-occurring disorders and for planning treatment for this population. For a detailed description of these assessment tools, see Chapter 5.

A great deal of effort in the 1990s also was put into developing materials for increasing knowledge and skills of mental health and substance abuse professionals working with clients with co-occurring disorders. Federal, state, and individual treatment agencies supported staff training programs; more and more national, regional, and local conferences focused on the topic; literature concerning how to effectively treat this population made its way into professional journals and books; and videotapes were made for training purposes. Professionals skilled in treating co-occurring disorders acted as supervisors and trainers for therapists without these skills. As a result, the 1990s witnessed a significant increase in the number of treatment professionals capable of working effectively with individuals with co-occurring disorders.

Researchers and therapists working with this population quickly found that in addition to being numerous, individuals with co-occurring disorders were far from a homogeneous population. This population included individuals who had major substance use and mental health disorders that significantly impaired their ability to function independently, and those with less severe conditions who generally functioned fairly well in the community. The type and intensity of treatment offered to one client would not necessarily be appropriate for another client. As early as 1981, Pepper, Kirshner, and Ryglewicz reported that the substance use behaviors were different between younger and older individuals with major mental disorders. Since then a variety of subgroup models have been proposed (see Chapter 5 for an overview of these models). Currently, the most commonly used model differentiates subgroups based on intensity of symptoms and their impact on functioning level. These models have made a significant contribution to understanding the heterogeneity of this population and have promoted the development of flexible treatment plans.

Outcome research also began to document effectiveness of treatment when modifications were made for the special needs of this population. In 1990 few research articles had been published concerning the treatment of individuals with co-occurring disorders, but by the end of the decade, over fifty studies had been published in national journals, with many local communities completing their own studies on the effectiveness of their treatment services. See Chapter 11 for a detailed description of this research.

The 1990s also witnessed the beginning of standardization of treatment approaches for individuals with co-occurring disorders. In 1994, the Center for Substance Abuse Treatment (CSAT, 1994a) published *Treatment Improvement Protocol (TIP 9)* on providing treatment services for individuals with co-occurring disorders; this *TIP* became the most requested of the series, with an updated edition scheduled for publication in late 2003. Furthermore, in 1998, the Center for Mental Health Services (CMHS) published standards of care for this population and the American Society of Addiction Medicine's (ASAM, 2001) criteria for substance abuse treatment placement now includes placement criteria for individuals with co-occurring disorders. Based on the work of a managed care consensus panel sponsored by the CMHS, Minkoff (2001) proposed a model system—the Comprehensive, Continuous, Integrated System of Care (CCISC)—which brings the mental health and substance abuse systems together to develop a comprehensive and integrated system of care for all individuals with substance abuse and mental disorders.

## CURRENT CONDITIONS AND THE FUTURE

Many integrated treatment services for individuals with co-occurring disorders have been initiated throughout the nation during the last ten years, yet many communities still lack them and very few have a full range of services for individuals with co-occurring disorders throughout the continuum of care. Treatment is provided often in a patchwork and ineffective manner, further complicated by the fact that most professionals still lack the knowledge and skills necessary to provide integrated treatment. In addition, universities are not adequately preparing new professionals to treat this population. Though tremendous progress has been made in developing specialized services and in training therapists to effectively work with this population, much still needs to be accomplished.

# Chapter 3

# Frequently Co-Occurring Axis I Psychiatric and Substance Use Disorders

The *Diagnostic and Statistical Manual-IV-Text Revision* (DSM-IV-TR), published by the American Psychiatric Association in 2000, describes all the mental disorders and their diagnostic criteria that are commonly accepted by the treatment, research, education, and insurance communities in the United States. The vast majority of these disorders are found on Axis I of the manual's diagnostic scheme. Axis I consists of 152 different mental health disorders and 114 substance-related disorders (V codes excluded). Conceivably, the mental health and substance abuse therapists might encounter any of these disorders while providing treatment to a multifarious caseload; however only nineteen mental disorders frequently co-occur with substance use disorders, and substance-related disorders can be clustered into three major types. The purpose of this chapter is to describe the frequently co-occurring types of mental health and substance use disorders that substance abuse and mental health therapists might encounter in their clients and discuss how this co-occurrence can affect both the client and treatment.

The nineteen Axis I mental disorders that the substance abuse therapist will frequently encounter when providing substance abuse treatment fall into seven major diagnostic categories: mood disorders, anxiety disorders, psychotic disorders, attention-deficit and disruptive behavior disorders, eating disorders, dissociative disorders, and impulse-control disorders. The substance-related disorders that the mental health therapist will most frequently encounter are categorized as abuse, dependency, and substance-induced. Substance abuse and mental health therapists need to be knowledgeable in identifying and intervening with these disorders if they are to be effective in treating their multifarious caseloads.

## SUBSTANCE-RELATED DISORDERS

Substance-related disorders are classified as either substance-induced disorders or substance use disorders. Substance-induced disorders have the same symptoms as a mental health disorder, for example, psychosis, but are the direct result of alcohol or other drug use. The symptoms of the vast majority of these disorders will significantly decrease or cease soon after the use of the substance has been discontinued, but the symptoms can cause a confusing diagnostic picture while use continues. A detailed discussion concerning methods to differentiate between substance-induced disorders and true co-occurring disorders is presented in Chapter 5.

Substance use disorders encompass either a substance abuse disorder or a substance dependency disorder. The DSM-IV lists eleven categories of substances: alcohol, amphetamine, caffeine, cannabis, cocaine, hallucinogen, inhalant, nicotine, opioid, phencyclidine, and sedative-hypnotic or anxiolytic. The use of these substances can result in a diagnosis of abuse, dependency, or induced disorders except for nicotine, which does not have an abuse diagnosis, and caffeine, which has neither an abuse nor a dependency diagnosis. An individual can have both abuse and dependency disorders concurrently as long as the disorders result from different substances (e.g., alcohol dependency and cannabis abuse).

### Substance Abuse Disorders

These disorders are characterized by a pattern of use that causes problems in a particular life sphere. Four criteria are used to diagnose this disorder: substance use that causes problems with work, school, or home; use in recurrent situations that are physically hazardous (e.g., driving while intoxicated); use that results in recurrent legal problems; or use that causes recurrent social problems. The diagnosis requires multiple recurrence of at least one of these symptoms during a twelve-month period.

### Substance Dependency Disorders

These disorders are characterized by a loss of control regarding how much of a substance an individual will use at a single time, abnormal thoughts of and cravings for the substance when it is not being used, and continued use even when individuals expect negative consequences. The amount and frequency of use is not as important as these characteristics.

The seven criteria for substance use dependency are: the presence of tolerance (the need for more of the substance to get the desired effect); withdrawal (physical problems when the substance is discontinued); use of larger amounts of the substance than was intended; unsuccessful efforts to control use; considerable time spent to obtain and use the substance; important life activities given up or reduced in order to use the substance; and continued use despite knowing that it is causing problems. Substance dependency is diagnosed when at least three of these symptoms are present during a twelve-month period. Individuals can have multiple dependency disorders (such as alcohol dependence and cocaine dependence).

### Treatment Implications

Although the mental health therapist's clients might use any substance, the vast majority use caffeine, alcohol, nicotine, marijuana, or cocaine, in descending order of popularity. The use of all of these substances can initially reduce some of the psychiatric symptoms that mental health clients experience, but will make them worse in the long run. Keep in mind that almost everyone uses drugs to feel good. Thus many individuals with mental health disorders use these drugs as a form of self-medication or to be more easily accepted into a peer group. However, the mental health therapist needs to help clients understand that the side effects of any use will ultimately make their condition worse. In addition, what may begin as an age-appropriate behavior or an attempt to reduce unpleasant symptoms can develop into dependence if the individual is genetically predisposed to such a condition. At this point, the substance use disorder takes on a life of its own in addition to its interaction with the mental health disorder, further complicating treatment.

The mental health therapist must assess for substance use in the client and develop an understanding of what role it plays in the management and presentation of the client's mental health symptoms (see detailed discussion of appropriate instruments and assessment issues in Chapter 5). The mental health therapist's assessment must also include decisions concerning the client's type of substance-related diagnosis, so she can identify the level of treatment intensity needed to achieve abstinence. Without abstinence, the client will not be able to maximize functioning capacity, because all use results in some increase in psychiatric symptoms. However, when these substances are used to help manage symptoms, the mental health therapist must be able to offer other methods of symptom management that are as effective, less destabilizing, and can be reasonably employed by the client if she is to be successful in promoting abstinence. When the mental health therapist encounters substance dependency, she must be prepared to deal with abstinence issues that will arise in treatment, such as withdrawal, cravings, and denial of the disorder, and be willing not to interfere with natural legal, financial, social, or non-life-threatening physical consequences of use.

## *MOOD DISORDERS*

Mood disorders are the most common Axis I disorders that co-occur with substance use disorders. These include major depressive disorder, dysthymia, bipolar disorder, and cyclothymia. Thirty-two to 41 percent of individuals in the general population with these disorders has been found to have a co-occurring substance use disorder (Kessler et al., 1994 and Regier et al., 1990). Individuals with bipolar disorder have the highest rate of co-occurrence (56 to 71 percent), and roughly one-third of individuals with major depressive disorder and dysthymia have co-occurrence rates of 27 to 41 percent and 31 to 40 percent, respectively. Cyclothymia was not examined in either study. Studies of substance abuse treatment programs found that 34 to 60 percent of clients had a co-occurring mood disorder (Khantzian and Treece, 1985; Ross, Glaser, and Germanson, 1988; Rounsaville et al., 1982). Studies of mental health programs have found co-occurrence rates of 24 to 60 percent (Lambert, Griffith, and Hendricksen; 1996; Schuckit, 1983). The following section includes a description of these disorders, their diagnostic criteria, and treatment issues that mental health and substance abuse therapists face when treating clients with these co-occurring disorders.

## Major Depressive Disorder

Major depressive disorder has a lifetime prevalence rate in the general population that ranges from a low of 5 percent for men and a high of 25 percent for women. Women are diagnosed two to three times more often with this disorder than are men. Although this disorder can begin at any age, the average age of onset is in the mid-twenties. Major depressive disorder also appears to have a strong genetic basis, as it is up to three times more common in individuals who have first-degree biological relatives with this disorder. The more depressive episodes individuals have, the more likely it is that they will experience additional episodes.

Nine criteria are listed for this disorder in the DSM-IV-TR: feeling depressed most of the day nearly every day; inability to experience pleasure from pleasurable events; marked weight loss or gain; inability to sleep or sleeping too much; increased (agitation) or significantly reduced physical activity; low energy levels nearly every day; feeling worthless or inappropriately guilty; difficulty concentrating or making decisions; and recurrent thoughts of death or suicide. At least five of these symptoms must be present for a two-week period to constitute a diagnosis of this disorder.

## Dysthymic Disorder

Dysthymic disorder has a lifetime prevalence in the general population of about 0.6 percent and is diagnosed equally in both women and men. Dysthymia often has an early onset—in childhood, adolescence, or early adulthood—and it often co-occurs with major depressive disorder. The disorder is more common in individuals with first-degree biological relatives who have either major depressive disorder or dysthymic disorder. Individuals who experience dysthymia prior to the onset of major depressive disorder often continue that level of mood impairment between major depressive episodes.

The six criteria for this disorder in the DSM-IV-TR are poor appetite or overeating; sleeping too little or too much; low energy or fatigue; low self-esteem; poor concentration or difficulty making decisions; and feelings of hopelessness. To diagnosis this disorder at least two of these symptoms must persist most of the day over a two-year period and the symptoms cannot be absent for more than a two-month period. For children and adolescents the mood can appear as irritability, and symptoms need only be present for a one-year period.

### Bipolar Disorders

Two categories constitute bipolar disorder, formerly called manic-depressive illness. Individuals with bipolar I disorder experience full manic episodes and individuals with bipolar II disorder experience a hypomanic episode, that is, the symptoms are similar to a manic episode but not severe enough to result in impairment or hospitalization. The lifetime prevalence in the general population for bipolar I disorder is from 0.4 to 1.6 percent, and for bipolar II the prevalence rate is approximately 0.5 percent. Bipolar I disorder is diagnosed equally in women and men, while bipolar II is diagnosed more frequently in women. The average age of onset for bipolar I disorder is twenty; within five years, 5 to 15 percent of individuals with bipolar II disorder will experience a full manic episode. Both disorders are more common in individuals with first-degree biological relatives who have major depressive disorder or bipolar I or II disorders.

The symptoms of a manic episode are: inflated sense of self; decreased sleep; more talkative than normal with pressured speech; moving quickly from one idea to another (clients often report it as racing thoughts); easily distracted or unable to stay focused; increased activities or movement; and excessive involvement in pleasurable activities that have a high potential for harm (such as spending money or sex). To diagnose a manic episode, at least three of these symptoms must be present for at least a week. Individuals with bipolar I disorder experience at least one manic episode, with most also experiencing a major depressive episode. Individuals with bipolar II disorder experience major depressive episodes and at least one hypomanic episode.

### Cyclothymic Disorder

Cyclothymic disorder has a lifetime prevalence rate in the general population that ranges from 0.4 to 1 percent. Women and men are equally diagnosed with this disorder, with onset usually in adolescence or early adulthood. The disorder is more common in individuals who have first-degree biological relatives with bipolar I disorder.

Individuals with cyclothymic disorder have an increased risk of developing bipolar I disorder.

This disorder manifests itself as chronic fluctuating periods of depressive and hypomanic symptoms, with neither set of symptoms severe enough to allow for a diagnosis of a major depressive or manic episode. The key for diagnosing this disorder is identifying numerous periods of depressive and hypomanic symptoms that are never absent for more than two months over a two-year period for adults and a one-year period for children and adolescents.

### Treatment Implications

The high co-occurrence of substance use and mood disorders should not be surprising since alcohol and other drugs alter mood. Individuals with mood disturbances will naturally be drawn toward substances that can at least temporarily relieve some of their symptoms. Kessler et al. (1994) found that 89 percent of individuals in the general population who had co-occurring mood and substance use disorders reported that the symptoms of the mood disorder predated the symptoms of the substance use disorder. Thus substance abuse and mental health therapists may have a client with a bipolar disorder who uses alcohol to reduce manic symptoms, or a client with dysthymia who uses cocaine to reduce feelings of depression. Of course, these substances will ultimately make the mood disorders worse because the withdrawal effects of alcohol or cocaine are the same as the symptoms of the disorders (depression is a withdrawal symptom of cocaine) and will intensify a client's discomfort. The client, of course, will ignore the long-term consequences in order to get some immediate relief from the symptoms of the mood disorder.

Thus to help individuals with co-occurring mood disorders achieve the treatment goal of abstinence, therapists must help them to more effectively manage their mood disturbances. Most persons with mood and substance use disorders find it very difficult to maintain abstinence when mood disorder symptoms are present for extended periods of time (Hasin et al., 1993). Treatment for mood disorders usually involves, in addition to talk therapy, the use of a mood-regulating medication. Thus the substance abuse therapist, in addition to providing traditional substance abuse treatment interventions, will also promote medication compliance. To do so, the client needs to acknowledge the mood disorder that needs such treatment and understand what medication can and cannot do. Individuals with long-term substance abuse histories often initially find mood-regulating medications ineffective. These individuals are used to substances, such as alcohol or cocaine, inducing an immediate and significant altered state. Medications, on the other hand, can require up to several weeks to reach a therapeutic level. Since their purpose is to normalize mood, during the early days and weeks of use the individual who is used to instant gratification feels no change. He therefore concludes that the medication is not working. Mental health and substance abuse therapists need to educate their clients about what to expect when they begin using mood-regulating medications and help clients make the connection that a decrease in their psychiatric symptoms and substance cravings is related to the effects of their medication.

## ANXIETY DISORDERS

Although not as common as mood disorders, a significant number of individuals with anxiety disorders have a co-occurring substance use disorder. Twenty-four to 38 percent of individuals with anxiety disorders in the general population have been found to have a substance use disorder (Kessler et al., 1994 and Regier et al., 1990). The most common anxiety disorders that occur with substance use disorders are post-traumatic stress disorder, panic disorder, social phobia, obsessive-compulsive disorder, and generalized anxiety disorder. Rates for these disorders range from 23 to 45 percent, with post-traumatic stress disorder having the highest rate and social phobia the least. Studies of substance abuse treatment programs found that 29 to 62 percent of clients have co-occurring anxiety disorders (Ross, Glaser, and Germanson, 1988; Wallace, 1986; Weiss and Rosenburg, 1985).

### Post-Traumatic Stress Disorder (PTSD)

Post-traumatic stress disorder (PTSD) has a lifetime prevalence rate in the general population of approximately 8 percent and is more common in women than men. The disorder can occur at any age following a traumatic event (such as witnessing a violent death). The symptoms usually occur within three months of the event but occasionally do not manifest themselves until years later. The intensity of the symptoms usually varies over time. Individuals with first-degree biological relatives that have depressive disorders have greater rates of PTSD.

Three key processes are present with this disorder. First, the traumatic event is persistently reexperienced in at least one of five ways: as intrusive images or thoughts; dreams; reliving the experience in feelings or actions; intense psychological distress resulting from seeing, hearing, or smelling something that reminds the individual of the event; or a physiological response to similar environmental cues. The second process involves attempts to avoid situations that remind the individual of the traumatic event. This needs to occur in at least three of seven ways: not talking about or suppressing feelings about the event; not going to places similar to where the event occurred; not being able to remember the event; a marked decreased participation in outside activities; feeling detached from others; restricted feelings; and having a sense of a foreshortened future. The third process involves an increase in the arousal state, as evidenced by two of five symptoms: difficulty falling or staying asleep; outbursts of anger; difficulty concentrating; hypervigilance; and an exaggerated startle response.

### Panic Disorder

Panic disorder can be present with agoraphobia (the fear of public places) or without agoraphobia, but always includes a panic attack. With a lifetime prevalence rate in the general population in most studies of 2 to 4 percent, its normal onset is in adolescence, although it can develop as late as the mid-thirties. The disorder is normally chronic but the frequency and intensity of symptoms vary among individuals. Some individuals have frequent attacks while others may have significant periods of time between episodes. Panic disorder is eight times more frequent in individuals who have a first-degree relative with this disorder.

The thirteen symptoms listed for a panic attack in the DSM-IV-TR are: accelerated heart rate; sweating; trembling; shortness of breath; a feeling of choking; chest pain; nausea; feeling dizzy; a feeling of unreality; fear of going crazy; fear of dying; feelings of numbness; and chills or hot flushes. The key for making a diagnosis of a panic disorder is that at least four of these symptoms develop abruptly and reach a peak within ten minutes.

### Social Phobia

Studies concerning the lifetime prevalence rate of social phobia disorder in the general population have found rates that range from 3 to 13 percent. It is more common in women than men and its onset is usually during adolescence. The symptoms of this disorder are usually lifelong but their intensity often changes over time. Life changes, such as a job that requires public speaking or an increase in meeting strangers, can increase the symptoms. The disorder is more frequent in individuals with first-degree biological relatives who also have social phobia.

Social phobia is the presence of a marked and persistent fear in one or more types of social situations (such as public speaking). Individuals with this disorder fear that their actions will be humiliating or embarrassing. The affected individuals realize that their fear is unreasonable and either attempt to avoid problematic situations or endure them with intense anxiety. For individuals under age eighteen, the symptoms must persist at least six months before a diagnosis can be made.

### Obsessive-Compulsive Disorder

Obsessive-compulsive disorder has a lifetime prevalence rate in the general population of approximately 2.5 percent. Its onset is usually during adolescence or early adulthood. In adulthood, men and women are diagnosed with this disorder at approximately the same rate, but males are more commonly diagnosed during adolescence. The symptoms are usually lifelong, steadily progressing for some individuals, while others have only episodic symptoms. The disorder occurs more often in individuals who have first-degree biological relatives with the disorder.

Obsessive-compulsive disorder manifests itself through either obsessions or compulsions. *Obsessions* are recurrent and persistent thoughts or impulses that cause anxiety and are not representative of real-life worries. Individuals try to ignore or suppress these thoughts and recognize that the thoughts are not a product of an intentional conscious process. *Compulsions* are repetitive behaviors (e.g., hand washing) or mental activities (e.g., counting) that an individual feels driven to do, are clearly seen as excessive, and are aimed at reducing distress or preventing a dreaded but unrealistic event. These activities also take more than an hour per day and interfere with social functioning.

### Generalized Anxiety Disorder

Generalized anxiety disorder has a lifetime prevalence rate in the general population of approximately 5 percent and is diagnosed in slightly higher rates in women than men. In most cases, the disorder begins in childhood or adolescence, although sometimes not until after the age of twenty. Its symptoms increase and decrease over time, but usually intensify during times of stress. Although the genetic origin of this disorder is unclear, anxiety is commonly observed in identical twins (rather than in just one twin) and in individuals who have a first-degree biological relative with major depressive disorder.

The DSM-IV-TR lists six symptoms for this disorder: feeling keyed up or on edge; easily fatigued; difficulty concentrating; irritability; muscle tension; and difficulty getting or staying asleep. To make a diagnosis of generalized anxiety disorder, at least three of these symptoms must be present more days than not for at least six months.

### Treatment Implications

Many individuals with anxiety disorders turn to drugs with sedative qualities such as alcohol, tranquilizers, or marijuana to help reduce their anxiety. Thus the substance abuse therapist will find that many clients smoke marijuana daily as a means to control their anxiety or binge drink periodically to deal with the return of anxiety symptoms. As with mood disorders, these substances help initially to reduce the symptoms of the disorder, but ultimately make them worse because of the withdrawal effects.

A common problem in treating individuals with co-occurring anxiety disorders is that almost all the medications that can effectively control the symptoms of these disorders also have high abuse potential. The Center for Substance Abuse Treatment (CSAT) (1994a), recommends a three-step approach to medication. The first step involves the use of nonmedication treatment techniques such as therapy, biofeedback, or acupuncture. If that does not work, the second step involves prescribing a medication with low abuse potential; only the third step involves the use of medication with a high abuse potential. Thus in treating clients with a co-occurring anxiety disorder, the therapist's approach is to first help the client recognize that the anxiety comes from an anxiety disorder that needs special treatment and is made worse by continued drug use. He then needs to help his client develop some behavioral techniques (such as breathing exercises) that help modulate some of the more severe symptoms and explore the use of medication with a low abuse potential.

Should these methods fail and the client is unable to maintain abstinence because of the anxiety symptoms, the therapist needs to develop, jointly with a doctor, a treatment plan that includes a medication of potential abuse, but also includes safeguards that reduce the risk of abuse. Safeguards include a demonstrated commitment of self-discipline on the part of the client to use these medications as prescribed and a limited access to the medication. Clients can demonstrate self-discipline by maintaining abstinence for thirty days even with symptoms of anxiety, the continued use as prescribed of an antianxiety medication with low potential of abuse even if it is perceived as not being helpful, or using a medication of high abuse potential as prescribed while having urine screening to confirm abstinence from other drugs. These and other methods used to confirm self-discipline must be matched with a realistic assessment of the client's ability to accomplish them. One client might have already demonstrated self-discipline in a variety of ways in treatment and is so understanding of her disorders that she can be realistically expected to use the medication appropriately with little monitoring. Another client might have demonstrated little impulse control and have difficulty tolerating any discomfort; she would need to demonstrate the ability to self-regulate a drug appropriately prior to being prescribed this type of medication. The key for the therapist is to identify the right type of intervention so that the client can be successful in demonstrating self-discipline. Regardless of the type of client, these medications need to be prescribed in a very controlled manner for an extended period of time. Some clients may be given medication only for a few days at a time while another might be given a prescription for thirty days. If the client claims to lose the medication or admits to abusing it, the therapist would need to discuss these issues and assess if additional medication should be prescribed, but ensure that no medication is taken until the next scheduled dose. Therapists working with clients with anxiety and co-occurring substance use disorders have to continuously compare the risk of medication abuse with the ability of an individual to maintain abstinence while anxiety symptoms persist.

## PSYCHOTIC DISORDERS

A significant number of individuals with psychotic disorders also have co-occurring substance use disorders. In the general population, research has found that 47 percent of individuals with these disorders have a co-occurring substance use disorder (Regier et al., 1990). Although the intensity of their mental disorder often excludes them from traditional substance abuse treatment programs, these individuals are two to four times more likely to be in these programs than would be expected based on the frequency of occurrence of psychotic disorders in the general population (Hesselbrock, Meyer, and Keener, 1985; Powell et al., 1982; Ross, Glaser, and Germanson, 1988). In addition, mental health professionals who traditionally work with this population report that 30 to 54 percent of their clients with these disorders have co-occurring substance use disorders (Damron and Simpson, 1985; Drake and Wallach, 1989). The two most common psychotic disorders that occur with substance use disorders are schizophrenia and schizoaffective disorder.

### Schizophrenia

Schizophrenia has a lifetime prevalence rate in the general population that ranges from 0.5 to 1.5 percent. The onset is usually in late adolescence to the mid-thirties, and is often diagnosed earlier in men than women. The symptoms of this illness are usually lifelong. For some individuals, symptoms increase with age and for others symptoms remain steady throughout their lives. Individuals with first-degree relatives with schizophrenia are ten times more likely to develop this disorder. There are five subtypes of this disorder. The three that most commonly co-occur with substance use disorders are paranoid type, undifferentiated type, and residual type.

This disorder's symptoms, as listed in the DSM-IV-TR, are often referred to as positive (productive) or negative (deficit) symptoms. The positive symptoms are delusions (e.g., an individual believes that he is a CIA agent or believes that helicopters are following him), hallucinations (most commonly, hearing voices), disorganized speech (e.g., each sentence may make sense but when several are put together there is no coherent thought), and disorganized or catatonic behavior (e.g., staying in one fixed posture). Negative symptoms include little expressed feeling, having few thoughts expressed as words, low motivation, poor grooming, social withdrawal, and cognitive defects. The key for making a diagnosis of schizophrenia is that at least two of these symptoms are present for a significant portion of time during a one-month period. Individuals with schizophrenia (paranoid type) have delusions and/or auditory hallucinations that are usually persecutory or grandiose in nature. Individuals with schizophrenia (undifferentiated type) experience psychotic symptoms but are not paranoid, disorganized, or catatonic, while individuals with schizophrenia (residual type) do not have prominent delusions, hallucinations, disorganized speech, or grossly disorganized behavior, but rather continue to evidence negative symptoms.

### Schizoaffective Disorder

The lifetime prevalence rate of schizoaffective disorder is not currently known; however, it appears to be less common than schizophrenia. The usual onset of schizoaffective disorder is in early adulthood, with the symptoms usually persisting through an individual's lifetime. The disorder is more commonly diagnosed in women than in men. The two subtypes of this disorder are bipolar type, which includes a manic episode and often a major depressive episode, and depressive type, which includes a major depressive episode. Individuals with relatives with this disorder are at increased risk of developing schizophrenia or mood disorders.

Diagnosis of schizoaffective disorder requires that the symptoms of schizophrenia be present during either a major depressive and/or a manic episode. In addition, the individual needs to have delusions or hallucinations for at least two weeks when a major mood episode is not present. Essentially, this disorder is a combination of symptoms of major mood disorders and schizophrenia that are present together at times, and not at other times. However, the symptoms of schizo-phrenia are present most of the time.

## Treatment Implications

The use of alcohol and other drugs can significantly increase the symptoms of psychotic disorders while greatly reducing the effec-tiveness of the antipsychotic medications. Even small amounts of al-cohol and other drugs can destabilize some individuals with these disorders and result in hospitalization. Individuals with psychotic disorders may use alcohol and other drugs to temporarily mute symp-toms, such as hearing voices, or as a means to connect with a peer group, which otherwise would not be available to them because of their odd behaviors. Individuals with schizoaffective disorder may use these substances to help manage their mood disturbances. Although the mental health therapist encounters more individuals with co-occurring psychotic and substance use disorders than the substance abuse therapist, he too must be prepared to assess and provide treat-ment to individuals with psychotic disorders.

Because individuals with these disorders are often excluded from traditional substance abuse treatment settings, the substance abuse therapist usually encounters individuals who have just recently devel-oped psychotic symptoms and who have not yet been diagnosed with them. If the symptoms have been identified, the client, his family, or the intake therapist may have attributed them to the substance use. For the substance abuse therapist to effectively treat this client, he must have access to psychiatric assessment and medication services. If the assessment identifies a psychotic disorder, medication would be necessary and the substance abuse therapist would have to help the client work through any denial that he or his family may have con-cerning the psychotic disorder, and work to promote medication compliance. Moreover, depending on the client's level of impair-ment, the substance abuse therapist must decide which treatment groups his client can participate in and what level of individual treat-ment or case management the client needs (see Chapters 6 and 7 for a detailed discussion of these issues).

## DISRUPTIVE BEHAVIOR DISORDERS

Disruptive behavior disorders normally begin in childhood or early adolescence; young persons with disruptive behavior disorders develop substance use disorders at much higher rates than those without. The three disorders of this category that have significant rates of co-occurrence with substance use disorders are attention-deficit hyperactivity disorder, conduct disorder, and oppositional defiant disorder. Kessler et al. (1994) found that approximately 60 percent of individuals with conduct disorder in the general population had a co-occurring substance use disorder. Neither attention-deficit hyperactivity nor oppositional defiant disorder was studied for co-occurrence with substance use disorder in the large studies of the general population. However, studies of clinical populations have found significant rates of all three of these disorders co-occurring with substance use disorders. Carroll and Rounsaville (1993) found that 35 percent of adult cocaine abusers seeking treatment had co-occurring attention-deficit hyperactivity disorder. Wilens et al. (1994), in their review of literature concerning the co-occurrence of substance use and attention-deficit hyperactivity disorders, found a 24 percent mean co-occurrence rate in the individuals in the studies' samples, while Caton et al. (1989) reported that 67 percent of the clients in an inpatient psychiatric facility with a diagnosis of conduct disorder also had a co-occurring substance use disorder.

### Attention-Deficit Hyperactivity Disorder (ADHD)

Attention-deficit hyperactivity disorder occurs, estimates report, in 3 to 7 percent of school-age children. ADHD is diagnosed more frequently in males than females and usually is first diagnosed in elementary school. Its symptoms normally decline in late adolescence, though some individuals experience all or some symptoms into early adulthood. Individuals with ADHD are more likely to have first-degree biological relatives with this disorder.

The symptoms fall into the categories of inattention or hyperactivity-impulsivity. An individual might have the symptoms of one of these or enough symptoms for a diagnosis of both conditions. The nine criteria for inattention in the DSM-IV-TR, of which six are required for a diagnosis, are: failure to pay close attention to details; difficulty sustaining attention; seeming not to listen when spoken to;

failing to finish tasks; difficulty organizing tasks; avoiding engaging in tasks requiring sustained mental activity; losing things necessary for a task; being easily distracted, and forgetful. The nine symptoms for hyperactivity-impulsivity, of which six are required for a diagnosis, are: fidgeting and squirming; leaving one's seat when being seated is expected; running and climbing excessively; difficulty playing quietly; acting as if driven by a motor; talking excessively; blurting out answers before questions are completed; difficulty awaiting one's turn; and interrupting or intruding on others. For a diagnosis of ADHD, an individual must have six symptoms for each disorder. In addition, for both disorders, symptom onset must be before the age of seven and persist for at least six months.

### Conduct Disorder

Lifetime prevalence rates of conduct disorder in the general population range from 1 to 10 percent, and it is more commonly diagnosed in males than females. Onset can occur as early as preschool; however it is most commonly first noticed between middle childhood and middle adolescence. Onset is rare after age sixteen. The vast majority of individuals who develop this disorder after age ten become well-adjusted adults though some will meet the diagnostic criteria for antisocial personality disorder (see Chapter 4). If onset is before age ten, the likelihood of meeting the criteria for antisocial personality disorder increases. Both genetic and environmental factors appear to influence the development of conduct disorder.

The fifteen symptoms of this disorder are categorized into four major categories in the DSM-IV-TR: (1) aggression to people and animals (e.g., bullies, initiates fights, uses a weapon, is cruel to people or animals, uses force to steal something, or forces sexual activity); (2) destruction of property (e.g., deliberate fire setting or destruction of property); (3) deceitfulness or theft (e.g., breaking into property, lying to obtain something, or shoplifting or forgery); and (4) serious violations of rules (staying out late without parental permission before age thirteen, has run away at least twice, or is often truant before age thirteen). At least three of these symptoms in the past twelve months are needed for a diagnosis and at least one symptom must be present during the past six months. In addition, the diagnosis of this disorder can only be given to an individual over the age of eighteen who does not meet the criteria for antisocial personality disorder.

## Oppositional Defiant Disorder

The lifetime prevalence rates of oppositional defiant disorder in the general population range from 2 to 16 percent. It is diagnosed more frequently in males before puberty but about equally between males and females after puberty. Onset is often before age eight and seldom occurs after early adolescence. The onset is usually gradual and may take years to fully develop. Some children with this disorder later develop conduct disorder but the majority does not. Like conduct disorder, both genetic and environmental factors appear to promote its development.

The eight symptoms of this disorder in the DSM-IV-TR are: often loses temper; often argues with adults; defies or refuses to comply with adults; deliberately annoys people; blames others for mistakes or misbehavior; easily annoyed by others; often angry and resentful; or often spiteful or vindictive. For a diagnosis, at least four symptoms must be present during a six-month period. If the individual meets the criteria for conduct disorder or antisocial personality disorder the diagnosis of oppositional defiant disorder cannot be made.

## Treatment Implications

Alcohol and drug use is common among young persons whose behaviors are associated with conduct or oppositional defiant disorders. In some ways alcohol and other drug use is considered a norm among peer groups who choose not to follow societal norms. Young persons with ADHD often turn to substance use as a way to reduce some of their hyperactivity symptoms or as an escape from the discomfort of doing poorly in school. Both substance abuse and mental health therapists, if they work with adolescents or young adults, find that a significant number of their clients have these disorders co-occurring with substance use.

The most important focus of the mental health and substance abuse therapists' interventions with individuals with these disorders is setting clear treatment expectations and boundaries. Individuals with either conduct or oppositional defiant disorder will consciously attempt to break the rules of treatment, and those with ADHD also will break the rules because of impulsivity or lack of attention. Regardless of the client's intention, substance abuse and mental health therapists must set clear rules and, if the rules are broken, enforce consequences immediately if they are to create a successful treatment setting for clients who have disruptive behavior disorders.

Medication can be effective in reducing the symptoms of ADHD; however it does have an abuse potential, though individuals with ADHD who find medication helpful usually don't abuse it. In addition to medication compliance, however, mental health and substance abuse therapists also have to monitor whether their clients are giving or selling their medication to others. Medication normally does not play a significant role in the treatment of conduct disorder and oppositional defiant disorders.

### DISSOCIATIVE DISORDERS

Although dissociative disorders affect only a small portion of the general population, two have significant rates of co-occurrence with substance use disorders: dissociative identity disorder (multiple personality disorder) and depersonalization disorder. The co-occurrence of dissociative disorders with substance use disorders was not part of the two large studies of the general population, the ECA and NCS; however several studies of treatment populations have found significant rates of co-occurrence. Dunn et al. (1995) reported that 18 percent of clients in an inpatient substance abuse treatment program met the diagnostic criteria for a dissociative disorder. Ross, Kronson, and Koensgen (1992) found that 39 percent of a substance abuse treatment population met the diagnostic criteria for a dissociative disorder and 14 percent met the diagnostic criteria for dissociative identity disorder. Hutzell and Eggert (1990) reported that 2 percent of a substance abuse treatment population met the diagnostic criteria for dissociative identity disorder. In a study of individuals recently detoxified from alcohol and other drugs, Wenzel et al. (1996) found high dissociation scores and speculate that dissociation might have been a residual effect of their substance use.

### Dissociative Identity Disorder

No definitive research estimates the lifetime prevalence rate of dissociative identity disorder in the general population, although researchers find it much more commonly diagnosed in women than men. Little is known about its normal range of onset, however, it is estimated that approximately six to seven years pass between its onset and its diagnosis. Its symptoms appear to manifest themselves less after individuals move into their late forties, although substance abuse or uncommon stress can aggravate symptoms. Several studies report that individuals with this disorder are more likely than the general population to have first-degree biological relatives with the disorder.

The DSM-IV-TR notes three symptoms for this disorder: the presence of two or more distinct identities in the same person; the ability for at least two of these identities or personalities to take control of behavior; and the inability to recall important personal information that is too extensive to be explained by ordinary forgetfulness. For a diagnosis, all three symptoms must be present and not caused by either substance use or a general medical condition.

### Depersonalization Disorder

As with dissociative identity disorder, no definitive research estimates the lifetime prevalence rate of depersonalization disorder in the general population. Diagnosed twice as often in women than men, the disorder appears to develop, on average, at age sixteen, although onset can occur in childhood and adulthood. The symptoms of this disorder can last for seconds or years and may wax or wane or occur episodically although they usually persist through a lifetime. Little is known concerning family patterns of this disorder.

The symptoms listed in the DSM-IV-TR are: persistent experiences of feeling detached from one's own mental processes or body; and during these episodes an individual's ability to determine what is real and what is not real remains intact. Many individuals have had one or two of these experiences in their lives, especially after a traumatic or stressful event. For a diagnosis, however, this experience must recur regularly and cause the individual ongoing difficulties.

## Treatment Implications

Individuals with dissociative identity disorder may find that some personalities use alcohol and other drugs while others do not. Because some personalities are unaware of others, the client may test positive for drugs but deny use and actually have no memory of the drug use. Although clients with other mental disorders may intentionally attempt to conceal substance use from the therapist, this may not be the case for a client with dissociative identity disorder. Clients with depersonalization disorder may use alcohol and other drugs to help manage the discomfort from the symptoms they experience. Medication traditionally plays a small part in the treatment of these disorders.

## EATING DISORDERS

Eating disorders that co-occur with substance abuse are bulimia nervosa and anorexia nervosa. Both involve excessive concern with weight and body image. Neither was examined in either of the two large studies of the general population; however several studies of treatment populations have found significant rates of co-occurrence of substance use and eating disorders. Bulik (1987) found that more than 60 percent of clients with bulimia nervosa had either an alcohol or drug use diagnosis; Jonas et al. (1987) found that 22 percent of cocaine abusers calling a hotline met the criteria for bulimia nervosa; and Holderness, Brooks-Gunn, and Warren (1994), in their review of studies examining this co-occurrence, found a median rate of 26 percent. Herzog, Nussbaum, and Marmor (1996), in their review of studies examining the co-occurrence of anorexia nervosa and substance use disorders, reported rates ranging from 12 to 21 percent.

### Anorexia Nervosa

This disorder has a lifetime prevalence rate in the general population of less than 1 percent but it is ten times more common in women than men. The disorder normally develops in mid- to late adolescence and rarely occurs after age forty. The course of the disorder varies greatly among individuals. Some individuals have only one episode while others experience symptoms in varying degrees for years. Individuals with anorexia nervosa are more likely to have first-degree biological relatives with this disorder or with a mood disorder.

The four criteria listed for this disorder in the DSM-IV-TR are: refusal to maintain normal body weight (less than 85 percent of expected weight for age and height); fear of becoming fat although underweight; undue emphasis on body weight and self-worth combined with denial of the seriousness of the low body weight; and missing at least three consecutive menstrual cycles if past puberty. All symptoms must be present for a diagnosis. There are two types of this disorder: the *restricting type* in which an individual maintains the low body weight by not eating, and the *binge-eating/purging type* in which an individual maintains low body weight by self-induced vomiting or the misuse of laxatives, diuretics, or enemas.

### Bulimia Nervosa

The lifetime prevalence rate of bulimia nervosa in the general population is from 1 to 3 percent. Most studies find that at least 90 percent of individuals with this disorder, which usually has an onset in late adolescence or early adulthood, are women. For some individuals the symptoms persist but usually diminish over time; for others the symptoms are intermittent. Several studies find that individuals with bulimia are more likely to have first-degree relatives with this disorder, mood disorders, and substance use disorders than individuals who do not develop this disorder.

The diagnostic criteria for bulimia nervosa in the DSM-IV-TR are: recurrent episodes of compulsively eating a significant amount of food in a short period of time and feeling a lack of control during the episode; use of self-induced vomiting, laxatives, diuretics, enemas, fasting, or excessive exercise to prevent weight gain; binge-eating episodes at least twice a week for three months; self-worth unduly influenced by body shape or weight; and these activities do not occur exclusively during episodes of anorexia nervosa. All of these symptoms must be present for a diagnosis.

### Treatment Implications

Individuals with these disorders often abuse substances, especially stimulants, but also over-the-counter appetite suppression aids and laxatives, to promote weight loss or to suppress appetite. Thus substance abuse and mental health therapists must assess and monitor for the abuse of both prescribed and nonprescribed medications when working with individuals with these disorders. They also may find that the symptoms lay dormant or occur only infrequently when their clients are experiencing the full symptoms of a substance dependency disorder. However, when clients achieve abstinence these symptoms often recur in full force as the result of having to deal with the stress of early recovery. Therapists may find that a client with bulimia nervosa will use her ability to purge as a method of reducing the effectiveness of Antabuse therapy. Mental health and substance abuse therapists also must carefully monitor the impact of substance use on already compromised body systems of individuals with these disorders and move quickly toward hospitalization when necessary. As with dissociative disorders, medication traditionally plays a small part in the treatment of eating disorders.

## IMPULSE CONTROL DISORDERS

Only one of the impulse control disorders, pathological gambling, tends to significantly co-occur with substance use disorders. Its level of co-occurrence with substance use disorders has not been studied in the general population but studies of treatment populations find significant rates. Castellani et al. (1996) found that 14 percent of homeless veterans with substance abuse problems had co-occurring pathological gambling disorder; Rupcich, Frisch, and Govoni (1997) reported in a study of clients in substance abuse treatment facilities that 14 percent were probable pathological gamblers and an additional 11 percent reported gambling problems.

### Pathological Gambling

The lifetime prevalence rate of pathological gambling disorder in the general population ranges from 0.4 to 3.4 percent, with men more commonly diagnosed than women. Onset normally occurs in early adolescence in males and in later life for females. One may socially gamble for years before the disorder actually develops. The symptoms, which may be episodic or occur regularly and which may intensify during periods of depression or stress, usually persist throughout an individual's lifetime. Individuals who pathologically gamble are more likely to have parents with this disorder.

The DSM-IV-TR lists ten symptoms of this disorder: preoccupation with gambling; need to increase amounts gambled; repeated unsuccessful efforts to control gambling behavior; restless or irritable mood when attempting to reduce gambling activities; use of gambling to improve mood or avoid problems; returning the next day to get even after losses; lying to others about gambling activities; participating in illegal activities to get money for gambling; jeopardizing significant relationships to continue gambling; or relying on others to help with financial difficulties caused by gambling. At least five of these symptoms are required for a diagnosis.

### Treatment Implications

An environment that includes alcohol and other drug use is common in situations in which pathological gambling occurs. In addition, the use of such substances impairs judgment and reduces impulse control and thus can reduce the ability of a client to successfully manage his symptoms. The characteristics of this disorder are very similar to substance dependency disorders and many of the treatment approaches are similar, especially the technique of avoiding people, places, and things that are associated with the disorder. Currently, medications play a small role in its treatment. During intake assessments, mental health and substance abuse therapists seldom ask about the symptoms of this disorder. Therapists need to include questions about pathological gambling when they conduct intake assessments and monitor for the disorder's symptoms during the treatment process.

## CONCLUSION

Nineteen Axis I mental disorders frequently co-occur with substance use disorders. Thus the substance abuse therapist must be knowledgeable about how to assess and treat these disorders and how they may affect substance use disorders, while the mental health therapist must assess for, and when necessary, treat substance use behaviors and understand how substance use can affect psychiatric symptoms. The next chapter will discuss the co-occurrence of substance use disorders and personality disorders, which are coded on Axis II of the DSM-IV-TR diagnostic scheme.

# Chapter 4

# Personality Disorders That Frequently Co-Occur with Substance Use Disorders

Individuals with a personality disorder and a substance use disorder can be among the most challenging clients. Even individuals with severe mental illness can have a co-occurring personality disorder that compromises the recovery from their substance use disorder more directly than does the Axis I disorder. In one staff meeting, a man who was diagnosed with schizoaffective and alcohol dependence disorders was described as stable in his psychiatric symptoms and abstinent from alcohol. Yet he was still making impulsive and extremely poor decisions about relationships, supportive employment, and housing. His decisions and behaviors, which were putting him at risk for relapse and for increased psychiatric symptoms, were consistent with the characteristics of borderline personality disorder. Personality disorders often only come to light during the course of treatment but must be vigorously addressed when diagnosed if long-term stability is to be achieved.

## *PERSONALITY DISORDERS: DEFINITION*

Personality disorders are diagnosed when personality traits are inflexible, maladaptive, and cause impaired functioning across a wide range of personal and social situations. Individuals with a personality disorder are locked into long-standing cognitive, affective, interpersonal, and impulse control patterns that lead to repeated antagonistic, disruptive, and self-defeating experiences (DSM-IV-TR). Personality-disordered individuals have trouble responding flexibly and adaptively to the inevitable changes and demands of everyday life (Frances, First, and Pincus, 1995). Instead, they utilize maladaptive behaviors, called "survivor behaviors," that have helped them to survive in past situations (Ries, 1994).

Another way of looking at personality disorders is to view them as personality immaturity (Ryglewicz and Pepper, 1996). The diagnostic criteria for personality disorders refer mainly to behaviors, especially behaviors that annoy other people. If a three-year-old lies, gets frustrated easily, tests limits, and lives in the present with no thought to the past or future, we consider the behavior as normal for his age. However, when a twenty-five-year-old behaves this way, it is entirely inappropriate. Treatment for individuals with personality disorders involves helping them develop more age-appropriate behaviors.

Personality disorders are the extreme end of personality characteristics. Few individuals with substance use and mental disorders have no traits of a personality disorder. However, traits do not define a personality disorder. Chapter 5 discusses how some behaviors resulting from substance use look like personality disorders. Finally, individuals with severe trauma histories may also demonstrate behaviors that appear to be personality disorders, when in fact, they are the result of the trauma.

Estimates of the number of adults in the general population that have a personality disorder range from 10 to 18 percent (Benjamin, 1993; Gunderson and Gabbard, 2000). A personality disorder as defined by the DSM-IV-TR is an enduring pattern that deviates from individuals' culture in two or more of the following ways: cognition, affect, interpersonal functioning, and impulse control. *The International Statistical Classification of Diseases and Related Health Problems,* Tenth Revision (ICD-10) (World Health Organization, 1994) describes the same four areas but adds *need gratification* to the concept of impulse control. Cultural competence is a vital component in understanding personality disorders because behaviors in one culture may be deemed unacceptable and deviant while supported by another.

## *PERSONALITY DISORDERS AND CO-OCCURRING SUBSTANCE USE AND MENTAL DISORDERS*

Benjamin (1993) and Nace (1990) contend that more than half of the adults in mental health and substance abusing populations have personality disorders while Tyrer, Casey, and Ferguson (1988) cite studies indicating that 69 percent of individuals with alcohol dependence have personality disorders. They also note that 45 percent of individuals with schizophrenia have personality disorders. According to Nace (1990), the most severe levels of substance abuse are associated with character pathology rather than with serious mental illness. Individuals with a personality disorder are more vulnerable to substance abuse, experience greater benefit from the effects of drugs, and are more likely to abuse substances at an earlier age and use multiple substances with greater frequency than individuals without a personality disorder.

Beck et al. (1993) notes that when a personality disorder contributes to drug use, the pattern becomes more compulsive and rigid. Once the alcohol or other drug use begins, personality-disordered individuals are more likely to continue using and develop full-blown dependence. These individuals are also more vulnerable to relapse and have more difficulty working cooperatively and collaboratively with service providers. Richards (1993) views persistent dependence as related to failures in self-regulation. The most important mediator of self-regulation is the personality. Personality pathology leaves these individuals vulnerable to addiction as they substitute alcohol and other drugs for affect management, self-esteem, resilience, and adaptability.

The DSM-IV-TR divides personality disorders into three clusters. The symptoms in each cluster often overlap or are very similar. Thus a client with a personality disorder may also exhibit symptoms of other disorders in that cluster. Although any personality disorder might co-occur with a substance use disorder, the antisocial and borderline personality disorders in Cluster B are most common. The remainder of this chapter describes each of these personality disorders within its cluster and how these disorders can impact substance use and treatment.

## *CLUSTER B PERSONALITY DISORDERS*

Individuals with Cluster B personality disorders are characterized by their dramatic, emotional, or erratic behaviors (DSM-IV-TR). Four personality disorders fall in this category: antisocial, borderline, histrionic, and narcissistic personality disorders.

### Antisocial Personality Disorder (APD)

The essential feature of APD is pervasive disregard for, and violation of, the rights of others. These individuals fail to conform to social norms; they are often deceitful and manipulative for personal gain. They may be impulsive, fail to consider the possible consequences for their behavior, and tend to be extremely irresponsible and show little remorse for their actions. They are inclined to blame their victims for being foolish or deserving their fate. Individuals with APD lack empathy and have inflated views of themselves. They may have superficial charm but are easily incited to violence (DSM-IV-TR).

Usually, individuals with APD get treatment only after an encounter with the criminal justice system. Once in treatment, individuals with APD who understand the utility of changing behaviors that create legal problems may change. The prognosis is better for those who can experience anxiety, depression, or attachment. If individuals insist, on the other hand, that their problems are caused by other peoples' behaviors or expectations, the prognosis is substantially less optimistic.

Individuals with APD are specifically prone to substance abuse and addiction because of their need for a high level of stimulation (Richards, 1993). The co-occurrence of a substance use disorder with APD is very high. The NIMH epidemiological study found a co-occurrence of 84 percent (Regier et al., 1990); the National Comorbidity Survey found 79 percent (Kessler et al., 1994); and Black and Larson (1999) reported that up to 75 percent of individuals with APD show early and lasting symptoms of alcohol dependency, and as many as half abuse other drugs. Many individuals with APD engage in a polydrug pattern of use involving alcohol, marijuana, heroin, cocaine, and methamphetamines. The illegal drug culture is exciting to these individuals; it makes the world a fast-paced and dramatic place that enhances their self-image. Overall, individuals with APD tend to prefer stimulants, e.g., cocaine and amphetamines, when available (Ries, 1994).

The APD treatment service provider must be incorruptible. Many of these clients do not experience or understand empathy and do not experience gratitude or appreciation toward service providers. They use and manipulate others and take pleasure in any triumph over a clinician who wavers from the strict boundaries of professional ethics or the treatment contract. By being tough minded and exacting, clinicians can win the respect of clients with APD (McWilliams, 1994). To do this, the service provider must be uncompromisingly direct by being clear, straightforward, keeping promises, making good on any statements of negative consequences, and persistently addressing and identifying reality. To effectively treat the APD population, a clinician needs to be active, directly confront APD thinking patterns, attitudes, denial, or minimization of antisocial behaviors, and address specific illegal behavior. However, not all individuals with APD may be appropriately treated in a non-contained environment. This includes individuals who: have a history of sadistic and violent behavior, show absolutely no remorse, exhibit intelligence that is two standard deviations from the mean, have no history of attachments, and who intimidate experienced service providers (without overt intimidation from the individuals with APD) (Meloy 1996). Treatment needs to help these individuals learn to tolerate feelings and conflict without the use of substances, reduce regression and acting out, and develop adaptive behaviors to deal with frustration and impulse control. The philosophy of the twelve-step recovery model can also be helpful for developing responsibility for self, honesty in dealing with feelings, sensitivity to both the needs and the feelings of others, avoidance of impulsive actions, and the ability to tolerate stress and painful feelings (O'Malley, Kosten, and Renner, 1990).

### Borderline Personality Disorder (BPD)

The essential feature of borderline personality disorder is pervasive instability of interpersonal relationships, self-image, and affect. Individuals with BPD tend to be impulsive and to make frantic attempts to avoid real or imagined abandonment. Separation or rejection can lead to profound changes in self-image, affect, cognition, and behavior (DSM-IV-TR).

In treatment, individuals with BPD may show rage, intense moodiness, make extraordinary demands for attention, test behavior, and behave in self-damaging ways. They can provoke feelings of helplessness and rage in service providers who need regular supervision in order to deal therapeutically with these clients. No therapists are so experienced or talented that they do not need this supervision. In addition to therapists' monitoring their own feelings, Sperry (1995) also suggests that service providers be active in identifying, confronting, and directing client behaviors; maintain a stable treatment environment; and show BPD clients the connection between actions and feelings and how self-destructive behavior is ultimately ungratifying.

Millon (1996) notes that individuals with BPD exhibit drug-seeking behavior as they are particularly vulnerable to the escape offered by alcohol and other drugs. Real-world interaction triggers multiple interpersonal crises and overwhelming negative affects. Drugs can, ostensibly, offer relief from BPD turmoil and emptiness. Drugs offer a way of coping; they can block out sensations of pain, discomfort, or negative affect. These individuals will use almost any drug or route of administration to their own worst advantage. They often abuse prescribed medications which they may hoard for suicide attempts.

Another issue regarding drug use or abuse for individuals with BPD is related to their intolerance for being alone and the intensity of their relationships. These individuals often use drugs and alcohol as part of their needed contact with others and their drug of choice is related to whatever substance is used by their social contacts. Recovery in these situations will be dependent upon linking addicted clients with BPD to a strong support network that fosters abstinence.

Gunderson and Links (1996) offer five basic treatment principles for working with individuals with BPD:

1. Identify, confront, and treat co-occurring substance abuse disorders (individuals with BPD have an extraordinary risk for suicide when substance use disorders are untreated).
2. Learn to differentiate nonlethal self-harm from true suicidal intent.
3. Stress that treatment is a collaborative enterprise; service providers are neither omnipotent nor omniscient.
4. Manage countertransference.
5. Seek consultation. Do not provide service in isolation.

Linehan (1993a) states that clients in BPD treatment must learn how to modulate their emotions. This requires four major abilities: (1) Inhibiting inappropriate behavior related to strong negative or positive affect, (2) self-regulating physiological arousal associated with emotions, (3) refocusing attention in the presence of strong emotions, and (4) organizing self for action in the service of an external, nonmood-dependent goal. If alcohol and other drugs are given up, clinicians need to check for other compulsive behaviors that may be used as substitutes, e.g., compulsive sexual behavior, gambling, spending, and eating.

Treatment of co-occurring disorders for individuals with BPD must address the function of the substance while developing strong substitutes that can sustain recovery behaviors and abstinence. These substitutes include involvement in self-help groups, affect management, medication compliance, cognitive self-calming techniques, and daily contact with sponsors. The treatment modality of choice is group because it most effectively addresses transference issues and is compatible with fostering affect management techniques, life management skills, and recovery community involvement.

## Histrionic Personality Disorder (HPD)

The essential feature of histrionic personality disorder is pervasive and excessive emotionality and attention-seeking behavior. Individuals with HPD are uncomfortable if they are not the center of attention (DSM-IV-TR). Such individuals, because of their interpersonal skills and inclination to seek approval by pleasing others, may initially look like the proverbial "dream" clients. However, they are usually seeking relief from a crisis in their lives and the accompanying depression. Once the crisis is resolved the depression dissipates and their motivation for change wanes or disappears.

Individuals with HPD are prone to substance use disorders because they seek easy escape from pain, deny negative consequences, and fail to observe or accept responsibility for the impact of their behavior on others. For individuals with HPD, alcohol and other drugs serve as an alternative to behaving as an adult. They use drugs to self-soothe and as an alternative to facing life problems. Millon and Davis (1996) state that individuals with HPD may abuse because the substances can lower their inhibitions and allow them to act out in stimulus-seeking ways, and by disinhibiting control of their impulses, absolve them of personal responsibility or guilt for behavior.

Drugs of choice for these individuals not only include antianxiety agents and stimulants but also any drug that is fashionable within their social context. Peers can also influence these individuals in their choice of places and circumstances to use, route of administration, and even which treatment centers to attend. Drugs or alcohol may also play a significant role in their sexual and romantic behavior. Richards (1993) notes that individuals with HPD often demand special treatment. They are inclined to become star group members or problem children due to relapse. They may also, consciously or not, view service providers or their group and their drug(s) of choice as jealous lovers fighting over them and for their allegiance.

### Narcissistic Personality Disorder (NPD)

The essential feature of narcissistic personality disorder is pervasive grandiosity, need for admiration, and lack of empathy. Individuals with NPD routinely overestimate their abilities and inflate their accomplishments. They assume that others see them this same way and are surprised when the admiration they seek is not forthcoming. They are also inclined to undervalue the contributions or skills of others (DSM-IV-TR).

Individuals with NPD often enter treatment for depression and tend to perceive their difficulties as not related to their own behavior. Depression for these individuals is often precipitated by a crisis that punctures their narcissistic grandiosity and reflects the discrepancy between NPD expectations or fantasies and reality (Beck and Freeman, 1990). They resist reality-based feedback and may flee the treatment setting if they are not sufficiently affirmed and comforted with an inflated view of themselves. Over time, it is nearly impossible to avoid disappointing these clients because if service providers respond negatively to the NPD self-aggrandizing or arrogance, even nonverbally, these individuals perceive the criticism and experience it as rejection. NPD treatment needs to focus on increasing behavioral responsibility, decreasing cognitive distortions and dysfunctional affect, and developing new attitudes (Beck and Freeman, 1990).

Individuals with NPD are secretive about but vulnerable to substance abuse because alcohol and other drugs can give them feelings of dominance and well-being (Benjamin, 1993); the experience of wholeness and vitality (Rodin and Izenberg, 1997); a mistaken and erroneous way to achieve significance and avoid a painful clash with reality (Sperry and Carlson, 1993); license to engage in the overall narcissistic pattern of self-involvement and self-indulgence (Beck and Freeman, 1990); a high level of stimulation (Richards, 1993);

and immediate relief from personal discomfort and a sense of self-importance and power (Beck and Freeman, 1990). The belief that they are unique and special serves to insulate these individuals from the recognition that they have developed a reliance on drugs. They maintain the grandiose belief, sometimes in extraordinary circumstances, that they are in charge of their addiction (Richards, 1993).

Successful treatment for individuals with NPD needs to address how addiction actually violates their sense of superiority; encourage appropriate dependency (on people rather than drugs); help develop tolerance for sad or uncomfortable affect; increase an acceptance of personal limitations; and also foster their emotional connection to others (Richards, 1993). Involvement in a twelve-step program can be quite beneficial for these individuals. In AA, entitlement is confronted with humor and insight. Generous support is offered, but with gentle pressure to confront the problem (Benjamin, 1993).

Individuals with NPD are particularly prone to relapse. They are inclined to be free of the fear of relapse or believe that they can re-engage in controlled use because of their new knowledge about addiction. Once in relapse, individuals with NPD have significant trouble returning to treatment due to shame and humiliation (Richards, 1993). However, should they return to treatment the positive impact of relapse for these clients is the acceptance of human limitations and the need for help from others to remain abstinent.

## CLUSTER A PERSONALITY DISORDERS

Individuals with Cluster A Personality Disorders are characterized by behaviors that appear odd or eccentric (DSM-IV-TR). Three personality disorders fall into this category: paranoid, schizoid, and schizotypal personality disorders.

### Paranoid Personality Disorder (PPD)

The essential feature of paranoid personality disorder is pervasive distrust and suspiciousness of others. Individuals with PPD tend to interpret the motives of others as malevolent and assume that others will exploit, harm, or deceive them. Compliments tend to be interpreted as criticism, e.g., a compliment on a new outfit may be interpreted as criticism of how they usually dress. Even offers of assistance may be interpreted as meaning that these individuals are helpless or inappropriately in need of help. Although these individuals may appear cold, they can often be hostile, stubborn, and sarcastic (DSM-IV-TR).

Control is a mitigating factor in individuals with PPD who engage in substance use. They may resist drug use because they do not want the loss of control that accompanies intoxication, withdrawal, and the physical effects of drug use. They may also resist drug use because of their intense sense of mistrust and vulnerability accompanying drug acquisition and use.

If individuals with PPD get past the distaste for losing control, they may be attracted to drugs that help them feel stronger and more formidable in defending against others. In particular, they may like the sense of personal power that cocaine and amphetamines can provide. Drugs that intensify the paranoid dynamic of self-aggrandizement include cocaine, marijuana, amphetamines, and alcohol. Meissner (1994) proposes that the more fragile the individuals with PPD, the greater their need for stabilization from external sources such as drugs. Substance use can be the answer to being "someone"; it can be a way to take control of the uncontrollable. Meissner suggests that alcohol and other drugs can protect against the direct experience of vulnerability, weakness, inferiority, and inadequacy. If alcohol or cocaine, for example, can reinstate the paranoid defenses and control feelings of despair and worthlessness, addiction becomes a substantial risk. These individuals also may be attracted to using drugs in forbidden settings to resist any infringement on their "sacred autonomy" (Richards, 1993). For example, they may use alcohol or other drugs in treatment settings to emphasize that they will do what they want, not what others want.

In treatment, direct and/or early confrontation will provoke hostility and escalate dysfunctional defenses that can prompt the individuals to quit treatment. Providing education on drugs and alcohol, however, may instead prompt these clients to recognize their problem and acknowledge that they do not want these substances to harm them—without igniting any paranoid defenses. Such individuals generally are inclined to work toward abstinence to free themselves of external constraints, i.e., the presence of probation officers or treatment providers. The therapist, however, can point out to these clients how autonomy deteriorates from escalating alcohol and other drug use and how their alcohol or drugs have betrayed them; revealing this personality structure can be enlisted to work toward abstinence. Matano and Locke (1995) note that clients with PPD in alcoholism treatment have difficulty relinquishing autonomy and control to a treatment program or a "higher power" as in Alcoholics Anonymous.

### Schizoid Personality Disorder (SPD)

The essential feature of schizoid personality disorder is pervasive detachment from social relationships and restricted expression of emotions in interpersonal situations. These individuals appear to be indifferent to intimacy and do not appear to gain much satisfaction from being part of a family or a group. They prefer solitary activities and appear indifferent to the approval or criticism of others (DSM-IV-TR).

In treatment, clients with SPD challenge service providers, not with hostility, distrust, or aggression, but with a lack of a response. They do not reciprocate feeling for feeling; they are not responsive to the kinds of emotional leverage used between people when one is attempting to influence the other. Their apparent freedom from internal pressure to do as others do or to follow the rules made and enforced by others can form a barrier to effective treatment. Individuals with SPD feel no particular need to confront service providers when they disagree, and they will often be treatment compliant. However, they remain quietly committed to their own course of action, e.g., using drugs the day they are released from an alcohol and drug or dual diagnosis treatment program.

Goals that address drug and alcohol use must be realistic. Individuals with SPD are inclined to consider their drug use to be nobody's business but their own. They may not directly argue but they will quietly resist behavioral guidelines they do not like. They may simply wait for the service providers or the treatment program to be out of their lives so they can resume behavior that they never intended to discontinue in the first place. Some individuals with SPD will only consider a treatment goal that reduces the danger or the negative consequences of drug use, e.g., harm reduction techniques.

Treatment must address the development of sufficient social support to foster abstinence without overpowering these individuals with an intolerable level of intimate contact with others. They may thrive in twelve-step meetings if their behavior is socially appropriate enough to be accepted in the self-help community. If not, they may need Dual Recovery Anonymous meetings where unusual behavior is better tolerated. Psychoeducation is vital to treatment because they most readily understand and accept information that is presented without intensity, pressure, or emotionally laden content. Motivational interviewing techniques addressing consequences of alcohol and drug use can be effective in providing these clients with the information they need to consider the possible benefits of abstinence.

### Schizotypal Personality Disorder (StPD)

The essential feature of schizotypal personality disorder is pervasive social and interpersonal deficits marked by acute discomfort with close relationships. An individual with StPD may have distorted thoughts and perceptions, act eccentrically, misinterpret casual incidents as having a particular meaning for themselves, and often, be preoccupied with paranormal phenomena. These individuals may feel they have special powers or magical control over others (DSM-IV-TR). Once in treatment, they may respond positively to an environment structured to allow them greater personal and interpersonal success. They are not inclined to prefer the isolation that comes from their social anxiety, but rather, value a setting in which they can successfully connect with others.

Individuals with StPD may have difficulty establishing connections to obtain illegal drugs, but if they do, are extremely vulnerable to exploitation and abuse or violence. These individuals may be attracted to psychedelics; marijuana, LSD, and peyote can all promote a fantasy state that is far from the troubling real world. Walant (1995) suggests that LSD can provide weird perceptual distortions that can actually alleviate anxiety about personal strangeness that is not drug induced. Alcohol may become a drug of choice because it is readily available. With the capacity of alcohol to disinhibit, individuals with StPD may drink to heighten their capacity for fantasy and unusual beliefs about who they are and what they can do. Any use of alcohol or drugs can destabilize individuals with StPD.

Treatment must address the development of sufficient social support to foster abstinence without overpowering these individuals with an intolerable level of interpersonal contact. Individuals with StPD do not tolerate confrontation well. When uncomfortable, they can effectively withdraw, distract themselves, or disrupt the treatment process. In spite of their interpersonal vulnerability, individuals with StPD often have an internal, rather quirky, resistance to what they may perceive as pressure from others. They may thrive in twelve-step meetings if their behavior is socially appropriate enough to be accepted by the self-help community. If not, they need to attend specialized meetings for individuals with co-occurring disorders.

## CLUSTER C PERSONALITY DISORDERS

Individuals with Cluster C personality disorders are characterized by anxious or fearful behaviors (DSM IV-TR). The three personality disorders that fall in this category are: avoidant, dependent, and obsessive-compulsive personality disorders.

### Avoidant Personality Disorder (AvPD)

The essential feature of avoidant personality disorder is pervasive social inhibition, feelings of inadequacy, and hypersensitivity to being negatively evaluated. Individuals with AvPD avoid work or school activities that involve significant interpersonal contact. They fear criticism, disapproval, or rejection. They frequently describe social and occupational problems and are rarely able to develop a strong social network that can help them through personal crises (DSM-IV-TR).

Individuals with AvPD risk developing a substance use disorder if they find comfort through alcohol or other drug use. Unfortunately, their pain is so apparent that some psychiatrists may be more inclined to prescribe benzodiazepines for these individuals than for those with other personality disorders. Individuals with AvPD may find that tranquilizers promote an internal sense of peace they have never known. Thus, they may persistently seek a continuing supply of these drugs which induce a calm they cannot provide for themselves.

Richards (1993) suggests that treatment for individuals with AvPD must consider the function of their addiction, including their drug of choice, within the context of their personality psychopathology. These individuals may gain some sense of control with their addictive behavior, despite negative consequences. Alternatively, they may attempt to cope with external reality with chemical courage or drug-induced self-confidence. Either way, these individuals modify their troubled feelings without influencing the causes of such feelings. They view their addiction as a magical solution to the pain of life (Peele, 1985). As such, they will be very resistant to the loss of their drug(s) of choice.

Involvement in a recovery community (see Chapter 10) can be very helpful for someone with AvPD. These communities are by nature accepting, noncritical, and do not force membership until the individual is ready. Such an atmosphere can allow individuals to feel safe enough to develop social ties. However, they need a great deal of assistance to overcome their anxiety about attending such groups, such as having a longtime member accompany them on their initial visit, arranging to arrive late and leave early until they can tolerate being with others, or whatever else increases their comfort.

### Dependent Personality Disorder (DPD)

The essential feature of dependent personality disorder is an excessive need to be taken care of, which leads to submissive and clinging behavior. These people may fear separation, have difficulty making decisions, and perceive themselves as being unable to function adequately without help from others. Individuals with DPD are often pessimistic and characterized by self-doubt; they tend to belittle their abilities and assets, seek others to dominate and protect them, and avoid jobs requiring responsibility (DSM-IV-TR).

Individuals with DPD do not seek treatment because they are *too* dependent. In fact, they like being dependent (Kantor, 1992). Instead, they usually complain of anxiety, tension, or depression (Turkat, 1990). The goal of treatment is for the individuals to recognize their dependent patterns and the high price they pay to maintain them. Clients with DPD must build strength rather than foster neediness (Benjamin, 1993).

For individuals with DPD, alcohol and other drugs offer an easy, passive way to either deal with or escape from problems (Beck and Freeman, 1990). The external search for self-comfort, security, and self-regulation makes these individuals quite vulnerable to drug use. Alcohol and other drugs offer individuals with DPD anxiety management, release and emotional expression, a substitute solution to unmet interpersonal needs, and an escape from competency demands (Richards, 1993).

Little progress can be made if the controlling partners of these individuals are not included in treatment. Individuals with DPD cannot achieve and maintain abstinence while living with or in a dependent relationship with an actively using partner. Although NA or AA contacts are easy for these individuals to make, there is no assurance that they will seek out and attach to the healthier and more sincere members of their groups. They can often be prey for more aggressive or narcissistic people in any system. If individuals with DPD are in relationships with nonusing partners, they are likely to drink or drug in secrecy and isolation. In these cases, sedative hypnotics and alcohol are likely to be preferred as they are either legal or can be obtained from physicians.

### Obsessive-Compulsive Personality Disorder (OCPD)

The essential feature of OCPD is a preoccupation with orderliness, perfectionism, and control. Control is maintained by painstaking attention to rules, trivial details, procedures, lists, and schedules (DSM-IV-TR).

Individuals with OCPD often enter treatment because their productivity or cognitive skills are slipping. They complain of depression and an inability to be productive. These individuals appear to be particularly sensitive to natural changes in cognitive skills due to normal aging (Turkat, 1990). Individuals with OCPD also may seek treatment because of psychophysiological difficulties, such as psychosomatic disorders related to the problems they have in discharging tension. They may also experience severe anxiety, immobilization, impotence, and excessive fatigue (Millon, 1981).

The potential for loss of control involved in intoxication, dependence, and withdrawal may protect individuals with OCPD from substance use disorders. They may also avoid the illegal and high-risk behaviors involved in the use of street drugs. One pattern of alcohol and drug use, however, may seem to enhance self-control and personal productivity that may be tempting for individuals with OCPD. It begins as a means to manage fatigue and loss of concentration during the course of the workday. At first, caffeine is used to boost energy during the day; the impact of the caffeine is then moderated at night with wine to induce sleep; the next morning is greeted with the need for caffeine to get started. This is such a common pattern that it does not seem to merit much attention, but when individuals with OCPD adopt it, over time they tend to need stronger uppers and downers to manipulate their capacity to work and sleep and the use of amphetamines and narcotics or benzodiazepines becomes a much more serious concern.

Treatment for individuals with OCPD must include teaching new and constructive ways to deal with excessive drive and feelings of tension, fear, dread, and anger without compulsivity. In treatment, individuals with OCPD are good at following advice, accepting guidelines, and responding well to programmatic efforts that require note taking, records, measurements, and specific steps or sequences. Psychoeducation (for both personality issues and drugs) is important for these individuals to avoid stimulating resistance (Richards, 1993). They are likely to attend twelve-step meetings when required. However, service providers need to be alert to the remarkable capacity that people with OCPD have to evoke annoyance and rejection from others. Clients may need help in learning how to utilize support groups well and to connect to a sponsor who will be both tolerant and patient.

## *CONCLUSION*

Although substance use disorders most frequently co-occur with Cluster B personality disorders, therapists working with substance use and mental disorders may encounter any of these disorders. To ensure treatment success, learning to identify these disorders early in treatment and address them thoroughly is important. Some of the symptoms of substance use disorders can mirror the symptoms of these disorders, and service providers will need to differentiate substance-induced symptoms from personality disorder-induced symptoms in developing a treatment plan. Chapter 5 will discuss methods of assessment.

# Chapter 5

# Assessment

Although numerous instruments are used to diagnose mental health disorders and substance use disorders, their accuracy often comes into question when an individual presents with symptoms of both substance use *and* mental disorders. Hence therapists working with multifarious caseloads must often develop treatment plans before obtaining a clear and complete diagnostic picture. This chapter provides an overview of the issues involved in conducting assessments of individuals presenting with multiple symptoms, and offers ways to obtain the information necessary to develop an effective treatment plan for individuals with a mixed diagnostic picture.

In addition to a standard psychosocial history, a comprehensive assessment for individuals presenting with mental health and substance abuse symptoms involves collecting information about seven additional areas of concern. These are: the level of the substance abuse problem; differentiation of substance-induced psychiatric symptoms from true co-occurring disorders; identification of the client's co-occurring disorders subgroup; consequences of substance use; motivation that contributes to continued substance use; the history of treatment or recovery by the client or family members; and identification of the level of treatment intensity that the client is able, willing, or can be mandated to participate in.

Furthermore, when working with a multifarious caseload, therapists must be able to use two different types of diagnostic processes (see Figure 5.1). The traditional process can be used with individuals who have only a substance use or a mental disorder. This involves conducting a comprehensive assessment using existing instruments or techniques that should in most cases lead to an accurate diagnosis of a particular substance use or psychiatric diagnosis. The diagnosis then sets the basis for the development of an appropriate treatment plan. However, when both the symptoms of a substance use and mental dis-

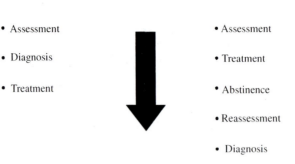

**TRADITIONAL**

- Assessment
- Diagnosis
- Treatment

**MODIFIED**

- Assessment
- Treatment
- Abstinence
- Reassessment
- Diagnosis

FIGURE 5.1. Assessment Paths

order are present, an accurate diagnosis is not always possible initially, so a modified diagnostic process must be used. It begins with identifying the psychiatric and substance use symptoms and treatment interventions to address these symptoms. The goal of the substance-use interventions is abstinence. When abstinence is achieved and maintained for an extended period of time, the client is re-assessed to obtain a clear diagnostic picture. Thus for some clients the assessment process leads to a clear diagnosis and treatment plan, while for other clients the assessment leads to a treatment plan, which later leads to a clearer diagnosis. Mental health and substance abuse therapists must be able to use both of these assessment paths when working with a multifarious caseload.

## IDENTIFYING A SUBSTANCE USE PROBLEM

We have found eight assessment or screening instruments useful in identifying substance use or mental disorders in individuals who have co-occurring disorders. The following is a description of each instrument and its effectiveness with this population, based on the research.

### Addiction Severity Index (ASI)

The addiction severity index, developed by McLellan et al. (1980), is used to identify the types and severity of problems caused by alcohol and other drug use. It was not designed to make a diagnosis but to measure changes in the severity of these problems during and after treatment. Lehman et al. (1996) found the ASI helpful in identifying substance use problems in a psychiatric population. Appleby et al. (1997) found it helpful in identifying substance use problems in a population with mental health disorders but not nearly as effective in identifying their level of psychiatric severity; Eland-Goossensen et al. (1997) also found a similar pattern.

## The CAGE Questionnaire

Developed by Mayfield, McCleod, and Hall (1974), this four-item questionnaire was designed to detect alcohol dependence. Two affirmative answers indicates an 85 percent chance of alcohol dependence. Drake et al. (1990) found this instrument more sensitive in detecting current and lifetime alcohol dependence in individuals with schizophrenia than the Michigan Alcoholism Screening Test (MAST) (see as follows).

## Chemical Use, Abuse, and Dependence Scale (CUAD)

This instrument, developed by McGovern and Morrison (1992), was tested for validity and reliability with a population who presented with many different substance use disorders and many different co-occurring mental disorders. The instrument is at a minimum a two- item questionnaire (denies alcohol or drug use) or at a maximum an eighty-item questionnaire (four drugs are being used). It provides severity and diagnostic information for each drug used and is based on DSM-III-R criteria.

## Clinician Rating Scales

Introduced by Mueser et al. (1995), these clinician rating scales were initially designed to help case managers working with individuals with serious mental disorders monitor substance use and treatment requirements. Two scales are used. The alcohol and drug use scales measure the type of alcohol and drug use pattern that a client has demonstrated over the last six months; and the substance abuse treatment scale measures the stage of treatment that the client had participated in during the last six months. The scales are based on

DSM-III-R criteria but were designed to be easily modified when those criteria change.

### *Dartmouth Assessment of Lifestyle Inventory (DALI)*

Rosenberg et al. (1998) developed this instrument specifically for individuals with a major mental disorder. It is composed of eighteen questions, fifteen questions taken from several other substance abuse assessment instruments were found valid for this population. The instrument addresses the use and effects of alcohol, marijuana, and cocaine.

### *Diagnostic and Statistical Manual (DSM)*

This diagnostic manual of the American Psychiatric Association (APA) has undergone three revisions since its third edition allowed the diagnosis of co-occurring disorders in 1980. The most recent revision, the DSM-IV-TR, is the commonly accepted diagnostic scheme now in use. It contains more than 100 substance-related disorders (see Chapter 3). The diagnostic criteria for these disorders have changed little since the introduction of the DSM-III-R in 1987. Drake et al. (1990) found that the Structured Clinical Interview for the DSM-III-R (SCID) was less effective than either the Michigan Alcoholism Screening Test (MAST) or the CAGE Questionnaire for identifying current alcohol dependence in individuals with schizophrenia.

### *Michigan Alcoholism Screening Test (MAST)*

This instrument was developed by Selzer (1971) and is composed of twenty-four questions, each scored from one to five points. A total of five or more points indicates that an individual has an alcohol dependence disorder. Toland and Moss (1989) found that the instrument can produce false positives with individuals who have schizophrenia because of confusion over alcohol-dependence symptoms versus schizophrenia symptoms. Drake et al. (1990), while studying the same type of population, found the MAST more sensitive in detecting lifetime alcohol dependence than current alcohol dependence.

### Urine, Blood, Hair, Breath, and Saliva Testing

These tests are used for detecting recent alcohol and other drug *use*. They do not indicate whether the individual is addicted. Although the previously mentioned assessment tools rely either on self-report or actual observations of a particular behavior, these tests actually measure the presence of the drug itself in the body. With the exception of hair tests, most drugs can be detected in the body only up to seventy-two hours after use, and the usage must be of a detectable level. However, these tests can provide important information concerning the recent use of alcohol and other drugs that may not otherwise be obtained through self-report or third-party observation and should always be part of an initial or ongoing assessment process.

None of these assessment methods alone provide all the information that therapists need to develop a comprehensive treatment plan; however, they can provide very helpful information in developing a diagnostic picture and an appropriate treatment plan.

## DIFFERENTIATING SUBSTANCE-INDUCED DISORDERS FROM CO-OCCURRING DISORDERS

Initially, therapists should assess whether the psychiatric symptoms are the result of a mental disorder or of the alcohol or drug use. As discussed earlier, this is never an easy decision because almost all symptoms of alcohol and drug intoxication and withdrawal mirror symptoms of mental disorders. In reality, therapists may not be completely sure of the origin of certain symptoms until long-term abstinence is achieved; however, they can ask certain questions of clients and significant others to help clarify the diagnosis.

Following are four very useful questions to sort out substance-induced disorders from co-occurring Axis I disorders (see Chapter 3):

1. *Did the psychiatric symptoms predate the onset of the substance use?* Kessler et al. (1994) found that the vast majority of individuals with mood disorders and co-occurring substance use disorders report that the symptoms of their mood disorder predated their substance use disorder by, on average, four years. Many clients, however, are poor historians and thus this information may be more accurate when obtained from family members or longtime friends.

2. *Is there a history of similar mental disorders in the client's biological family?* Many of these disorders appear to have a genetic basis and are more common in biological relatives than in the general population (see Chapter 3).

3. *Is the onset of symptoms within the normal age range?* Although exceptions occur, most mental disorders have a normal age range for symptom development (see Chapter 3). Thus if a forty-five-year-old, with no history of psychotic symptoms, suddenly begins to exhibit such symptoms, a therapist needs to rule out either a substance-induced disorder or a medical condition before assuming that a psychotic disorder is present.

4. *Does a significant change occur in the psychiatric symptoms after two or more weeks of abstinence?* Though it normally takes an extended period of time for all the symptoms of a substance-induced disorder to disappear, a significant reduction of symptoms generally occurs within two weeks of abstinence from most drugs. At times, when co-occurring disorders are present, symptoms may actually increase after a period of abstinence because the substance use had helped to reduce some of the symptoms. A good two-part question to ask clients is, *Have you ever gone a period of time without using?* and if so, *Did your psychiatric symptoms get better or worse?* Although only abstinence or the availability of long-term treatment records can form a clear diagnostic picture, answers to these questions can allow a therapist to make some good assumptions concerning the clients' treatment needs.

As with Axis I disorders, clients actively using alcohol and drugs who present with symptoms of personality disorders (see Chapter 4) can also present a confusing diagnostic picture. Six of the seven symptoms of antisocial personality disorder, for example, could be substance induced; three of the nine symptoms of borderline personality disorder could be substance induced; and three of the eight symptoms of histrionic personality disorder could be substance induced (see Box 5.1). Although substance use is a commonly associated trait for individuals with these disorders, an individual could be diagnosed with a personality disorder when in fact the behavior is the result of substance use. As Gerstley et al. (1990) points out, the diagnostic criteria of personality disorders are primarily based on behavioral symptoms that can also result from other disorders. Studies find significant disparities between individuals who meet the diagnostic

---

**BOX 5.1. Personality Disorder Symptoms**

**Antisocial Personality Disorder (6 of 7 Criteria)**

(1) Repeatedly behaving in ways that are grounds for arrest
(2) Lying, conning
(3) Impulsivity
(4) Irritability (fighting, assaulting)
(5) Reckless disregard for the safety of others
(6) Irresponsibility (failure to keep jobs or meet financial obligations)

**Borderline Personality Disorder (3 of 9)**

(1) Impulsivity
(2) Intense mood changes
(3) Problems with anger

**Histrionic Personality Disorder (3 of 8)**

(1) Inappropriately sexually seductive or provocative
(2) Theatrical and exaggerated expression of emotion
(3) Easily influenced by others

---

criteria for a personality disorder as the result of their substance use but who, in fact, do not have one (Rounsaville et al., 1983; Woody et al., 1985).

When clients present with symptoms of personality disorders and have co-occurring substance use disorders, three questions should be asked:

1. *Did the personality behaviors predate the onset of substance use?* Since the onset of behaviors associated with these personality disorders normally predates substance use, the answer to this question from family members or childhood friends can provide valuable information.

2. *How frequent are these behaviors?* Since the behaviors result from a fixed, rigid view of the world, they would occur frequently if not daily if they were the result of a co-occurring personality disorder.

3. *Does a personality change occur when under the influence of alcohol or other drugs?* A statement, such as, *"He is such a nice guy when he doesn't drink,"* is very common and would indicate a marked personality change during substance use.

As with the symptoms of Axis I disorders, these questions do not guarantee diagnostic clarity but can help the therapist begin to make some educated assumptions concerning the type of treatment a client needs.

## SUBGROUPS OF INDIVIDUALS WITH CO-OCCURRING DISORDERS

Because individuals presenting with substance use and psychiatric symptoms are a very heterogeneous population, separating them into more homogeneous subgroups can make treatment planning much more effective. Pepper, Kirshner, and Ryglewicz (1981) divided individuals with serious mental disorders into two subgroups: younger individuals who used alcohol and drugs and had spent little time in state hospitals and an older group that used only alcohol, if they used at all, and had spent significant time in psychiatric hospitals. Schuckit (1985) based his subgroups on when the psychiatric symptoms began in an attempt to differentiate substance-induced disorders from co-occurring disorders. Cloninger (1987) described Type I alcoholics who had a later onset of the disorder with little pathology in the family and Type II who had an early onset with one or both parents demonstrating antisocial behaviors.

As the understanding of this population grew, other subgroup models were introduced, reflecting an increase in knowledge about the variety of considerations needed for effective treatment planning. Blackwell, Beresford, and Lambert (1988) proposed a five subgroup model that was based on the presence of alcohol and/or psychiatric disorders. Sandberg, Greenberg, and Birkmann (1991) proposed four subgroups of individuals with co-occurring disorders based on why they used alcohol and drugs. Lehman (1996) proposed a five subgroup model based on the types of substance use disorders, mental health disorders, medical problems, and social problems that affected the client. Hien et al. (1997) proposed a three subgroup model based on which disorder was primary.

The subgroup models that we find most helpful in managing multifarious caseloads are based on the intensity of an individual's substance use and psychiatric symptoms. Two such models have been proposed: one by Ries (1993) and the other by the Metropolitan Washington Council of Governments (COG) (1995) (see Table 5.1). Each model breaks this population into four subgroups based on similar criteria.

The advantage of these models is that they are based on the level of symptoms and the impact of these symptoms on the individual. Because the same disorder can impact individuals in many different ways, basing treatment subgroups primarily on the types of disorders present often does not reduce the heterogeneity of this population. One individual with an alcohol dependency disorder and a major depressive disorder might have only short periods when depressive and alcohol symptoms are present and have a job, a family, and be fairly self-sufficient. Another individual with the same disorders might have extensive periods of time with those symptoms and be unable to hold a job, maintain intimate relationships, or have a peer support network. The level of symptoms and the ability to function independently are very different for these individuals. The two most important questions for treatment planning, then, are which clients can be treated together and what level of services is needed? Our experience shows that functioning level is the best guide for both these questions. In general, the functioning level is best predicted by the intensity of the client's symptoms. Although no current subgroup model can accurately and quickly classify the treatment needs of all individuals with co-occurring disorders, the use of any of the models will begin to create more homogenous treatment populations.

TABLE 5.1. Subgroup Models

| Ries Subgroup Model | COG Subgroup Model | MH Symptoms | SA Symptoms |
|---|---|---|---|
| 1 | 3 | Low | Low |
| 3 | 2 | Low | High |
| 2 | 4 | High | Low |
| 4 | 1 | High | High |

## CONSEQUENCES OF SUBSTANCE USE

Substance use can both increase and decrease psychiatric symptoms at the same time or in a sequential pattern. The mental health therapist may have a client with a psychotic disorder who is less socially anxious when he smokes marijuana but at the same time experiences an increase in auditory hallucinations. The substance abuse therapist may have a client who often returns to either alcohol or cocaine use when her depressive symptoms become too uncomfortable, but then she experiences an even deeper depression for a period of time after she discontinues the use of these drugs. Although this information can be obtained from client self-reports or clinical observations, the therapist's best source of information is from family members, peers, or other treatment professionals.

The impact of substance use can be categorized in three different ways: mild to moderate impairment, major impairment, or decompensation.

### Mild to Moderate Impairment

The client may experience a mild decrease in cognitive, emotional, or behavior management, which in fact, may not be readily noticed by either the client or those around him. Impairment usually needs to be pointed out by direct feedback or awareness from psychoeducational interventions. For example, a client experiences increased anxiety or negative thinking after using alcohol; a client reports an increase in hearing voices after a relapse to cocaine use.

### Major Impairment

Defined as a major decrease in cognitive, emotional, and behavior management, the elevated impairment is readily noticeable to the client and those around him. The symptoms of the mental disorder are significantly increased but not to the point that emergency, residential, or hospitalization services are needed. However, increased services are usually needed and can be provided by an outpatient therapist or case manager. For example, a client with a psychotic disorder experiences significant increases in delusions, hearing voices, or paranoid ideation after using alcohol and marijuana; another client becomes severely depressed after drinking alcohol.

## *Decompensation*

Decompensation is defined as a significant decrease in cognitive, emotional, and behavior management to the point that the client's ability to take care of himself is greatly diminished. Impairment is readily and immediately noticed by those around the client and almost always by the client. The intensity of the psychiatric symptoms is such that they require immediate intervention strategies, such as emergency stabilization in either a residential or hospital setting. For example, after the use of LSD, a young adult with schizophrenia becomes so delusional and paranoid that her safety and that of others around her comes into question; an individual with major depressive disorder becomes so depressed after the use of cocaine that he is unable to get out of bed, leave the house, or take care of his basic eating and grooming needs.

In almost all cases any alcohol or drug use increases an individual's psychiatric symptoms to some degree, during both intoxication and withdrawal; however the exact extent of this impact differs greatly among clients. For some, a small amount of a drug used for a short period of time can cause decompensation, while others can use large amounts of a drug over a long period of time and experience only mild impairment. The primary purpose for assessing for this impact is to determine the urgency, type, and intensity of treatment needed. An individual who experiences mild impairment can be targeted for psychoeducation or outpatient treatment groups that can move him slowly toward abstinence and recovery, while an individual who decompensates when using substances needs more intensive and immediate types of interventions.

## *MOTIVATION FOR CONTINUED SUBSTANCE USE*

To effectively intervene with the substance use behaviors of individuals with co-occurring disorders, understanding how clients believe their alcohol or drug use benefits them is important. Without this knowledge, developing interventions that have any real meaning for clients will be very difficult. This information is usually obtained from client self-reports or clinical observations, although third-party reports can also be useful.

Individuals with mental health disorders continue their substance use for a variety of reasons. The most common are: to seek symptom relief; reduce social discomfort; seek peer acceptance; self-harm; manage time; deny the existence of a mental disorder; or avoid withdrawal. Clients use one or more of these reasons to continue their substance use. The following section describes examples of each and suggests intervention strategies.

### Symptom Relief

Often referred to as self-medication, the client uses alcohol or other drugs to help manage symptoms of a mental disorder. The individual may use marijuana to reduce some of the symptoms of an anxiety disorder or drink alcohol to reduce some of the manic symptoms of a bipolar disorder. The client may be unaware that he has a mental disorder or he believes that these drugs are more effective or acceptable than prescribed medications. The therapist must work with the client and his doctor to find medications that are equally or more effective if the abused substance is to be discontinued.

### Reduction of Social Discomfort

Individuals with mental health disorders often experience discomfort among other people, varying from mild anxiety to full-blown paranoia. Using drugs or alcohol may reduce a variety of symptoms for short periods of time, such as anxiety in individuals with social phobia; paranoia or hearing voices in those with psychotic disorders; or the need to isolate by individuals with major depressive disorder. Since most individuals want to socially interact with others, individuals with disorders that interfere with this interaction often experience alcohol and other drug use as beneficial, not problematic. The therapists must increase their clients' ability to manage their symptoms in social settings through either more effective use of medication, or skill training. They also need to increase the clients' awareness of how alcohol and drugs actually make their symptoms worse in the long run, thus defeating their original purpose for using them.

## Peer Acceptance

Using alcohol or other drugs as a way of establishing contact with, or being part of a peer group is called *peer acceptance*. Many individuals with major mental disorders often seem odd or strange to others and find themselves isolated, avoided, or ridiculed. However, they may be more readily accepted into a drug-using peer group that is based solely on having drugs to share or the willingness to use them. For example, an individual with schizoaffective disorder buys alcohol and marijuana so that a group of individuals will spend time with her at her apartment; or an individual with schizophrenia hangs out with a group of homeless individuals whose only requirement for entry into their group is that he has alcohol or drugs to share. Alcohol and drug use thus serves as a means of facilitating peer contact and feeling that one is part of a group. The therapist must work with the client to develop social networks that accept him for who he is and do not require substance use to be accepted. Promoting a client's participation in a psychosocial rehabilitation center and self-help groups are methods of helping him develop new peer networks.

## Time Management

Individuals with mental disorders that severely impact their ability to form extended social networks, maintain employment, develop and maintain intimate relationships, and in general reduce their interest in things, often have a significant time void to fill; as a result, they may turn to using alcohol and other drugs to occupy the time. For example, an individual with schizophrenia who uses a substance spends a great deal of time looking for, purchasing, managing the altered state, and then recovering from its effects. Alcohol and drug use can be an organizing agent for individuals with extensive periods of time with nothing to do; thus the therapist has to help the client find other satisfactory activities if substance use is to be discontinued.

## Self-Harm

Many individuals with mental disorders are very unhappy with their lives and at times either consciously or unconsciously wish themselves dead; however, for personal or religious reasons, they do not see suicide as an option. The use of alcohol and other drugs to inflict injury or produce a potential danger to oneself is an alternative. Furthermore, some individuals, because of past traumatic experiences such as sexual abuse, may use substances as a means to continue what they now perceive as their natural state of victimization. Because alcohol and other drugs have many potentially serious physical affects, their use can serve as a means of punishing oneself, or slowly shortening one's life. For example, an individual with major depressive disorder and an extensive history of heart disease in his family uses alcohol and cocaine regularly as a means to passively and prematurely end his life. Another client with post-traumatic stress disorder, resulting from an extensive history of sexual abuse, and borderline personality disorder is only able to reduce her self-mutilating behavior by increasing her substance use. Therapists working with such clients must help them find some meaning in life and effectively deal with their mental disorder, or help them work through their need to victimize themselves.

### Seeking to Deny the Existence of a Mental Disorder

For many individuals the stigma associated with having a mental disorder is much greater than the stigma associated with having a substance use problem. Therefore, alcohol or other drugs may be abused to deny the existence of the mental disorder. Their symptoms, such as apathy, depression, anger, anxiety, feeling different from others, or thinking other people are looking at them can then all be attributed to substance use. For example, a client with co-occurring schizoaffective disorder and alcohol and cocaine dependency disorders tells herself there is nothing wrong with her by attributing the paranoid ideation, depression, and anxiety to the alcohol and cocaine use. This client's therapist has to work on helping the client accept her mental disorder if the substance use disorders are to be managed effectively.

### Avoiding Withdrawal

Individuals with mental disorders can also become physically dependent on alcohol and other drugs and need a specific level of the substance in their bloodstream to avoid withdrawal symptoms. When withdrawal symptoms begin, an individual will initiate drug-seeking behavior, that is, locating and using that drug to the exclusion of everything else. For example, a client with an anxiety disorder who has become addicted to a benzodiazepine medication by taking more than prescribed will experience an increase in anxiety and other withdrawal symptoms once he runs out of the medication. At that point he will put pressure on his current doctor to prescribe additional medication or seek out new doctors for additional prescriptions. Detoxification from the drug is necessary before substantial treatment or recovery can occur.

## HISTORY OF APPROACH TO TREATMENT AND RECOVERY

Taking a history of how individuals or members of their families have approached treatment and recovery in the past can also be helpful in developing treatment plans for individuals with co-occurring disorders. It can give insights into how open or resistant an individual might be to treatment, what treatment approach might be most acceptable to them, and what level of outside support might be available to help guide the clients through this process. An individual or family member might have approached treatment and recovery in one or several of six different ways.

### None

Since the onset of the symptoms of the mental health and substance use disorders, the individual has not been able to manage symptoms effectively for any significant period of time. Also there is either no history of these disorders in the family or family members with these or similar disorders have also never managed them effectively. For example, a client with borderline personality disorder and alcohol and cocaine abuse disorders enters treatment for the first time, and has family members with untreated substance use disorders.

### Relapse Cycles

An individual has effectively managed his symptoms for significant periods of time, but then has periods (not a one-time, one-day event) of failing to do so. This pattern needs to occur at least twice to be a relapse cycle. For example, a client with narcotic and alcohol dependence disorders and co-occurring generalized anxiety disorder has been abstinent and takes a nonaddicting antianxiety medication that, combined with some behavior management techniques, controls the anxiety effectively. However, every nine months to a year, the client uses narcotics and discontinues his medication for a period of three to six months. He then returns to treatment, begins his medication, and achieves abstinence.

### Achieved Stability Only in a Controlled Environment

Some individuals effectively manage the symptoms of co-occurring disorders only when living in a controlled environment (such as a residential program, jail, hospital, etc.). Once the individual returns to the community he returns to alcohol and drug use and fails to manage his psychiatric symptoms effectively. For example, a client with major depressive disorder and alcohol abuse disorder has a long history of multiple hospitalizations resulting from medication noncompliance and alcohol use. During these hospitalizations the client becomes stable, but when released soon returns to alcohol use and does not take her medication as prescribed.

### Achieved Abstinence and Stability with Assistance

An individual effectively manages the symptoms of co-occurring disorders with the assistance of others. Normally, this assistance comes from mental health or substance abuse treatment professionals and/or self-help groups but occasionally religious organizations, friends, or families perform this role. For example, an individual with bipolar disorder and a co-occurring alcohol dependence disorder received treatment for both disorders in either a mental health or substance abuse treatment system and achieved abstinence and psychiatric stability as the result of this treatment.

### Achieved Stability Without Assistance

An individual effectively manages the symptoms of co-occurring disorders without the assistance of others. Though this method is not often seen by treatment professionals because these individuals seldom enter treatment systems, a number of individuals do learn to manage the symptoms of less severe mental health disorders and substance use disorders without the assistance of others. For example, an individual with attention-deficit hyperactivity disorder who abused alcohol and other drugs during adolescence and early adulthood has learned to compensate for his impairments and decided by his mid-twenties to discontinue his substance use.

### Family History of Recovery

How family members of a client have dealt with mental health and substance use disorders can play an important role in predicting how an individual will approach treatment and recovery. Family members might have approached this issue in any or all of the ways previously listed. When no history of treatment or recovery is present in the family, the client must find her own way with no guidance and possibly no support from her family. In those instances the client must develop a peer network that can provide this guidance and support. When other members of the family have pursued a particular course to treatment and recovery, the likelihood is greater that the client will also be most comfortable with that path. However, when family members have pursued more than one course of treatment and recovery, finding out whom the client is most similar to in the family becomes important, because that often indicates the preferred course for that client. The history of treatment and recovery in the family can provide valuable information concerning how a client might prefer to approach abstinence and psychiatric stability.

## MATCHING TREATMENT NEEDS
## WITH TREATMENT POSSIBILITIES

After a comprehensive assessment, the therapist must decide on the type and intensity of treatment to offer the client. This decision is based on four factors: needed treatment; available treatment; treatment the client is freely willing to participate in; and leverage and influence available to promote an unwilling client to participate in treatment. Although the best type of treatment for an individual can usually be readily identified, that treatment service may not be available for an individual with co-occurring disorders, or she may be unwilling to participate in it. Few individuals voluntarily enter treatment for their substance use disorders. Thus the use of leverage (family demands, court orders, etc.) or influence (encouragement from important family members, friends, or even a therapist) becomes necessary in influencing individuals with co-occurring disorders to participate in treatment. The art of treatment placement with this population requires a thorough examination of each of these factors and the placement of clients in a type of treatment that assures their participation and comes closest to matching all their treatment needs. Retention in treatment is the key variable for long-term success by these clients (see Chapter 13).

> The substance abuse therapist, following the completion of a comprehensive assessment, finds that he has a client with alcohol and cocaine dependency disorders who is unlikely to stop using these substances without time away from their availability. This client also demonstrates the symptoms of bipolar II disorder. He has been referred to treatment after receiving his second driving while intoxicated (DWI) charge.

The ideal treatment plan includes placement first in a detoxification center, followed by an evaluation for bipolar II disorder and medication if needed. A residential treatment program and then a period of time in an outpatient aftercare program would follow. The referral agency of the criminal justice system is willing to support this plan and the client is willing to do what is necessary to avoid jail; however, the only residential treatment program available does not accept clients with bipolar disorder. The therapist would need to collaborate with the publicly funded detoxification center to allow his client to stay an extra two weeks so that his psychiatric symptoms can be stabilized with the medication, which also gives him a longer abstinence period before returning to the community. The substance abuse therapist then arranges to see his client several times per week on an outpatient basis. The therapist has thus addressed the symptoms of both disorders and maximized the level of treatment that was possible.

> The mental health therapist, after a comprehensive assessment, finds that she has a client with schizoaffective disorder who uses alcohol or marijuana more days than not, and who is frequently medication noncompliant. The client was brought to the agency by his family. He acknowledges that he might have a mental disorder and may need some help with that, but sees nothing wrong with

his substance use. The family is quite anxious about his well-being, but is very hesitant about making any demands on him concerning treatment.

An ideal treatment strategy would require medication compliance and abstinence from alcohol and marijuana. However, without any real leverage or influence to require this, the mental health therapist works on building a relationship with the client while encouraging him to attend psychoeducation sessions. The sessions define and describe mental disorders and the importance of medication in their treatment, and alcohol and other drugs and their impact on individuals who have mental disorders. By placing low demand on her client the mental health therapist greatly increases the chances of his participation in treatment. By promoting his participation in psychoeducation programs, she begins to provide the client with the necessary information for self-diagnosis of his major mental disorder, and helps him develop the motivation necessary to be medication compliant and abstain from alcohol or other drugs. The mental health therapist can also work with the family to increase their understanding of his disorders and help them become part of the treatment team (see Chapter 9).

## CONCLUSION

For some clients, an accurate diagnosis is only possible after an extended period of abstinence. The assessment tools currently available provide therapists with guidance concerning the extent and the nature of the problem but are not yet sophisticated enough to provide all the information needed to design an effective treatment plan. Thus assessment for individuals presenting with substance use and mental health symptoms must be an ongoing process. A lack of a clear diagnosis, however, should never prevent the onset of treatment. Treatment should be based on the information available but be flexible enough to change as new information is obtained. In addition, information concerning the impact of the substance use on psychiatric symptoms, reasons for continued substance use, and history of treatment and recovery are all important for effective treatment planning. The next three chapters will discuss how to use this assessment information to develop individual, group, family, and case management intervention strategies.

# Chapter 6

# Introduction to Treatment: Goals and Themes

The next four chapters focus on the primary treatment modalities used for clients with substance use and mental disorders. These intervention strategies are psychoeducation (Chapter 7), group treatment (Chapter 7), individual treatment (Chapter 8), case management (Chapter 8), family treatment (Chapter 9), and relapse prevention or symptom management (Chapter 10). This chapter reviews treatment goals for all the treatment modalities and examines treatment themes that arise frequently when working with individuals with co-occurring disorders regardless of which treatment modality is used.

## *TREATMENT GOALS*

Establishing treatment goals is one of the initial and most critical tasks that a mental health or substance abuse professional must undertake early in the treatment process. Goals give direction to treatment and provide benchmarks against which its effectiveness can be measured. Building on the treatment goals of a multifarious caseload outlined in Table 1.2, we have developed two overarching treatment goals for all individuals with co-occurring disorders: abstinence or nonproblematic substance use, and psychiatric and/or interpersonal stabilization. Because of their long-term needs to address reoccurring symptoms, individuals with serious substance use and/or serious and persistent mental disorders also need the goal of long-term participation in a community support network, such as Alcoholics Anonymous, Emotions Anonymous, or a psychosocial program. Many of these individuals may also have the goal of obtaining some form of employment or regular participation in volunteer activities. Work of any type generally increases life satisfaction and provides a reason for continued abstinence and psychiatric stability. Although additional treatment goals are often set, these goals are used for all clients with co-occurring disorders.

## TREATMENT THEMES

Individuals with co-occurring disorders consistently present ten themes in treatment regardless of the treatment modality used. The following is a description and example of each theme and suggestions for the goals of therapist interventions when encountering the theme.

### Theme One: Acceptance of a Mental Disorder

No one wants to have a mental disorder. Accepting the existence of a mental illness often means that an individual must change many life expectations. Having a mental disorder usually involves limitations.

John, a young man of twenty-two who lives with his parents, has been referred for treatment after being charged with driving while intoxicated. He is usually suspicious and gives only vague answers to questions. His parents report strange and sometimes threatening behavior at home. He has been prescribed an anti-psychotic, but his doctor doubts he is taking it. John insists that the medication is to help him sleep and that nothing else is wrong with him. When he comes to group, he says only that he wants to go to college. What he really wants is to be like other people his age, go to school, work, drink, and even drug with no adverse effects. He believes if he can just get a little more sleep his thinking will clear up enough to go to college.

Unfortunately, John has been diagnosed with schizophrenia. Before any of his career and life goals can be achieved, therefore, he needs to accept that he has this disorder and understand what he must do to stabilize its symptoms. Thus therapist interventions need to target John's understanding of mental illness, how substance use affects his symptoms, connect that his life difficulties result not from who he is but from an illness, and that his illness is treatable. Because he is so young, he may need therapy with other individuals in his age group. In groups, as the therapist supports the members' exploring the anger they have at the unfairness of being different, she can focus on the similarities in the group as well. These may include having similar symptoms, which helps the members to verbally admit that they experience hearing voices, for example, or have problems with the idea of taking medication. Through this process, John may come to accept that he has a disorder that he must work at managing.

### Theme Two: Acceptance of the Impact of Substance Use

Just as everyone else, individuals with mental disorders want to use alcohol and drugs in ways that do not cause them problems. In addition, many individuals with mental disorders find that using alcohol or other drugs may reduce their symptoms for awhile or help them feel more comfortable in social settings. Unfortunately, use of these substances ultimately makes their symptoms worse.

> Wayne insists during a group session that since he is not addicted to alcohol, his drinking does not cause him any negative consequences. In fact, he states that his girlfriend once mentioned that she thought he is more sociable after he has had a few drinks.

Of course this is only half the story. The therapist received a call from the girlfriend who expressed concern about Wayne's drinking. She indicated that he was OK if he had one or two drinks, but if he had more he began to appear paranoid and sometimes became verbally abusive or physically threatening. She reported that she had recently called the police because of this behavior. When this theme arises the therapist needs to target her interventions toward helping clients thoroughly examine all the benefits and consequences of their substance use. Acknowledging that the substance use may offer some benefits for the client often increases the client's willingness to also examine the negative consequences of this use. The therapist can facilitate other group members to share their experiences of denying the impact of their use on their symptoms and behavior. The ultimate goal here is to help clients paint a clear and honest picture for themselves of the benefits and liabilities of their substance use. In almost all instances such a picture points toward the goal of abstinence.

### Theme Three: Identifying What Is Normal

Individuals with mental disorders, especially those that cause serious impairments, often cannot differentiate normal moods or thoughts from those caused by their disorders.

When Sheila's brother is killed in a car accident, her depression increases significantly. Sheila, who had finally been stabilized on an antidepressant medication during the last year, worries that the medication is no longer helping control the symptoms of her major depressive disorder. She attributes the increase in her depression not to the death of her brother but instead to the return of her psychiatric symptoms.

When encountering this theme, the therapist needs to define normal thinking, feeling, and behaving for clients so they have benchmarks to help them differentiate the symptoms of their mental disorders from normality. In this instance, pointing out that anyone would experience significant depression when grieving for a loved one helps this client understand that she is not necessarily spiraling down into another major depressive episode but is most likely experiencing normal grief. The therapist also needs to encourage the group to support the client in taking care of herself so that her grieving does not necessarily trigger a major depressive episode.

### Theme Four: Differentiating Between Medication and Drug Use

Clients struggling with accepting their mental disorder or those who feel righteous in their early substance dependence recovery often view the use of medication as just a dependence on another drug.

Claire, who has two months of abstinence from marijuana after years of using it daily to help control her symptoms of anxiety, announces in a group that she is going to discontinue her nonaddictive antianxiety medication. She reports that she had been thinking about this for some time and that members of her Marijuana Anonymous group had all decided it would be best for her to be drug free. She just does not want to be dependent on another drug.

The goal of the therapist's intervention is to help Claire differentiate between medication and drug use by pointing out that the purpose of medication is to promote stability while the purpose of drug use is to attain an altered state. She can explain to the client that doctors prescribe medication, while clients take it upon themselves to use drugs depending on street availability. Medication goes through strict evaluative and quality control measures while drugs may go through a variety of adulterations by street dealers. When effective, medications reduce specific symptoms so the client can achieve normality, while drugs may reduce symptoms but destabilize the client in other areas. Finally, if the individual with both substance use and psychiatric disorders does not take her prescribed medication, the resulting discomfort may lead her back to drug or alcohol use.

### Theme Five: Dealing with Negative Client, Family, or Community Responses to the Symptoms of a Mental Disorder

Often, family members or persons in the community view individuals with substance use and mental disorders as lazy, unmotivated, and personally responsible for their condition. In fact, many clients also accept this view of themselves.

James is a group member who lives with his parents and takes medication to reduce his paranoid ideation that has caused past bizarre behavior and some legal problems. Although the client has accepted he has a condition that causes these feelings or thoughts, his family believes the past symptoms are the result of his previous drug use. Both the client and his family believe that medication will be needed for just a short period of time. Soon after he begins treatment, he experiences some mild side effects from the medication and both he and his family decide to discontinue its use. When his paranoid symptoms begin to return, his family confronts him about what they believe is his return to drug use, while he believes he just needs to think more logically in order to get rid of them.

When encountering this theme, the goal of the therapist's interventions is to help clients develop a broad understanding of how their disorders fully affect their functioning and how to communicate that effectively to those with whom the client lives, works, or encounters. In this instance the therapist works on increasing the client's understanding of exactly what disorder he has, what it means to have this disorder, and what needs to be done to manage it effectively. If possible, family sessions can focus on the same issues. If such sessions are not possible, then the therapist works with the client to develop the skills to communicate this information to his family and how to deal with their negative responses if they do not accept that he has a mental disorder. In group treatment, the therapist asks the other members to share how they handled similar situations.

### Theme Six: Dealing with the Victim's Role

Clients often see themselves as victims of their disorders and many are outraged and feel sorry for themselves because they believe they have little mastery over their life.

Kim introduces herself to the group by saying she was depressed because no one appreciates her, that people see her as just a mentally ill drug addict, and that the only jobs available to her are beneath her.

The therapist's goal in this instance is to help Kim manage her disorders instead of being a victim of them. Whenever Kim weathers a stressful situation without using alcohol or drugs, the therapist can verbally reinforce it. In pointing out Kim's successes, the therapist may help Kim feel more empowered and less victimized, thereby instilling hope in her client that she can learn to manage her disorders effectively. By helping the client design small attainable goals, the therapist shows her that change is possible. Having other group members describe how they have learned to manage their disorders more effectively can also be a source of inspiration. The therapist can provide the client with information on how to do things differently and give her opportunities to turn that information into behavioral skills in both group and community settings, which can increase the client's feelings of competency. However, clients who view themselves as victims will tend to initially resist these therapeutic interventions. Thus the therapist and the group will need to be both persistent and patient when working with such clients.

### Theme Seven: Dealing with Relapse and the Return of Psychiatric Symptoms

When clients relapse to substance use or experience an intensification of their psychiatric symptoms, they often experience guilt, a sense of failure, and fear that nothing has changed. In this case, the therapist's goal is to keep clients' hope alive by turning the relapse or return of symptoms into a learning opportunity, not only about what they might do differently next time, but also about how much positive change they have accomplished so far.

Sam has been sober for twelve months and three days. His depression has increased, he is unhappy at work, and he and his girlfriend just had a big fight. He cashes his paycheck and spends $400 on a motel room, cocaine, and alcohol. He is very chagrined the next day and believes he is a bad person who cannot stay sober.

Instead of initially examining why he relapsed, the therapist can simply ask what he has learned from this experience. The therapist also can focus on the fact that the client stopped after one day, and ask what he would have done in the same situation two years ago. This can help the client distinguish a slip from a relapse and allow him to acknowledge that his handling of this setback was a great improvement over how he handled such setbacks in the past. Thus the initial intervention highlights the strengths and positive changes that the client has made over time. When the relapse is framed as a learning experience, the therapist can help the client examine the issues that led up to it and develop plans for its prevention in the future. In the group setting, the therapist can facilitate the group members to support Sam's strength and efforts to limit the slip, and group members can discuss what they have learned from their slips.

### Theme Eight: Dealing with Suicidal Ideation

This theme arises when individuals have seriously considered or attempted suicide. Some individuals with co-occurring disorders struggle daily with thoughts of killing themselves. For example, Natasha reports in the group that she has been thinking about killing herself since yesterday.

The therapist needs to do a safety check first and decide whether the suicide risk is imminent. If not, then, as in the previous case of relapse (Theme 7), the therapist can ask why she has not killed herself yet, instead of initially focusing on why she wants to kill herself. By doing so the therapist can support her strengths and coping skills. Because it helps Natasha to know that she is not the only person who has to deal with such feelings, the therapist asks the group members how they have successfully dealt with suicidal ideation in the past. Doing so allows other group members the opportunity to share their past successes and express their reactions to hearing about another client's suicidal thoughts. Such a process engages the entire group in developing a solution for the problem and prevents group members from becoming isolated with their feelings. The therapist then helps Natasha and any other group member who has been severely affected by the information to develop an antisuicide plan until their next scheduled appointment.

### *Theme Nine: Dealing with Achieving More Stability*

Clients who have spent much of their life drinking, drugging, being mentally unstable, and going in and out of treatment facilities often find themselves ill-equipped to support themselves, socialize appropriately, and in general be responsible for their life. The idea of functioning in a healthy a way often overwhelms clients and becomes a trigger for relapse.

> Morris had been on the first generation antipsychotic medications for years, and had attained sobriety, but continued to have auditory hallucinations that interfered with his daily functioning. He was uncomfortable around other people and unable to work. When he was placed on an atypical antipsychotic medication, the voices were finally controlled, he was able to tolerate being in a room with others, and was being evaluated by vocational rehabilitation services for job training. Although his family and treatment providers were celebrating his significant improvement, Morris was becoming very anxious, and he was concerned that if he got a job he could no longer come to the psychosocial center. He would then be expected to handle everything on his own, which he knew he was not ready to do. Morris therefore stopped taking his medication, began drinking, and was hospitalized shortly thereafter.

The goal of the therapist's interventions when encountering this theme is to help clients develop a realistic view of their recovery and convey that each individual will change at his own unique pace and will not be asked to do more than he is capable of doing. The therapist can ask the other group members if they have felt like Morris, and together the whole group can support one another. The therapist also can help Morris figure out more direct ways to let people know how he is feeling (such as telling his case manager) without having to relapse. Once the reasons for Morris's relapse are identified, he can be assured that the psychosocial center will be available to him as long as he wants to go there and that *he* will decide his level of independence.

### *Theme Ten: Dealing with Mental Illness at Self-Help Meetings*

Individuals are often uncertain or uncomfortable about what to say about their mental disorders at self-help meetings such as Alcoholics Anonymous or Narcotics Anonymous (AA and NA) and thus have difficulty participating in these programs.

Pat reports that she does not want to go back to AA meetings anymore because people look at her funny and do not like her. On further inquiry, she reveals that she recently stood up in an AA meeting and shared that she is an alcoholic with bipolar disorder. Since then she has felt that some of the members are avoiding her.

The therapist's goal in this theme is to help the client understand the primary purpose of twelve-step groups and how to use them appropriately. This is essential because involvement in such groups is necessary for ensuring long-term recovery for most individuals with dependence disorders. In this instance, the therapist can help the client understand that the sole purpose of these groups is to help her deal with her addiction, not her mental illness. The therapist can acknowledge Pat's feeling that she is being shunned because of her illness, while also offering other reasons why AA members might avoid her. In addition, the therapist can point out that not everyone at that meeting reacted in that manner, that many individuals are not avoiding her. With the exception of self-help groups specifically for individuals with co-occurring disorders, such as Double Trouble or Dual Recovery Anonymous, clients should limit how much they share about their mental disorders unless the members have shown that they not only understand but also will not be overwhelmed by this information. Other members of the therapy group can be very helpful in sharing how they handle this dilemma, and suggest which AA or NA meetings in the community are more sympathetic to individuals with co-occurring disorders.

## *CONCLUSION*

The treatment goals discussed in this chapter can be used with each of the treatment modalities discussed in the next four chapters. Likewise the ten treatment themes will arise regardless of the treatment modality used. The next chapter will describe the most common treatment modality used for individuals with co-occurring disorders.

# Chapter 7

# Psychoeducation and Group Therapy

Group treatment is usually the treatment of choice for individuals with co-occurring disorders. Although many types of group treatment are used with various populations, this chapter examines the two types that are used most often to treat individuals with co-occurring disorders: psychoeducation and group therapy. The goal of psychoeducation is to increase awareness and help the client personalize the information presented, develop knowledge and skills, and motivate change through the use of lectures, written materials, audiovisual aids, self-disclosure, and other education and counseling techniques. The goal of group therapy is to provide a safe environment in which participants may share what they think, feel, and do. The goal is to plan for, implement, and evaluate the effectiveness of changes in behavior, emotional control, and thought processes that have been interfering with the individuals' functioning. This chapter describes how these two types of group treatment can most effectively be used with multifarious caseloads.

## *PSYCHOEDUCATION*

During the past thirty years almost all substance abuse and mental health programs have incorporated some form of psychoeducation into their treatment regimens. Although some psychoeducation groups are very structured with homework, role-playing, and tests, other psychoeducation groups are tailored to a more impaired population, requiring only that the individual attends, sits with others for a period of time, and not be too disruptive. Most clients in outpatient treatment, even individuals with unstable serious mental illnesses, have the minimal skills to participate in this type of lower-demand group. Psychoeducation takes many forms ranging from detailed courses in skill building such as dialectic behavioral therapy (Linehan, 1993b) for individuals with borderline personality disorder to simple, short informational sessions about a disorder or medication. In the 1970s, two factors promoted the inclusion of psychoeducation into the treatment mix. The first was the treatment community's philosophical shift to consumer empowerment (thus necessitating knowledgeable clients). The second was the increasing numbers of unmotivated court-mandated clients entering treatment who needed to understand why their behavior was problematic.

Following suit, most treatment models proposed for individuals with co-occurring substance abuse and mental health disorders also recommended use of psychoeducation as part of the treatment regimen (Minkoff, 1991; Noordsy and Fox, 1991; Sciacca, 1991). As with other substance abuse and mental health treatment models, the purpose and focus of psychoeducation can vary greatly for individuals with co-occurring disorders. Some models recommend making it primarily an educational tool that supports other treatment activities (Hendrickson, 1989; Ryglewicz, 1991). Other models use psychoeducation as the main intervention strategy for individuals not yet in treatment (Osher and Kofoed, 1989) or to prevent relapse (Weiss, Najavits, and Greenfield, 1999). Whatever the focus, the use of psychoeducation is now standard practice in mental health and substance use treatment.

## PROMOTING PERSONALIZATION
## OF PSYCHOEDUCATION MATERIAL

For psychoeducation to be effective it must provide participants with the opportunity to personalize the information. Personalizing, or connecting the information to real-life situations, greatly helps participants to see its relevance and retain the information presented. For clients to personalize material, the group leader must use open-ended and personal questions that require clients to connect the information to their own life experience but that do not in any way limit the range of their responses. After a lecture about the many different ways that substance use might affect the symptoms of mental disorders, the group leader may ask, "How did *your* substance use affect the symptoms of *your* mental illness?" Such a question is in no way abstract, but immediate and relevant to the material just presented. The question allows each individual to connect the lecture material in a variety of ways to their own personal experiences but does not force them to share with the group more than they are willing.

Clients are also more likely to personalize information when the content of lecture material can be varied depending on participant responses. For example, during a presentation on caffeine a client who suffers from severe anxiety reveals that he drinks two pots of coffee daily. Instead of just continuing her lecture about caffeine, the facilitator can explore what effect caffeine might have on his anxiety symptoms. In another instance, after one participant claims to have no negative effects from drinking, the facilitator can ask the group to share how alcohol affected their lives. Instead of fighting with this client about the merits of alcohol use, she uses the voices of other participants, who probably have more credibility with this client, to present the possible negative effects of this drug. In still another instance, a client shares that the police are out to get him. The facilitator, who knows that this client has recently stopped taking medication and is using marijuana again, shifts her lecture to the effects that alcohol and other drugs have on paranoid symptoms. She explores with this client and the other participants what their past experiences have been when using substances and not taking their medication as prescribed. Thus, modifying a lecture to respond to spontaneous comments from the participants personalizes the information by making it immediately relevant to a client's life experience.

## *PARTICIPANT LIMITATIONS IN PSYCHOEDUCATION SETTINGS*

Few individuals with mental health or substance use disorders enter a psychoeducation program without some impairment in their learning abilities. These learning liabilities may result from both cognitive impairments and/or the active symptoms of their disorders. Alcohol and drug use and mental health disorders often result in significant impairments in cognitive functions (Erinoff, 1993; Majewska, 1996; Parsons, Butters, and Nathan, 1987; Blume, Davis, and Schmaling, 1999). These impairments occur in attention maintenance and concentration, short-term memory, abstract thinking, problem solving, connecting separate facts into larger paradigms, processing and organizing new information, and adapting to new environments. In addition, clients may bring such symptoms as paranoid ideation, hallucinations, poor impulse control, labile emotions, or substance withdrawal to the psychoeducation setting. Therefore, traditional learning environments need to be modified for this population.

A variety of accommodations are useful for addressing these learning impairments. First, limit sessions to one hour whenever possible or ensure that a fifteen-minute break occurs every hour. Many participants find it difficult to sustain attention for longer periods of time. In addition, many clients participating in psychoeducation are still addicted to nicotine; thus withdrawal will normally begin toward the end of an hour. Second, keep the didactic or lecture portion of the presentation short, not longer than twenty to twenty-five minutes during any one-hour session, and constantly restate and summarize the information. Third, provide the information one piece at a time and before moving on ensure that the participants fully understand the presented concept. Asking participants to describe their understanding of the material just presented is a good way to measure their grasp of the information and to correct any misunderstandings. Fourth, provide the information in a variety of formats because one part of a participant's cognitive functioning may be more impaired than another. Also, each individual has a different learning style. Some people receive information better if it is presented visually, others respond better to information presented orally, while others learn more readily when written information is offered. Reinforcing the material with overheads, videos, descriptive stories, real-life events, and handouts can accomplish this. Handouts and visuals should always be concise, simple, and clear. Fifth, do not require clients to participate at first. To keep clients comfortable, therapists need to allow them to move around or leave the room for a short period if necessary, allow them to sit by themselves in the corner if they choose, and in general, let them enter the psychoeducation process when they are ready and in ways they choose.

## DESIGNING PSYCHOEDUCATION PROGRAMS FOR MULTIFARIOUS CASELOADS

The two key questions concerning the design of a psychoeducation program are: Who is it for? and What should be covered? The need for group cohesion drives the first question. We have discovered over the past twenty years that the key ingredient for ensuring cohesion in a group being formed out of a multifarious caseload is the level of impairment the client brings to the group. The impairment level directly affects the amount of support a client will need to maintain stability in the community. Also take into consideration the likelihood of the disorder or disorders becoming fully stabilized. An individual with co-occurring alcohol dependence and dysthymia is an example of a less-impaired client with two disorders but who responds well to treatment. Once these disorders are stabilized the individual should be able to live independently in the community with little support other than medication and self-help groups.

On the other hand, an individual with schizoaffective and co-occurring alcohol, cocaine and cannabis dependence disorders would be expected to have much greater impairment. Even if all the disorders are stabilized, which may be difficult, that individual will probably need some sort of community-based supportive treatment throughout most of his life. The issues that clients bring to group concerning symptom management, relationships, employment, and life in general are very different for each of these clients. Thus we recommend grouping clients according to their level of long-term impairments. This of course necessitates the availability of two psychoeducation groups; one for less-impaired individuals and another for more impaired individuals.

Once group membership is determined, the next question is what material should be covered? Fortunately, the material that needs to be covered for both groups of individuals is pretty much the same. At a minimum, the effects of the five most commonly abused drugs by both types of individuals—caffeine, alcohol, nicotine, marijuana, and cocaine—should be presented. In addition, material on narcotics, hallucinogens, amphetamines, sedative-hypnotics, or inhalants may be included depending upon how commonly these drugs are being used by the population at hand. Other important topics to include in a psychoeducation program are the concept of co-occurring disorders or how substance use and mental disorders affect each other; how substance use and mental disorders can increase the risk of involvement in the criminal justice system; overview of the symptoms and nature of substance use and mental disorders; overview of the treatment and the process of recovery for these disorders; and the impact that these disorders can have on the family. Box 7.1 presents a sample outline of such a psychoeducation program. Relapse prevention activities may also be presented; see Chapter 10 for a sample outline of a relapse prevention program for individuals with co-occurring disorders.

The real difference between these two types of groups is not the substance of the material presented but *how* it is presented. The presentation needs to be tailored to the specific needs of each group of individuals. For example, the same video on the effects of alcohol can be shown to both groups, but the subsequent discussion needs to be geared to the particular group's level of functioning. Less-impaired individuals can tolerate longer lectures and be expected to participate more in both class discussion and small group exercises, while more-impaired individuals usually need much more guidance and support in expressing ideas in a classroom setting. Less-impaired clients often find written exercises very useful, whereas more-impaired individuals will find it hard to tolerate anything that requires organiza-

---

**BOX 7.1. A Co-Occurring Disorders Psychoeducation Program**

Session 1     Overview of Mental Health and Substance Use Disorders

Session 2     Concept of Co-Occurring Disorders

Session 3     Alcohol and Mental Disorders

Session 4     Marijuana and Mental Disorders

Session 5     Cocaine and Mental Disorders

Session 6     Caffeine and Nicotine and Mental Disorders

Session 7     Other Drugs Commonly used Locally and Mental Disorders

Session 8     Addiction and Mental Illness

Session 9     Effects on the Family

Session 10    Overview of Treatment for Co-Occuring Disorders

Session 11    Overview of Recovery from Co-Occuring Disorders

tion, focusing, and quick thinking. The psychoeducation program for less-impaired individuals is often a closed group model, one series of sessions for a set amount of weeks, for example, ten sessions in five weeks. For more-impaired individuals, however, the set curriculum is often presented as an open group that allows participants to enter at any time, easily make up what they may miss, and stay for longer than one series. Other logistical issues, such as time, length, and location concerning these groups will also differ depending on the level of impairment of the participants. Group treatment logistics will be discussed later in this chapter.

## THE ROLE OF THE LEADER

Remember that participants in substance abuse treatment groups often are there involuntarily. They may be incarcerated or inpatients; participation may be a requirement of their probation; or they may be instructed to attend by their case manager before a certain service will be offered. Therefore the leader must be able to defuse their anger and resentment. This can usually be done by acknowledging that they are being forced into treatment and being clear with them about the number of sessions that they need to attend and any other requirements they must fulfill to complete the program. The leader must allow these members to participate at their own rate, and be clear with them about confidentiality issues and goals (Brown, 1998). The leader must also maintain a safe environment and make it the norm that craving or thoughts of using or self-harm that are triggered by anything seen or heard during the session will be addressed immediately.

## REASONABLE GOALS
## FOR A PSYCHOEDUCATION PROGRAM

Because psychoeducation is neither psychotherapy nor skill building, it has its own unique set of goals. For those who have substance abuse and/or mental health disorders, it is used to increase knowledge about the disorders; change false beliefs about the disorders; and motivate behavior change that helps clients to manage these disorders more effectively. In other words, psychoeducation can give the participant reasons and the desire to effectively use therapy or skill-building activities. For those who have already made positive changes, psychoeducation can help *reinforce these changes*. For example, a relapse prevention psychoeducation program can motivate an individual who has recently achieved abstinence to continue the behaviors she has begun and even learn ways to increase her recovery skills.

Upon first evaluation, in a caseload of individuals with various levels of impairment, a client's level of psychosis, ability to tolerate a group setting, or ability to manage impulses may not be initially observable. In this case, the clinician may want to assign the client to a psychoeducation group for an *extended assessment*. In a low-demand psychoeducation format, additional information for treatment planning can be obtained, such as ability to tolerate a group setting, level of paranoia, attention-deficit problems, and other behaviors that may not have been evident in the initial session.

## *GROUP THERAPY*

Group therapy can change how individuals think and manage their feelings and behaviors through their interactions with other group members and the group therapist. In most instances group therapy is the clinical treatment of choice for individuals with co-occurring disorders. The most effective type of group therapy for this population is based on the cognitive-behavioral model (Burns, 1999; Ellis, 1988; Olevitch and Ellis, 1999). Individuals with multiple disorders usually have deeply ingrained behavioral and thinking patterns that dramatically interfere with their ability to manage their disorders effectively. To learn how to better manage their disorders clients need to identify their ineffective cognitive and behavioral patterns and develop new thinking and behavioral skills. These new skills include how to correct negative thought distortions that lead to hopelessness and helplessness and to increase positive interactions with other people. With better interactions, individuals can develop trust, learn how to give and receive appropriate feedback and support from others, and modify their behaviors as they observe how others effectively handle difficult situations. These cognitive skills lead to a healthier sense of self (Gazda, Ginter, and Horne, 2001) and a greater sense of mastery over life; clients also gain a sense of themselves that is separate from their disorder. Such a differentiation provides them with the strength to make the changes necessary to manage their psychiatric and substance abuse symptoms. These changes are most easily accomplished in a group setting.

Several other factors also make group therapy an attractive treatment of choice whenever possible. Group therapy is cost effective because it allows clinical staff to effectively treat several individuals at a time. Almost all substance use and mental health issues can be treated effectively in a group environment. Almost all clients can eventually participate in this treatment modality, especially when groups are tailored to specific impairment levels. However, group therapy does not eliminate the need for other treatment modalities. Some clients need extensive individual treatment to prepare them for a group setting and others need individual and case management services in addition to group treatment (see Chapter 8). Many clients also need family treatment (see Chapter 9). Modalities other than verbal group psychotherapy may also be indicated. For example, psychodrama, art therapy, and other creative arts therapies can be extremely useful with individuals who are alexithymic, that is, they do not recognize feelings, which occurs often with individuals who have used alcohol and drugs to medicate unpleasant emotional states. The key is to use group treatment whenever possible and other modalities to deal with issues that cannot effectively be addressed in a group. However, before implementing group therapy for clients, decisions need to be made concerning membership, operating rules, and logistics.

## *GROUP MEMBERSHIP*

As with psychoeducation groups, the key variable, the glue that binds the group together, is ensuring that group members have *similar impairment levels*. Each time we have combined individuals with significantly different impairment levels into one group, one set of these individuals naturally select themselves out and leave the group. These clients have reported that they either felt that the group was asking too much of them or it was too elementary for their needs. As a rough rule we use the Global Assessment of Functioning (GAF) of the DSM-IV-TR for determining group placement, placing those with an expected normal GAF level of 60 or below in one group and those with a GAF over 60 in another group. Although the GAF measures are very subjective, they can be helpful as a starting point when combined with other information to determine the appropriate group for an individual.

*Current substance usage* is another important group membership concern. Should individuals who are still using drugs and alcohol be placed with individuals who are not using? The phases of treatment model suggested by Osher and Kofoed (1989) and others tend to place users in persuasion groups and nonusers into treatment groups. We find that we can combine users and nonusers in one group as long as the majority of members acknowledge that alcohol and other drugs cause them problems and that abstinence or a reduction in use is their goal. In that way the power of the group is working toward the goals of treatment. Research has shown that either model is effective in promoting change (Drake, McHugo, and Noordsy, 1993; Hendrickson, Stith, and Schmal, 1995); thus which model is used is really based on how comfortable the therapist is with the model and the number and type of clients and treatment resources available.

Finally, should individuals with co-occurring substance use and mental disorders be placed in specialized groups or be integrated into groups with individuals who have only substance use disorders? Substance abuse groups with members who have less impairment can include individuals with and without co-occurring mental disorders because the substance use disorder is usually the most disruptive one. Less-impaired group members with co-occurring mental disorders usually have milder forms of mood, anxiety, or personality disorders; thus their treatment issues can usually be addressed adequately without modifying the primary purpose of the group. However, we find that combining severely impaired individuals with and without co-occurring disorders is usually disruptive to the treatment process. For example, placing clients with only schizophrenia in a group with clients who have schizophrenia and substance use disorders makes the treatment goals too broad for effective group focus. One group member is attempting to manage one disorder while another group member is attempting to manage two or more interacting disorders. Thus individuals with major impairments should be placed in a group that focuses on co-occurring disorders, while those with no substance use problem should be placed in other groups that focus only on mental disorders.

# OPERATING RULES FOR THE GROUP

Ten issues arise frequently enough in treatment groups so that certain rules need to be established: confidentiality, timeliness, attendance and participation requirements, length of treatment, intoxication, threatening or violent behavior, respectfulness, contact outside the group, termination notice, and readmission requirements. Some rules apply equally to both types of groups and some are modified depending on the type of group. These rules are initially presented twice to new group members, once prior to entering the group and then again during the first group session.

## Confidentiality

Without trust, no one feels safe in sharing personal thoughts, feelings, and behaviors. Therefore, the rule is simple for both types of groups: What is said in here, stays in here. The only exceptions are mandated reporting requirements concerning such issues as imminent danger to self or others or child abuse. The client needs to be always informed before any information is discussed outside the group, even when a client has signed a release allowing the therapist to talk to the third party. If confidentiality is broken, all involved members need to address it immediately in the group setting. If a client breaks confidentiality a second time he is asked to leave the group.

## Timeliness

No group can really begin until all members have arrived, because late-arriving group members always disrupt the group process. Hence the rule for both types of groups is to be on time. We always shut the group room door at the exact scheduled starting time. Even very impaired clients can get to the group on time when this rule is vigorously enforced. If a member requests to enter the group a few minutes late, the group and the therapist decide if the lateness was unavoidable; sometimes buses are late and sometimes tires become flat. However, when clients are refused admittance, they are always encouraged to return to their next scheduled group. We believe such a rule reinforces the concept that the work occurring in the group is to be taken seriously.

### Attendance and Participation Expectations

Attendance and participation expectations are tied to the impairment levels of clients. Individuals with major impairments often have difficulty attending all scheduled groups because of reduced organizational skills and increased symptom levels. Though these clients need some flexibility when it comes to attendance, they still are expected to attend many more sessions than they miss. Clients who know they will miss a session need to inform the group therapist ahead of time. These groups can tolerate some level of inconsistency in attendance; however, very erratic attendance by a group member can be distracting and disruptive to the continuity of the group process; therefore, clients who do not attend on a fairly regular basis are removed from the treatment group and placed in a psychoeducation group. Psychoeducation groups are designed to tolerate erratic attendance; furthermore, clients can also use this group to demonstrate that they are ready to consistently attend a therapy group by attending four psychoeducation groups in a row. Individuals with less impairment, however, need to follow much stricter guidelines because they have the skills to attend scheduled sessions. They are expected to attend all scheduled sessions unless excused because of illness, family, or work emergencies, but even in those instances, the client is expected to call the therapist prior to the absence.

Expectations concerning the level of an individual's participation in the group also depends on his level of impairment. Individuals with less impairment are expected to share and give feedback to other group members on a regular basis almost from their first day in the group. The participation level of clients with greater impairment may vary greatly from group to group depending on their symptom levels. Thus the group leader must be sensitive to the varying moods and abilities of clients from day to day. Part of the art of running groups is to know when to actively encourage participation and when to respect a client's need to be silent. On some days, the only group participation requirement may be to come and stay in the group.

What is shared will also determine the effectiveness for both types of groups. If these groups are to be successful, the bulk of what is shared must be personal information, such as what clients feel, think, and do. If group members talk about world events or complain about the general unfairness of social services and legal systems, the group is not on task and personalization is not occurring. In these instances the therapist needs to redirect the group toward personalizing how their substance use or mental disorders are impacting them. The level of sophistication concerning how and what personal information is revealed will of course vary greatly depending upon a client's cognitive skills. The depth of the shared information is not as important as the focus of its content.

## Length of Treatment

Treatment usually needs to be longer for individuals who are more impaired than for those who are less impaired. However, the actual length of time a client participates in group treatment is usually the result of the interplay between what a client needs, is willing to do, and can be mandated to do. Clients who are mandated into treatment by a court, family, or other authorities need to know how long their "sentence to treatment" will be. Knowing this and exactly everything else that is expected of them from the beginning gives these clients some sense of control over their lives. They will have the data they need to choose either to complete the "treatment sentence" or to face the consequences for not doing so. For less-impaired clients who have a substance use disorder, we recommend that the minimum length of treatment be six months; for individuals with co-occurring disorders with major impairments, we recommend one year.

For the nonmandated client, the length of treatment normally is the client's choice. However, what a client is willing to do can often be influenced by the therapist. It is the therapist's role and responsibility to inform the client exactly how long an effective length of treatment should take. Clients might not choose that length, but at least they have the information necessary to make an informed choice. Also, such information often influences clients to commit to a longer time in treatment than they originally might have. Because a therapy group's process is disrupted when a new client attends only one or two groups and then drops out, clients should agree initially to attend a minimum of six sessions. Clients who are unable to commit to this minimum requirement can be referred to a psychoeducation group instead. In general, after clients meet either their minimum session requirement or commitment, they are free to leave the group or stay as long as they like. Occasionally, clients become dependent on the group and are fearful of moving on. When clients use group attendance as an excuse for avoiding involvement in other necessary community activities, the therapist may choose to limit how long the client can stay in the group, while at the same time working with the client to connect with other community-based activities that are designed for lifetime membership, such as self-help groups or a psychosocial center.

## *Intoxication*

We define intoxication as having used a nonprescribed drug or a drug in a nonprescribed manner during any part of the day prior to the beginning of a group. No member may be intoxicated during either type of group. Ideally, other group members should confront the intoxicated individual; however, if the group fails to perform this task, the therapist must make the intervention. While acknowledging how difficult abstinence can be at times, the group or therapist must ask any intoxicated individual to leave the group but encourage him or her to return drug-free to the next scheduled session. When the group fails to address the intoxication issue, the therapist must help the group members gain some understanding as to why they were unable or unwilling to perform this task and come up with a plan on how to do it next time.

## *Threatening or Violent Behavior*

If clients engage in such behavior, they are immediately removed from either type of group. If individuals have a history of such behavior, a three-factor assessment is conducted before admitting them to a group. These factors are the history and date of last incident; the relationship between the behavior and substance use or medication noncompliance; and what steps the client has taken since to prevent this behavior. A prospective member who has been violent in the last year is usually not admitted to a group unless the previous behavior was the direct result of intoxication or psychiatric symptoms that are now in full remission. The individual also needs to acknowledge that this behavior was inappropriate. Clients not meeting these criteria are monitored through individual or case management activities until they demonstrate their ability to refrain from such behavior in a treatment setting.

## *Respect*

It is important for every group member's sense of security in sharing personal information that all group members respond respectfully to one another. Members should refrain from name-calling or denigrating what another member is saying, also show themselves the same respect. Another operating principle in group is that only the client has the right to determine how painful symptoms are and what personal concerns are important enough to share with the group. An individual with major depression, asthma, and nicotine addiction is in just as much danger, if not more so, than a heroin addict with an anxiety disorder. The therapist must interrupt any attempt by a group member to make another feel that he must defend himself for bringing a personal issue to the group. Less-impaired individuals, who do not have certain personality disorders, generally readily accept and follow this rule; however, more-impaired individuals who have less-developed social skills, may need the reasons behind this rule explained to them and may need occasional reminders during the course of a group.

## *Contact Outside the Group*

Most traditional group therapy approaches discourage contact between group members outside the group. For groups of less-impaired individuals who normally have extended social networks, this is appropriate. However, enforcing this rule for groups of more-impaired individuals would be difficult and not necessarily beneficial. More-impaired individuals normally have multiple treatment needs and multiple treatment experiences. As a result, group members often know one another from a hospital, detoxification center, day treatment program, or residential setting. Clients often have known one another for years before joining the group and may be an important part of one another's social network. Therefore, contact between group members that supports their recovery outside the group (such as going to AA meetings or doing nondrug-related recreational activities together) is encouraged even though this heightens the risk of inappropriate social behavior outside the group (such as using drugs together or exacerbating symptoms). When outside activities between group members run counter to the goals of the group, they need to be addressed as soon as possible. Initially, it is usually a secret, however, eventually one of the group members will bring the information to the therapist privately. For example, Susan informs the therapist that Jose and Betty have been drinking together after the group sessions. The therapist works with Susan to bring the issue up in group, not from an accusatory position that their behavior is bad, but from a position of worry for them. Susan also needs to talk about how Jose and Betty's behavior is impacting on her own attempts to stay sober.

The therapist should take a noncritical approach, express concern for Jose and Betty, and frame the behavior as being far from abnormal for individuals with alcohol dependence. The therapist needs to take the position that keeping secrets about outside activities interferes with the effectiveness of the group and group members need to be honest about what happens outside the group. This intervention strategy makes the group a safe place to bring up such issues and communicates that honesty is expected from group members.

### Termination Notice

Members of both groups are asked to give two weeks' notice prior to leaving the group. Although this rule is almost impossible to enforce, it exemplifies organized and responsible behavior. In actual practice, individuals with less impairment follow this rule much better than those with greater impairment who tend to have fewer organizational skills and difficulty with such orderly behavior because their psychiatric symptoms often interfere.

### Readmission Requirements

Individuals with substance use and/or major mental disorders normally are admitted to treatment more than once (see Chapter 13). Readmitting a person to a therapy group depends on several factors: what level of treatment the client needs; what other services are available to the client; what has changed since the last admission; and anything that a client must agree to or demonstrate before regaining entry to the group. Normally, these demands are much higher for individuals with less impairment than for individuals with major impairment. For example, a client with alcohol dependence and generalized anxiety disorders who had never fully participated in his previous group and has a history of noncompliance with treatment might be required to participate in residential treatment, or to attend all sessions of the psychoeducation series and take Antabuse prior to being accepted back into an outpatient treatment group. On the other hand, a client with schizoaffective and cocaine dependence disorders with the same attendance history might only be required to attend four psychoeducation groups in a row prior to readmission. In general, treatment compliance is more difficult for this client because of his disorder and gaining entrance to a substance abuse residential program could be very difficult. Thus more-impaired clients need more flexible readmission criteria. Also, many clients who are severely impaired often voluntarily reenter co-occurring disorders' treatment groups even though their substance use is in remission. This is not the case for clients with less impairment. Some members of the severely impaired population intuitively know that they need longer-term treatment and support in order to maintain their positive changes. Hence readmission criteria for this population should be based more on treatment interest than length of stability and substance use remission.

## *GROUP LOGISTICS*

### *Frequency of Groups*

Research is not clear concerning how frequently an individual with a specific disorder should attend group treatment. However, at least for individuals with substance dependency or co-occurring disorders, research does indicate that longer stays in treatment are associated with better outcomes (see Chapter 13). Thus, ideally, groups should be offered in a way that promotes retention. Less-impaired clients whose disorders are more easily stabilized tend to benefit from groups held once per week. Clients whose disorders are more difficult to stabilize, and those who are isolated and need a sense of affiliation with a recovery community often benefit from multiple groups; ideally, groups should be offered daily, when possible, so that those who need more support have it available. Doing so matches clients' treatment needs with treatment opportunities, which increases the potential of treatment retention.

## Length of Groups

As with psychoeducation, the ideal length of treatment groups for more-impaired individuals is one hour, but less-impaired individuals can usually participate effectively in groups that last one and one-half hours. This is again a function of the client's level of concentration skills, attention span, communication skills, and ability to manage psychiatric symptoms and nicotine withdrawal.

## Location and Time of Groups

The appropriate location of a group is strongly associated with clients' ability to travel and adapt to new environments. Less-impaired individuals usually can attend a group that meets at a different site from other services they may be receiving because they have the skills and resources to travel between different locations. They often have an automobile or can easily use public transportation. More-impaired individuals, however, often do not have private transportation and may have difficulty using public transportation. Thus treatment groups for more-impaired individuals need to be held where the clients are already receiving the bulk of their services; this maximizes ease of access and hence the potential of treatment retention. For example, it *is* possible for a client with schizophrenia to take the bus from the psychosocial rehabilitation center to another agency office for her co-occurring disorders group, but the chance for regular attendance is slim. Better to offer such a group *at* the psychosocial rehabilitation center.

The time of day that the groups are held depends upon the needs of these two groups of individuals. Less-impaired individuals usually need evening groups because of work commitments. More-impaired individuals are usually not employed and need to have their days more organized. In addition, their symptoms sometimes make coming out after dark difficult, hence daytime groups are usually most advantageous for them. However, some less-impaired individuals do work evening hours and some more-impaired individuals are involved actively in the workforce or volunteer activities, so it is helpful to have available at least one daytime group for the less impaired and one evening group for the more impaired.

## Size of Groups

The functioning level of group members also affects the number of participants that should be placed in a group. The ideal size of a group for more-impaired individuals is between four to eight members. Because of the limited verbal skills of some members, a group of less than four often has limited material with which to work. Also a very small group can increase the level of anxiety or paranoia in some individuals because they feel pressure to share more than they want. Some clients need a large enough group to hide in emotionally but still feel safe in. A group with more than eight members can overwhelm some of these individuals because of too much stimulation or because the time is inadequate for all the members to share important issues. However, the attendance patterns of more-impaired clients are often erratic; thus with up to ten members in a group, one can expect four to eight to attend. Less-impaired individuals usually can be expected to attend groups regularly and make connections about their own situation through problem-solving discussions with other clients. These skills and the length of the group usually allow a somewhat larger group of ten to twelve members.

## Number of Group Leaders

Individuals with more impairment tend to have more active symptoms and are more crisis prone than individuals with less impairment. These groups should be co-led. Usually, many issues and symptoms present themselves concurrently, which makes it very difficult for a single clinician to attend to everything happening in the group. Also, if a group member experiences suicidal or major psychiatric symptoms during a session, having two leaders allows one to leave the group with the client in crisis while the other leader can stay and help the remaining group members process their reactions to the event. Usually, groups composed of less-impaired individuals do not need coleaders to address the issues that arise in the course of treatment. However, other issues could necessitate the need for coleaders, such as therapist inexperience and the need to have gender, culture, or race represented by a group leader. These issues should also be considered when choosing coleaders for the more-impaired groups.

# A TYPICAL GROUP SESSION
# FOR MORE-IMPAIRED INDIVIDUALS

This group consists of Elaine, diagnosed with alcohol dependence, major depressive disorder, and post-traumatic stress disorder; Jackie, diagnosed with schizoaffective disorder, alcohol dependence, and cocaine dependence; Frida, diagnosed with schizophrenia, cocaine dependence, and borderline intellectual functioning; Sara, diagnosed with schizophrenia, alcohol dependence, and bereavement; Charles, diagnosed with schizoaffective disorder, polysubstance dependence, and personality disorder not otherwise specified (NOS) with narcissistic and antisocial features; and Walter, diagnosed with bipolar disorder and alcohol dependence.

Frida is new to the group, so the therapists and the group members begin by introducing themselves to her. Group members say their name, what symptoms and behaviors they are working on, and a strength, such as "perseverance," or "my faith." Then Frida introduces herself to the group. The therapists next ask the members to list the rules of the group. Frida is then welcomed to the group.

Elaine begins by stating that she may move to California. Frida closes her eyes. Jackie stares off into space. Charles talks about his stay in California. The leaders ask Elaine to elaborate. She reports that the only way she can get away from her intrusive family is to drink alcohol or move very far away where they cannot control her. She describes their intrusive behavior. Jackie looks at the middle of the room and says, "I wouldn't let my brothers do that to me! No way!" The therapists then ask her why. She states that it is none of her brothers' business, and they better not come into her apartment without her permission. The therapists support Jackie's sense of boundaries. Sara says, "I'm not strong enough to stop them." The therapists suggest that Sara is *not yet* strong enough to stop them. The therapists wonder about what her past relationships were like. She thinks about it and decides they were like her brother, they wanted her to do whatever they wanted. Again she says she must move to California. The therapists ask her what kind of man she will find for a companion in California. She argues that she will not have a boyfriend in California. Jackie laughs. Charles says, "Of course you will; you always do." Sara agrees, and admits he probably will be just like her previous controlling, abusive boyfriends unless she learns to change and get stronger inside, so that she can maintain her boundaries without having to move far away. "I need to make changes inside me, not where I live." During the rest of the group time, the therapists get the group members to help Sara brainstorm what steps she might be ready to take to begin the process of being able to stand up for herself and set limits with her family. At the end of the session each member states how group was for them today, and the therapists again welcome Frida to the group.

Groups such as this often require therapists to be very active in keeping the discussion on task and soliciting feedback from other group members.

## A TYPICAL GROUP SESSION
## FOR LESS-IMPAIRED INDIVIDUALS

This group consists of Paula, diagnosed with alcohol dependence and dysthymia; John, diagnosed with cocaine dependence and generalized anxiety disorder; Michael, diagnosed with marijuana abuse disorder and attention-deficit disorder; Lee Ann, diagnosed with alcohol dependence and depressive disorder NOS; Harry, diagnosed with cocaine dependence and cocaine-induced mood disorder; Chuck, diagnosed with cocaine dependence; William, diagnosed with alcohol abuse disorder; Maria, diagnosed with marijuana and alcohol dependence; Wayne, diagnosed with alcohol and cocaine dependence; and Brenda, diagnosed with anxiolytic and alcohol dependence and anxiolytic-induced anxiety disorder.

The group begins with the therapist asking each member if they were able to achieve their abstinence or nonproblematic use goals for the past week. All but Lee Ann report achieving their goals. Lee Ann reports that she drank twice during the week. Once the members finish updating the group, Lee Ann begins to discuss her understanding of why she drank. She reports that she is not really sure why she used alcohol. Michael and Wayne quickly confront her about that statement. They tell her she drank because she is an alcoholic. Brenda, however, challenges Michael and Wayne: "Come on, it's just not that simple." The therapist then redirects the conversation by wondering out loud why their individual experiences lead them to such different conclusions. Each then describes why they believe they had relapsed in the past. Other members also share such experiences. Some describe their obsessions and cravings for drugs, and others talk about how the symptoms of their mental disorder contributed to a relapse. The therapist then asks Lee Ann: "Now that you have heard these other experiences, are there any you can identify with?" Lee Ann states: "There are parts of several experiences that I identify with." She then describes what happened during her relapse process. The discussion concludes with Lee Ann developing a new relapse prevention plan. The group concludes with each group member restating their abstinence or nonproblematic use plan for next week, and what plans they have to deal with any potentially risky situations they may face.

Such groups often only require that the therapist set the structure and pose questions that require clients to look at their own motivations and behaviors in order for the group to function and stay on task.

### CONCLUSION

Almost all clients in multifarious caseloads are able to participate in and benefit from psychoeducation and group therapy. When assigning clients from multifarious caseloads to these types of group treatment activities, the key for success is ensuring that clients have similar levels of impairment and that the education, treatment, and participation requirements vary according to levels of impairment. The next three chapters describe four additional treatment modalities that most of these clients will also receive: individual therapy, case management, family therapy, and relapse prevention. Modifications, based on impairment levels, are also presented for these intervention strategies.

# Chapter 8

# Individual Therapy
# and Case Management

Mental health facilities tend to use individual therapy and case management more frequently while substance abuse settings tend to use group therapy more often. Outcome studies show that each of these modalities is an effective treatment vehicle. Often the theoretical base, professional training, and type of treatment with which the therapist feels most comfortable determines the type of treatment modality used. The Task Force on Dual Diagnosis in Oregon (Walker, 2000) recommended a full range of treatment for individuals with co-occurring disorders, including opportunities for individual and group therapy and case management. A policy report on dual diagnosis from the Metropolitan Washington Council of Governments (1995) noted that some clients are initially too distrustful, fearful, or disorganized to participate in group therapy and thus need individual attention. This chapter does not promote one modality over another, but instead discusses how individual treatment and case management can be most effective with a multifarious caseload.

## *INDIVIDUAL THERAPY*

Daley and Zuckoff (1999) point out that people need to feel they have choices in the treatment they receive. Many individuals complain about and feel cheated by treatment programs that offer only group sessions. Individual sessions allow consumers with co-occurring disorders to work on issues they believe are too sensitive to bring up in group. Conversely, a therapist may want to discuss certain concerns with a client privately. An example is a group member who was observed going through trash cans for food. Although other group members would have been supportive, the client may feel humiliated if his financial situation were revealed to the group.

McGovern (1994) offers guidelines for individual treatment for clients with co-occurring disorders: individual therapy should be active, directive, and reinforce compliance with all treatment recommendations. Therapy should support sobriety and underscore the failure of self-medication. It should empower clients with responsibility for their own behavior and stress the combined effects of co-occurring disorders and set concrete rules for safe behavior. Individual therapy should recommend and encourage participation in recovery groups and in peer support groups.

In addition, Wallen (1994) adds these guidelines: individual therapy should monitor psychiatric symptoms and support client compliance with medication. Confrontation should be moderate and issues discussed in a concrete and straightforward manner. Individual sessions should foster the development of coping skills to deal with stress without the use of alcohol or other drugs. Individual therapy should support developing constructive ways to use time without using drugs and reinforce mature, responsible adult behavior. It also should promote and support involvement in constructive leisure activities, education programs, support groups, needed medical care, and returning to treatment after a relapse.

An example of how individual and group treatment can be integrated is to encourage clients in individual treatment to participate in group, focus on specific symptoms, and help clients be less guarded and defensive in group. Individual sessions also can focus on how a person could use a group to receive solicited helpful support from others. If a client participates fully in individual therapy and is still reluctant to engage in the group process, the reasons then become a focus in individual sessions. Also, the client might be given assignments, such as participating in every group for six consecutive sessions or bringing up a topic at the beginning of group on at least three different occasions and then use individual sessions to evaluate that experience.

Overall, individual therapy can be preparation for group therapy, adjunctive to group therapy, or an alternative for individuals who because of their symptoms cannot tolerate or participate effectively in group therapy. Six general guidelines to foster full client participation in both individual and group treatment are:

1. Do not allow individual sessions to compromise the group process. This might happen if clients only talk about significant issues in the individual session and remain distant and uninvolved in group.
2. Do not allow individual sessions to become a haven or a refuge from group treatment. Clients with co-occurring disorders must feel safe in treatment, but they must also be encouraged to risk knowing others and allowing others to know them as they work on both their psychiatric and substance use issues. Accordingly, individual sessions must not be much more supportive and congenial than group sessions.
3. Clinicians may sometimes find it useful to define group involvement as a higher skill than individual treatment. Clients may need individual therapy until they can "graduate" into being group participants. Clinicians may emphasize that the capacity to give in a group is healing and important to recovery from substance use and mental disorders.
4. Do not allow clients to attend individual sessions and skip group sessions. This may need to be confronted and the reasons explored, but it must not be allowed to continue unchallenged. In individual therapy the therapist might explore the issues that get in the way of the client using group treatment. Another approach is to provide one individual session for attending two consecutive groups.
5. Do not ally with clients against group expectation. No therapeutic alliance should be formed that allows clients to be "protected" from the group. Individual sessions can prepare clients to assertively challenge an unwanted expectation or demand within the group. However, this should be framed as fostering assertiveness with others rather than being protected from uncomfortable situations.
6. Discuss issues in individual therapy in terms of how they might be managed within the group.

As with group treatment, individual treatment requires the therapist with a multifarious caseload to address a wide variety of substance use and mental health issues. Regarding substance abuse, the individual therapist must teach the signs and symptoms of addiction; provide information on specific drugs; focus on craving and how to rechannel urges to use; encourage and motivate abstinence; monitor abstinence through the use of urine screens or other objective measures; hold the individuals accountable for their choices; assist in the identification of triggers and how alcohol and other drugs were used to cope with life's problems; assist in the development of new, effective, problem-solving strategies; introduce and strongly encourage participation in support groups; assist in recognizing and changing problematic attitudes and behaviors that may stimulate a relapse; and encourage the development of self-esteem. Other substance use factors relevant to the treatment process include dealing with anger, managing postacute withdrawal symptoms, addressing other compulsive behaviors, and discussing unhealthy relationships (Mercer and Woody, 1999).

On mental health issues, individual therapy must focus on psychiatric symptoms, medication and medication compliance, resolving conflict and working through trauma, understanding and changing destructive interpersonal behavior, educating about specific psychiatric disorders, urging acceptance of responsibility for managing the mental illness, facilitating the recognition of and changing problematic attitudes and behavior that may trigger a relapse or exacerbation of symptoms, developing effective problem-solving strategies, and encouraging participation in support groups. Therapy also may explore how patterns of destructive behavior toward self or others may derive from childhood survivor behaviors. In therapy, a client can learn how to change such patterns or give them up in the service of successful relationships and reduction of self-harm.

A checklist, developed by Daley and Thase (1994), can help monitor the effectiveness of individual therapy for clients with co-occurring disorders. It allows the therapist to evaluate each session to determine how successfully the co-occurring issues, which are viewed as two "no fault" biopsychosocial disorders with multiple causes, were covered. The checklist includes:

1. Support recovery from both disorders with a focus on craving and abstinence.
2. Provide feedback and confrontation about denial, self-defeating behaviors, strengths, and the connection between thoughts, feelings, and behaviors.

3. Provide information and education about psychiatric illness, addiction, and the relationship between these disorders.
4. Encourage participation in self-help groups, in getting and using a sponsor, and discuss resistance or negative views about self-help groups.
5. Encourage clients to participate in ongoing treatment as needed; assist clients to develop an emergency plan to deal with unexpected setbacks such as relapse in one or more disorders.

Therapy with clients who have co-occurring mental health and substance use disorders also requires a focus on and education about the impact of one disorder on the other, such as the impact of alcohol, other drug use, and abstinence on psychiatric symptoms. These interactions are not always as straightforward as a simple positive interaction, i.e., abstinence reduces the severity of psychiatric symptoms. At times, abstinence can reduce psychiatric symptoms but sometimes it can exacerbate them. If drug use was either medicating or masking depression, anxiety, or suicidal ideation, the therapist needs to pay particular attention in the early stages of abstinence to ensure client safety. Also, if drugs were diminishing severe social anxiety or fear of rejection, then abstinence makes it extraordinarily difficult to engage in constructive interaction or socialization.

## CASE MANAGEMENT

The term *case management* has many different meanings for many different people. At the turn of the last century, Mary Richmond, who envisioned a cadre of friendly visitors to help the worthy poor cope with illness, children, church, and saving and spending money, used the term social casework for these activities (Kahn, 1998). The 1963 federal Community Mental Health Centers Act included case management services for individuals returning to the community from state hospitals. The Community Support System developed by the National Institute of Mental Health in 1977 defined case management as a means to help clients navigate a fragmented social service system (Siegal, 1998).

For years, individuals with substance use disorders received case management-like services from the clergy and skid row missions, detoxification centers, and halfway houses. Initiatives undertaken by both the National Institute on Drug Abuse (NIDA) and the National Institute on Alcohol Abuse and Alcoholism (NIAAA) include projects that use case management to enhance substance abuse treatment. Case management is identified as one of the eight core substance abuse counseling skills, according to the National Association of Alcoholism and Drug Abuse Counselors (NAADAC). Managed care also uses the term case management to describe one of its activities to contain health costs (Siegal, 1998).

The Case Management Society of America defines case management as "a collaborative process which assesses, plans, implements, coordinates, monitors, and evaluates the options and services required to meet an individual's health needs, using communication and available resources to promote quality, cost-effective outcomes" (Cleary and Paone, 2000, p. 6). The American Nurses Association adds the goals of enhancing quality of life and decreasing fragmentation of care to its definition of nursing case management (Ling, 2002). Although the National Association of Social Workers (NASW) notes that there is no universally accepted definition of case management, they propose that it is a method of providing services that addresses both the client's biopsychosocial status and the state of the social system in which the case management is delivered (NASW, 1992). The Commission for Case Manager Certification (CCMC) (2000) proposes that case management is not a profession in itself, but an area of practice within the case manager's profession. Individuals performing case management activities are normally trained in some other profession, such as nursing, social work, psychiatric rehabilitation, or counseling.

Essentially, case management is defined by the agency that provides the service. Although its role varies from agency to agency, the common factor in all definitions of case management is the focus on connecting clients to needed resources and monitoring client progress in those services. The case manager is often seen as the central, unifying point of contact for clients receiving services from multiple sources. The CCMC notes that case management is collaborative and across disciplines and that it is a means for achieving client autonomy and wellness via advocacy, communication, education, resources, and facilitation.

## FUNCTIONS OF CASE MANAGEMENT

The literature generally agrees on the functions of case management, though models of case management vary. Traditional case management functions include: client identification, outreach, and engagement; assessment of treatment needs; treatment planning; implementation of the treatment plan; supportive counseling; linkage to treatment services; advocating for services; monitoring other service involvement; reassessment of service needs; and termination of services. Because case management models are designed to be comprehensive, many of these functions overlap with traditional functions provided by all therapists. Thus, this chapter will focus only on those functions not discussed elsewhere in this book but that need to be part of the treatment toolbox of any therapist working with a multifarious caseload.

### *Client Identification, Outreach, and Engagement*

Case management can be effective when it targets clients identified at risk (Cleary and Paone, 2000). Identification, outreach, and engagement are proactive functions in case management. The more intensive the case management model, the more focus there is on these activities. Individuals most in need of case management tend to be so disorganized due to their levels of dysfunction and severity of life problems that it's unlikely they would seek help on their own. Many clients with co-occurring disorders have the potential to "hit bottom" with increasingly severe psychiatric symptoms and hazardous substance abuse; intervention can prevent disability or further deterioration. For these individuals, case management involves reaching out to offer services in the most pragmatic way possible as a means of engaging the client for more focused intervention. For example, if a homeless individual with schizoaffective and alcohol dependence disorders needs socks or a warm blanket, the case manager provides a tangible form of assistance while connecting with the client and beginning to introduce other possible services. The goal of case management at this stage is to reduce personal and agency barriers that block admission to treatment (Montague, 2000).

## Linking to Treatment Services

The linkage function of case management can be particularly challenging when dealing with systems or programs that are disinclined to work cooperatively with one another. Programs may compete with one another for resources; disagree about approach to treatment; restrict their accessibility to an unwanted client population; be unavailable as they try to manage overwhelming demand for limited treatment resources; or insist that some preexisting problem be resolved before treatment can begin. When attempting to coordinate comprehensive treatment plans for clients in need of services from more than one agency, therapists may have to expend a great deal of time and energy to overcome these barriers.

In their attempts to link clients to services, therapists will need to work at the system level and so must become familiar with the admission criteria of agencies that their clients need. They will also need to develop personal relationships with staff of those agencies who can help explain the political dynamics of their agency and intervene when necessary to overcome an admission blockage. They also must be willing to return the favor and organize joint meetings to develop collaborative treatment plans.

## Advocating for Services

Connecting clients with needed services can be very challenging at times and the therapist may need to advocate for the client while they attempt to link the client to particular programs. Clients may need services from agencies whose admission criteria may be vague or exclusive concerning their disorders. Many clients with co-occurring disorders may resist going to these additional services or engage in threatening or obnoxious behaviors or attitudes.

In these cases, therapists need to be both patient and persistent with their clients and other treatment agencies. They need to very clearly explain to both the client and the agency why a particular service is needed. At times, therapists have to "make a case for their client" by emphasizing the client's strengths and providing the reasons why the client would be successful if accepted into the services, while never appearing to dump a very undesirable client on another agency. Therapists must emphasize that they will continue to also be involved with the client and in some situations play an active role in helping clients successfully use the additional services. Examples of their involvement may be driving the client to the service or accompanying and helping the client to initially adjust to the new service environment. Advocacy is both a verbal and a behavioral activity.

## Monitoring Other Services

Sometimes referred to as case coordination, this function involves monitoring the participation of clients in services provided by other staff or agencies and the ongoing quality of these services. Therapists need to be proactive and request reports, make phone calls, make site visits, sort out conflicting information, and make frequent observations of client behavior. Therapists with multifarious caseloads may monitor medication compliance and effectiveness, participation and effectiveness of additional mental health or substance abuse treatment, housing support, and work training or assistance services. The goal of this case management function is to ensure that individuals are participating in any additional services necessary to achieve their treatment goal and that the services are meeting the treatment needs of clients. This function also includes having to intervene with the client or on the system level when the client is not participating adequately or services are ineffective.

## Reassessing

This function is very critical for therapists with multifarious caseloads because many clients have disorders whose treatment needs can change very rapidly. Some individuals with psychiatric disorders can become stable or unstable quickly. Likewise individuals with substance use disorders can relapse and destabilize rapidly. Of course the destabilization of one disorder can quickly destabilize another disorder for individuals with co-occurring disorders. Thus the therapist may need to facilitate additional services very quickly by performing most of the previous functions effectively. On the other hand, a client may stabilize more rapidly than expected and may no longer need a specific level of service; in this case, the therapist will need to move that client into a less-intense level of treatment. This case management function requires constantly paying attention to how symptom levels match with treatment services and informing other treatment providers of these changes.

## MODELS OF CASE MANAGEMENT

Just as the type of case management services needed will vary from client to client, how the services are provided also will vary from client to client, from therapist to therapist, and from agency to agency. Case management models range from the brokerage model, which has little direct client contact and no provision of direct services to the assertive community treatment model, which provides treatment and services around the clock. The traditional models of case management are: brokerage, strengths, rehabilitation, clinical, intensive, and assertive community treatment case management. The following is a brief description of each, the intensity and frequency of client contact with each, and its range of interventions.

### Brokerage Model

This model is often thought of as pure case management. The case manager is not a direct service provider and has little contact with the client. Rather, he or she does assessment, develops a plan of intervention, makes referrals, and monitors outcome. An example of the brokerage model is discharge planning services for clients leaving psychiatric hospitals. The case manager brokers services for that client who may need housing, financial, psychiatric and addiction treatment, medication, and support group needs.

### Strengths Model

The strengths model of case management focuses on identifying and building on client strengths for independent living. The case manager seeks community resources and environmental situations in which the client can experience success, and works on developing a strong interpersonal relationship, called a partnership. This model incorporates many of the principles of competency-based treatment discussed in Chapter 1.

## Rehabilitation Model

Using the rehabilitation model of case management, the therapist does a functional assessment to identify the client's skill deficits to determine what services are needed for this proactive approach to skill building. The case manager, though actively involved with the client, does not provide direct service but interpersonal support, assistance with crises, and necessary referrals for needed services (Walsh, 2000).

## Clinical Case Management Model

The clinical case management model emphasizes the relationship between the client and the case manager as the vehicle for change. The clinical case manager integrates treatment with the coordination of services by addressing psychological difficulties that inhibit optimal functioning, intervening in the environment, and brokering resources (Balancio, 1994; Surber, 1994). The clinical case manager promotes change directly with the client, within the environment, and in the relationship between the client and the environment. Treatment focuses on reducing debilitating symptoms, maintaining psychiatric stability, and improving psychological well-being.

## Intensive Case Management Model (ICM)

ICM utilizes assertive and persistent outreach services, including therapeutic interventions to high-risk clients who do not otherwise receive much, if any, treatment, such as homeless individuals who have co-occurring disorders or are at very high risk for rehospitalization (Morse, 1998). A case manager has lower caseloads to allow for the frequency and intensity of services, twenty-four-hour availability, and active assistance in accessing needed resources. Sometimes the ICM is used when there are insufficient resources to support an assertive community treatment (ACT) program.

## Assertive Community Treatment (ACT) or Full Support Model

The ACT model has been more widely researched than other models and is widely disseminated throughout a number of states as a program for individuals with serious mental illness. The ACT model, which in some ways is similar to the ICM, emphasizes direct treatment and services, shared caseloads, and the use of an interdisciplinary team that includes a psychiatrist and a nurse (Morse, 1998). The assertive outreach is designed to coordinate and individualize care, which may be provided by an individual or a team, for people who are at risk for rehospitalization. The psychosocial aspects of ACT aim to help the individual stay motivated and involved in life and to optimize home life, help develop coping skills to meet the demands of community living, assist with housing and other practical needs, and provide cognitive behavior interventions that stay focused on medication compliance and symptom management (Hussain, 2000). Intervention goals focus on preventing symptom relapse to keep the client in the community (Walsh, 2000).

## *INDIVIDUAL TREATMENT AND CASE MANAGEMENT WITH A MULTIFARIOUS CASELOAD*

The key question a therapist faces when providing individual and case management services for clients in a multifarious caseload is, "How much individual therapy and case management is necessary?" A full-time employed client who has a normal social network and dysthymia disorder that is well-controlled by medication and is referred to treatment because of a driving-while-intoxicated charge requires very few individual or case management services. On the other hand, a client with alcohol dependence and schizophrenia and few social supports because of paranoia and poor social skills who is on the verge of becoming homeless after a short hospitalization and is eligible but has not yet applied for a variety of financial and housing assistance programs, will need a great deal of individual and case management services. The higher/lower functioning model described in Chapter 6 is a good predictor of how much individual and case management will be needed.

In these examples individual treatment for the first client may only involve two sessions: an initial session to establish a relationship and a treatment plan, and a final session in which the client and therapist review the client's progress toward the treatment goals. For many such clients, all subsequent treatment is done in a group setting.

The second client, however, will probably need a great deal of individual attention. The client may be unwilling or unable to initially participate in group treatment because of his or her psychiatric symptoms; thus those symptoms need to first be addressed individually. In addition, the housing and financial needs of this client will require a great deal of case management attention, which is also conducted individually. Although the treatment goals for both clients are abstinence and psychiatric stability, the amount of time spent in individual and group service settings will differ significantly for these two individuals.

In general, the more impaired the client, the more case management services he will need. The level of severity of symptoms is not only strongly associated with the number of services the individual will need but also how likely the individual is able to access those services on his own. One therapist estimated that seventeen forms had to be filled out, many by the individual seeking services, before that service was available to the client. Individuals with significant substance use or psychiatric symptoms rarely could do that on their own. The symptoms of certain disorders also may make a referral source uncertain about accepting an individual. Thus therapists will often have to advocate that a particular service admit the client or explore alternative placements. Also, as the number of symptoms increases, the more likely the client will appear demanding, noncooperative, or noncompliant. In such a situation many avenues for additional treatment, health care, or housing can close. Staff at referral agencies are not always sophisticated about these types of symptoms; the therapist will need to educate staff about the clinical meanings behind some of the behaviors that they will observe so that those agencies will use their rules to help the client succeed instead of using them to terminate or refuse services.

Therapists with multifarious caseloads who work in traditional treatment settings will primarily use the clinical case management model. Case management activities in those settings always occur in the context of ongoing treatment. Thus, therapists with multifarious caseloads must have the flexibility to move back and forth between providing therapy and case management functions, often within a single treatment session. In the second case example, during an individual session, the therapist may spend part of the session discussing with the client his paranoia and ways he can handle it more effectively, another part monitoring his medication compliance and its effectiveness, and yet another part helping the client fill out an application for housing assistance.

## CONCLUSION

Both individual treatment and case management are essential services that therapists working with multifarious caseloads must be able to provide to clients. How much and what type of these services are needed will vary greatly from client to client, but whenever possible, these services must be integrated with group treatment services. The next chapter discusses another treatment modality with which individual, group, and case management services must also be integrated: family therapy.

# Chapter 9

# Family Interventions

This chapter outlines the issues and intervention strategies involved in providing family support and treatment for individuals on a multifarious caseload. Families play a very important positive role in the treatment process when they support the treatment goals. Research substantiates this for individuals with substance use disorders, mental health disorders, and co-occurring disorders (Atkinson, Tolson, and Turner, 1993; Bellack and Mueser, 1993; Hendrickson, Stith, and Schmal 1995; Liberman et al., 1987; O'Farrell et al., 1992). Thus substance abuse and mental health therapists need to make every attempt to engage families in the treatment process.

This chapter describes the basic methods available to mental health and substance abuse therapists for working with the family or family issues and presents the overall treatment goal for these interventions and offers strategies that most effectively engage families in treatment. It discusses basic family treatment concepts needed for substance abuse and mental health therapists to work effectively with families and the normal stages that families pass through during the treatment and recovery process. Finally, the chapter covers common areas where families become stuck during this change process and offers interventions to help families overcome these stuck points.

## *FAMILY INTERVENTION METHODS*

Family interventions come in many forms and range from a single contact with one family member to long-term treatment with all family members. The six basic types of family interventions are family consultation, family psychoeducation, family support, couple therapy, family therapy, and examining family issues. Each has a particular purpose and more than one mode of implementation. Therapists often use more than one type of these interventions during the course of treatment.

### Family Consultation

This least-intensive family intervention consists of a brief consultation with family members to obtain important historical and current information about a family member to use in developing the treatment plan. It may be a one-time contact with one or more members of a family either by phone or face to face, in some instances it may be by e-mail or mail, or it can be periodic contact.

### Family Psychoeducation

Psychoeducation, which is generally presented in groups but can presented with individual family members, provides information about substance use and psychiatric disorders for family members in a manner that allows them to personalize the information, increase their knowledge, and promote motivation for behavior change. It covers the nature of these disorders, what effective treatment involves, and how these disorders can impact other family members. It also helps families better understand how their actions can promote or hinder recovery. Psychoeducation groups can be designed for a specific disorder or multiple disorders and can be ongoing (members can join at any time) or time-limited (all members join at the same time).

### Family Support

Offered in group format or with individual family members, family support helps family members in their daily dealings with their relative with substance use and/or mental health disorders. It is not designed necessarily to promote behavior change, but to provide family members an opportunity to discuss their concerns and frustrations in dealing with a family member with these disorders. When conducted in a group setting, this intervention allows families with similar issues to interact and support one another and reduce their sense of isolation in dealing with these issues. These groups can be ongoing or time limited and often include psychoeducation.

### Couple Therapy

Couple therapy, which requires participation of both members of a spousal or committed partner relationship, examines how mental health and substance use disorders affect the relationship and how each person contributes to the continuation or the reduction of the symptoms of these disorders by their behaviors or communication patterns. This type of therapy can take place in couple sessions, in occasional individual sessions when each member of the couple needs a session with the therapist alone to move the couple therapy forward, in couple groups, or in any combination thereof.

### Family Therapy

Family therapy focuses on issues that exist among the members of a family and requires participation by at least two members. Family therapy examines how mental health and substance use disorders affect the family and how each person contributes to the continuation or the reduction of the symptoms of these disorders. As with couple therapy, family therapy can take place in family sessions, occasional individual sessions, in multifamily groups, or in any combination thereof.

### Examining Family Issues

Family issues therapy focuses on family issues when other family members are unwilling or unable to participate in treatment. It provides the client with the opportunity to examine the dynamics of her family of origin or her current family for the purpose of identifying interactions that promote or hinder her recovery. It then helps her develop strategies to reduce the impact of the negative interactions. Family issues interventions are normally done in individual sessions, making use of such tools as family genograms; however, they can also be conducted in group settings.

### Goal of Family Interventions

Regardless of the type of client or family intervention used, the overall goal for any type of family intervention is to increase family interactions that promote abstinence or nonproblematic substance use and psychiatric and/or interpersonal stability.

## FACTORS THAT HINDER FAMILY INVOLVEMENT IN TREATMENT

Although any form of family intervention can help promote constructive family interactions, getting family members involved in the treatment process can be very difficult as family members often resist participation. The most common causes of resistance are: treatment is not part of the family's culture; denial of the disorder; a negative prior treatment experience; shame or guilt because a family member has the disorder (stigma); the need to balance multiple demands; or burnout resulting from having to deal with the individual and his disorder over many years. The following is a description of each of these factors.

### Treatment Is Not Part of the Family's Culture

Some families are not willing to expose their problems to outsiders. This may result from the ethnic culture of the family, from fear of anything government related (such as county services), or from a set of practices that have evolved as a norm in that particular family. This attitude, however, may not be universally applied to all helping professionals as some families find it acceptable to discuss family problems with a clergyperson, a spiritual advisor, or a special friend of the family, but not a therapist.

### Denial of the Disorder

Some families deny the family member's mental and/or substance use disorder. They may be uninformed; would not know what to do if the disorder were acknowledged; may be denying their own disorders; or generally believe that the symptoms are not the result of a disorder, but of sinful acts or poor self-discipline.

### Negative Prior Treatment Experience

Many individuals entering a treatment program have been in some similar treatment in the past, and their family may or may not have participated in that treatment. Regardless of their level of participation, the family will either have a positive, negative, or mixed view of the previous treatment. Families with negative or mixed prior treatment experiences generally will be more hesitant to participate in the current services. Negative views may stem from families perceiving that the former therapist cut the family out of treatment, refused to listen to their viewpoints, blamed the family for causing the disorder, or that the treatment was not as successful as the family had hoped.

### Shame and Guilt

Shame results from embarrassment that a family member behaves in a certain manner; guilt stems from the belief that this behavior is the result of something the family did or did not do. Both psychiatric and substance use disorders still have moral issues attached to them, and the general public tends to view behaviors associated with their symptoms as self-indulgence or poor self-discipline or some other character weakness. When the family believes this, they may avoid treatment because they are embarrassed by the family member's behavior. Families that are unaware of the biological origins of many of these disorders often look for some deep underlying psychological reason for these behaviors. Since all families have made mistakes raising children, they attribute these behaviors to their fault. Such guilt may prevent some families from participating in treatment.

### Multiple Demands

Families have many demands on their time and energy, including numerous pressures from family issues concerning other children, spouses, brothers, sisters, and parents and from systems outside of the family, such as work, school, church, neighborhood organizations, etc. When a therapist asks a family to become involved in treatment, he is in essence vying with many other demands on the family, and the family has to decide which demand is most important.

### Burnout

The family may resist treatment because they are emotionally drained from too many treatment failures, too many long nights, too many hopes dashed, and too much anger about nothing having changed. They also may have reached a point where they are concerned that if they continue to put the same amount of effort into dealing with the issues of one family member, the wellness of the other family members or the spousal relationship will suffer.

When substance abuse and mental health therapists encounter these barriers to family involvement, they need to be sensitive to and respectful of the family's resistance to their offers of help. However, they still need to try to involve the family in the treatment process in some manner, because that involvement will increase the chances of treatment success.

## PROMOTING FAMILY INVOLVEMENT

It is not possible to get all families involved in the treatment process; however, therapists can take several actions to overcome the barriers blocking family involvement. First, they must put any blame they may feel toward the family concerning what it has or has not done into the "circular file." All families have made mistakes and will continue to make mistakes in dealing with one another. However, few families do this to intentionally harm an individual member, but rather in hopes of helping them. The therapist's role is to help the family channel this desire into behaviors that can be more helpful in promoting effective management of mental health and substance use disorders.

Next, therapists need to get a consent to release information that allows them to talk to family members. Although this sounds obvious, few therapists routinely make requests for such releases of information, but instead wait until there is a crisis. The earlier that the release is requested in treatment—preferably as a normal part of the intake process, the greater the chance of obtaining it. Once the release is obtained the therapist is free to contact the family for a variety of reasons ranging from collecting additional information to inviting them to participate in treatment. However, before any contact is made, the therapist needs to inform the client of his intention to make contact and the nature of the contact.

When therapists approach a family that has not yet expressed an interest in being involved in treatment, they need to initially place few demands on the family's time. Initial contacts should focus only on the need for a consultation concerning their expertise about a particular family member. Therapists may emphasize that only the family can provide them with a complete picture of the family member. By initiating contact in this manner, the family is required only to provide information in a single meeting or even a phone call; however, such contact begins to establish a relationship between therapist and family.

During this initial consultation, substance abuse and mental health therapists should attempt to find out what the family is most worried about concerning the family member. They should also inform the family on how they or their agency can help with this concern. If a family is worried about suicide, for example, the therapist may discuss emergency services available and how they and the family might talk periodically about the level of suicide risk. Another family might be worried about what will happen to their young adult member with schizophrenia when his aging parents die. The therapist may discuss the support services available from their agency or in the community. Still another family may worry about their family member being arrested for drug use and going to jail; the therapist can discuss what the family can do to make it more difficult for the member to continue to use drugs, or how they can promote treatment involvement. She can also emphasize that courts often place individuals convicted of such offenses in treatment programs instead of jail. By identifying and beginning to address the family's concerns, the therapist becomes an important resource to the family instead of another burden on their time.

Once substance abuse and mental health therapists identify a family's concerns and discuss available services, they can then emphasize that treatment is much more likely to succeed when the family is involved; that they need the family's help and participation to make a difference. Therapists can do this by reviewing the research about how family involvement increases the chances of success and/or by giving examples from their own work of how family involvement made a difference. Therapists should match their requests for family help with their clinical judgments about what the family might be willing to do. The goal of this intervention strategy is to establish some form of ongoing contact with the family. Accordingly, therapists will give the family a variety of ways to be involved, ranging from regular family sessions to having permission to call the family again in the future for another consultation.

The key to increasing the likelihood that families will participate in psychoeducation is to keep such programs *undemanding* and *easily accessible*. The programs may be presented in an ongoing basis to allow families to join at any time and easily make up missed sessions. Some therapists find, however, that if families know the psychoeducation series is short term, such as six weeks long, they may be more willing to commit their time.

Finally, therapists must always view family engagement in treatment as an ongoing process that often requires multiple contacts before one or more members of a family are willing to participate in the treatment process. They must be patient and persistent in their efforts to engage the family. The outcome of such efforts can only contribute to the greater likelihood of treatment success.

## IMPORTANT FAMILY TREATMENT CONCEPTS

Once therapists are able to engage all or portions of the family in the treatment process, they need to keep several important concepts in mind when working with family members.

### The Family As a System

The action of any individual in the family has impact on all members of the family. Thus it is not always necessary to have all members of the family in treatment to promote family change. When the parents of a client respond differently to his alcohol use and refusal to take his medication as prescribed, the client will respond differently. Likewise, if a client achieves abstinence and medication compliance, his family will respond to him differently. Thus change in one part of the family system necessitates some form of change in all parts of that system.

## The Family As the Client

In sessions where therapists are working with more than one member of the family, they must understand that their client is the *family,* not the individuals in it. As a result, the goal of these sessions is to help the *family* make changes; they must avoid being more concerned about one member than another. Therapists who have less experience moving back and forth between individual and family interventions tend to overalign with the family member with whom they work most often. This change in focus must be clearly stated to the family and demonstrated in the therapists' actions if their family interventions are to be successful.

### Identified Patient

This is a family therapy concept that views the symptoms of one member of the family as an expression of some issue in the family. Although this may be the case when a teenager acts out because of problems between parents, it has been unfairly used to blame families for causing substance use and major mental disorders. Therapists can be more effective by identifying how the family has organized itself regarding mental health and substance use disorders; support interactions that promote symptom reduction; and intervene when interactions increase symptoms. For example, when family members increase their expressions of anxiety with the family member with schizophrenia, the symptoms of schizophrenia are exacerbated (Leff and Vaugh, 1985; MacMillan et al., 1986). Thus the family is not the cause of the disorder, but their actions impact it, and some of these actions need to be modified to promote recovery.

### First-Order Change versus Second-Order Change

The ultimate purpose of therapists' work with families is not only to change what they do but also to change the rules by which they operate. First-order change involves doing something different, such as no longer attempting to hide the fact that a family member has alcohol and depressive disorders, but instead pushing that individual to get medication and substance abuse treatment. Although change has occurred in the family, the rules by which they operate have not. The family is still responsible for making something happen, not the individual with the disorder. Second-order change involves changing the family rules, such as encouraging and supporting medication compliance and treatment for the individual, but also encouraging other family members to move on with their own lives whether or not the individual with the disorder engages in treatment. In this instance the responsible person becomes the individual with the disorder. This is not to imply that first-order change is not important, for it paves the way for second-order change; however, it is important that therapists recognize it as a midpoint, not an end point.

### Family Cutoffs

In some instances, a family member with a substance use or mental disorder will stop having contact with other family members, or the family will refuse to have contact with her. This cutoff is caused by frustration or anger or as a way to avoid conflict. Therapists need to help the family understand that just because contact between family members is broken, the emotions attached to these relationships are still problematic. Unless these emotional relationships are resolved, the individual with these disorders will have difficulty sustaining long-term recovery or establishing healthy ongoing relationships. Therapists need to promote resolution of such a cutoff by supporting constructive contact among family members when possible, or when constructive contact is not possible, helping an individual resolve her emotional issues with family members.

### United Family Front

A united family front is an agreement among all family members on how to approach a particular problem. A united family front is generally considered essential if family decisions are to be implemented effectively. However, in many instances therapists find that not all members of a family agree with a specific course of action. In those instances the therapists must either help the family work toward a consensus or help the family support a decision even if they disagree with it. For example, one parent may believe that a little marijuana use is OK for someone with an anxiety disorder but the other parent believes in total abstinence. Even though the one parent does not believe in total abstinence, he could support his wife's wishes just because parents should support the executive authority of each other. Doing so does not require a family member to pretend to agree with something (which is always quickly figured out by other family members), but still allows that member to support the position taken by the family.

### Circular Causation

Therapists often observe that a family continues to do the same things repeatedly. This regular cycle of actions and reactions that leads to no change is called circular causation. Therapists need to identify such cycles in a family and offer different ways to react at any point in that cycle.

A client with bipolar disorder and alcohol abuse disorder returns home after a hospitalization and for awhile takes her medication as prescribed, attends treatment regularly, and abstains from alcohol. The family's position at discharge was that for her to live at home, she had to follow that treatment plan. However, after a month she begins to miss a few treatment appointments, then does not always take her medication, and still later begins to drink occasionally. This behavior becomes more frequent and she experiences a full manic episode and must be hospitalized. Throughout the process the family threatens to ask her to leave but fails to follow through on those threats, thus reducing the consequences of treatment noncompliance. After the third cycle, the therapist points out the pattern to the family and helps them develop a different action plan for any point in this cycle, such as not allow their daughter to come home after the hospitalization and insist that she move into a group home; or after the first missed appointment, missed medication, or drinking episode, require her to intensify her treatment or move out.

It matters less what is done differently or when, just that the pattern be broken.

### The Family As Case Managers

Regardless of the level of services that therapists, their agency, or other professionals provide a client, therapists need to recognize that in most instances it is the family who will provide the bulk of the support needed by individuals with substance abuse and psychiatric disorders. Thus in reality the primary case manager for many clients will be the family. It will be family members who help financially, advocate for public and private programs, help in filling out forms, assist in securing housing, drive to meetings, help resolve conflicts, or just hold the client's hand and offer love and support. In fact, research finds that families of individuals with a major mental illness and a substance use disorder spend approximately 16 percent of their annual income supporting the family member and twice as much time providing care and support to that person than they do for their other children (Clark and Drake 1994). Therapists need to acknowledge this contribution when working with families and offer them the same respect they offer other professionals working with a client.

## A MODEL FOR IDENTIFYING FAMILY CHANGE

Having a conceptual model to follow can help guide therapists through the change process with families. Such a model needs to have both an end point at which treatment is aimed and predictable phases and steps that families go through as they move toward this end point. Such a model helps therapists anticipate potential stuck points during the change process and allows them to identify and track a family's changes. Figure 9.1 presents a very helpful conceptual model that defines eight distinct phases through which most families pass before achieving a balance between personal and family support needs. Each phase involves emotional, cognitive, and behavioral activities by the family. Often family members do not move through these phases at the same time or in the same way. At times, some members or entire families become stuck in a particular phase and need help to move to the next phase. The model is based on the belief that the process of change is usually two steps forward and one step backward. In other words, the family makes a breakthrough in what they are able to do or in their understanding of the issues, but time is needed to assimilate and consolidate this change before moving to the next phase. This period of time often appears to be a step backward. A description of the eight phases of this model follows.

### Phase One: Denial and Minimization

Family members may deny that an individual member has a particular substance use or mental disorder, or significantly minimize its impact. This denial may be the result of a lack of knowledge, a family culture or belief system that does not accept the existence of such disorders, guilt based on the belief that the symptoms are the result of

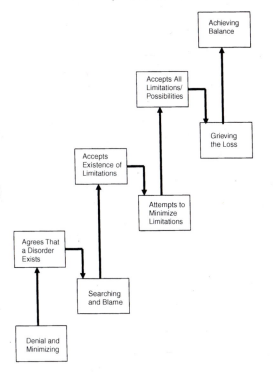

FIGURE 9.1. A Model of Family Change

something the family did or did not do, or an attempt by other family members to deny that they too have that disorder. In this phase family members typically will not be supportive of the treatment activities.

Peter, age thirty-three, who has an alcohol dependence disorder and a co-occurring dysthymic disorder, has a long history of maintaining abstinence for periods of time but then relapsing. Although he acknowledges that feeling depressed contributes significantly to the relapses, neither he nor his family believes he has a mental disorder for which medication could be helpful. Both believe that the depression comes from his frustrations with abstinence and that the relapses could be prevented if he would just put more effort into working his Alcoholics Anonymous program.

An intervention strategy for such a family would involve increasing their knowledge about depression and dysthymia in particular. It is unlikely that such a family would initially be willing to participate in a formal family education program, but they might be willing to read a pamphlet research something on the Internet. Rather than get into a power struggle with the family or ask the family to keep their minds open concerning the existence of the disorder, the therapist might suggest that the family approach the information only as a research project. The therapist might also use any anxiety that the family feels as a way to encourage the family to seek more information. The therapist might ask them to predict what would happen if the relapses continued to occur and what would be the downside of a trial of medication; he might also point out additional health, legal, or social problems that the family is failing to identify. In general, the therapist tries to promote an increase in knowledge and question the wisdom of maintaining the status quo.

### Phase Two: Acknowledging the Existence of the Disorder

This phase involves family members acknowledging the existence of a particular substance use or mental disorder. Figure 9.1 shows acknowledgment as an upward movement (two steps forward). Family members finally accept that the member has a substance use and/or mental disorder. However, at this point the family is still unclear why the disorder has occurred and does not realize the disorder's implications for both the family and family member. In this phase, family members may not be willing to participate in treatment, but they usually are open to obtaining information about the disorder.

### Phase Three: Searching and Blaming

This phase involves family members attempting to understand why the disorder has occurred. Figure 9.1 shows this phase as a downward movement (one step back). Often, finger-pointing or guilt occurs, suggesting that someone in the family or something the family has done has caused this disorder. Family members tend to feel anxious and confused about what this means for them. Although the family may not be willing to participate in formal treatment at this point, they are likely to be willing to participate in psychoeducation activities. To move to the next phase, the family must develop a clear understanding of the disorder, recognize its symptoms, its potential consequences, and its impact on both the targeted family member and the rest of the family.

## *Phase Four: Accepting the Existence of Limitations*

This phase involves family members coming to the realization that these disorders place limitations on all members of the family (two steps forward). Family members typically express anger and frustration and dismay at the unfairness of the situation. A clearer picture of what the individual and the family must face begins to take focus. However, the family does not yet fully understand or accept all of the limitations that they will encounter.

## *Phase Five: Trying to Minimize the Limitations*

This consolidation phase involves family members attempting to minimize or negate the impact of these disorders (one step back). Typically, the family continues to push the family member of concern to do what he cannot do, such as drink normally, maintain a highly stressful job, or be symptom-free all the time. This phase also often involves the family experimenting with different treatments in order to find a cure. This pushing and treatment seeking is usually caused by the family's anxiety and fear that their lives will be totally disrupted by this disorder. To move on to the next phase, the family must develop a balanced view of the disorder that involves understanding which symptoms can be effectively treated and which symptoms will just have to be managed.

## *Phase Six: Accepting All the Limitations and the Possibilities*

This phase involves family members accepting the fact that their family member will not be able to do certain things, but that does not mean that they or the family member cannot have a full and meaningful life (two steps forward). This phase usually involves a sense of loss but also a sense of relief. In this phase the family usually comes to see themselves as partners in the treatment process and begins to understand the paradoxical reality that by accepting these limitations, many possibilities previously unnoticed become available.

## *Phase Seven: Grieving the Loss*

In this phase, family members fully experience the loss of some of the dreams they had for their family member; they feel the sadness of this loss, but also gain a sense of serenity about it. Their anger is gone. Families in this phase can be very helpful to other families in peer support groups. The movement to the final phase is usually marked by a sense of optimism for what the future holds for both the family and the member with the disorder.

### *Phase Eight: Achieving Balance*

In this phase the family members actively address their own needs while at the same time provide appropriate assistance to their family member. Each member is clear that they have certain responsibilities to their family member, but they are also free to have a satisfying family and personal life. Although a crisis (such as a relapse to drug use or the intensification of psychiatric symptoms resulting from a stressful life event) may require members to periodically take on more responsibilities, the setback is viewed as a temporary situation and not as a threat to their personal happiness.

## *STUCK POINTS IN THE FAMILY CHANGE PROCESS*

Families commonly get stuck and need help with the change process in one or several ways, which include behaviors, attitudes, perceptions, or emotional reactions. Getting stuck may occur at any time during the family's journey toward acceptance and understanding, but it most often occurs in the beginning phases of adjustment or during a crisis. A description of each stuck point and suggested interventions to help the family move to the next phase of adjustment follows.

### *Nonacceptance of the Disorder*

Peter, discussed previously, has an alcohol dependence disorder and a co-occurring dysthymic disorder and periodic relapses. His family views his depression merely as a result of frustrations with abstinence. The family would probably benefit by reading more about depression and dysthymia. As discussed in Phase One, the therapist should not get into a power struggle with the family about the existence of the disorder, but provide information or sources of information, question them about the consequences of continued relapses and health, legal, or social problems the family may be failing to recognize, and ask what the family has to lose if the family member of concern tried medication.

## The Family Blames Itself

Family members believe that something they have done or not done is the cause of the family member's symptoms. They do not deny the existence of a problem, but they have not yet connected the symptoms as an identifiable disorder. This stuck point is similar to the previous one, except that the problem is fully acknowledged and the family is more open to outside help.

Maurice is a twenty-year-old with schizoaffective disorder and co-occurring cannabis abuse disorder who suffers from paranoid delusions, which are greatly exacerbated by his marijuana use. These delusions interfere with his ability to function appropriately in a work or school setting. His parents, who divorced when he was fifteen, attribute his poor social functioning to the impact of the divorce and his ability to split them when they try to present a united front concerning the need for him to find work or go to school.

Again, an effective intervention for this stuck point is to provide information, except at this point the family may be more open to participating in a formal psychoeducation program.

Sometimes, the family actually has done something that may have intensified the affected member's symptoms, such as allowing physical or sexual abuse to continue. In such cases, the therapist needs to help the family face the truth, forgive themselves, acknowledge their past actions to the affected member, and deal with the present.

However, some families feel such a need to be in control of all things that affect them that they accept too much blame or responsibility for what has happened. In this case, the therapist not only has to provide information but also needs to help the family identify those things over which they have some control and those things over which they do not. Such control issues often stem from the anxiety that develops in growing up in a family that was unpredictable and chaotic. Many clients with substance use and psychiatric disorders have parents who grew up in such families. Using a genogram to map out family-of-origin issues can often help the family identify the source of these control issues so they can begin the work of managing them more effectively.

## Resistance to Treatment Involvement

Family members sometimes resist or undermine the participation of a family member in treatment. The family acknowledges the existence of the problem but does not believe that treatment is the appropriate course of action.

Twenty-six-year-old Susan, who has cocaine dependence disorder and co-occurring borderline personality disorder, has just been released from a psychiatric unit after a suicide attempt. Her family acknowledges that she has limited emotional control and is addicted to cocaine. However, they believe treatment will just give her more excuses for continuing her behavior and they have decided that she needs to find a nutrition counselor who will modify her diet to balance her brain chemistry.

In this situation, therapists should not object to the family trying to help in their own way; rather they should reinforce the family's good intentions and also ask what they would do next if their plan does not work. In such cases therapists can be most effective if they take on a consultative role with the family by being there when the family needs them and asking the family hard questions concerning the effectiveness of their plan. Part of the strategy is to get the family to agree ahead of time that they would give treatment a try if their method fails. Such a strategy allows the therapist to establish a non-adversarial relationship with the family, but at the same time have input into the family decision-making process.

## Fear of Change

Sometimes the family resists doing anything different for fear that change will make things worse. In many ways this is a realistic fear not only because unplanned changes by the family can exacerbate the situation, but also because even well-thought-out changes and demands may trigger an increase in dysfunctional behavior in the individual with a disorder. Thus things often do get worse before they get better.

Bill, twenty-nine, who has bipolar disorder and co-occurring alcohol dependence disorder, often discontinues his medication when his manic symptoms begin to appear. Eventually he becomes psychotic and threatening and has to be hospitalized. This has occurred many times. The family continues to allow him to come home after each event and makes few demands on him concerning medication compliance. The family fears that if they do not let him come home or if they make too many demands on him he will end up manic and homeless and will get hurt or harm someone else.

This family needs permission that they need not be totally responsible for their family member's behavior. They too have a right to a safe and stable home life. Involvement in support groups or family therapy can provide them an outlet to express their fears and receive feedback concerning how others effectively manage such situations. The therapist needs to help these families view change from a long-term perspective and not be too reactive to a particular behavior or response. Presenting the family with the phases of this change model can be helpful in giving them a sense of where they are and where they need to go. They also need help to understand that the changes necessary for their family will take time and a great deal of practice.

### *Anxiety Regarding a Potential Death*

Anxiety regarding a potential death is the extreme view of the previous stuck point. This too is a realistic fear because individuals with substance use and mental disorders face many health and other physical risks. At this stuck point the family is hesitant to make demands on the individual because they fear such demands would drive him away from the family and result in his death.

Wanda, age twenty-nine, has opioid dependence disorder and co-occurring social phobia disorder, and lives with her parents. She uses several doctors to obtain narcotics for a vague pain disorder and seldom leaves the house. She takes more medication than is prescribed and when she periodically runs out, she turns desperately to her family and threatens to harm herself if she does not get some relief from her pain. They then help her make arrangements to obtain more medication. They know she is addicted, but are afraid to make any demands on her because they fear she will kill herself without these medications.

When families experience these kinds of fears, they need to be confronted with the question of what will happen if they continue to do nothing. The answer, unfortunately, is that the family's ultimate fear may become a reality. Wanda may accidentally take an overdose of her medication and die. The therapist can then ask how the family would feel if they learned that there was something they might have done but did not do. The key to this intervention is showing how *not doing* something is worse than *doing* something. This is seldom a quick process and requires the therapist to make many suggestions concerning what the family might do and then help them evaluate the risks and benefits of each. Often, hearing how other families have dealt with similar situations can be even more effective than just listening to what the therapist has to say. Thus, involvement in family support groups or participation in psychoeducation programs can be very helpful.

### One-Shot Approach

The one-shot approach stuck point involves the family attempting to find the perfect treatment or a cure. The family is often angry that disorders have developed and feels that it just is not fair that their family member has it. They have difficulty accepting that the disorders may be lifelong and life changing. They want the symptoms gone and the family exactly as it was before the disorder's onset. Few individuals with co-occurring disorders will experience that type of recovery.

Casey, an eighteen-year-old with major depressive disorder and co-occurring marijuana dependence disorder, has been having trouble remaining free of depressive symptoms since he was thirteen years old. He has used marijuana since age fourteen and finds that it helps reduce his depressive symptoms while he is high. He no longer uses it daily but does when his depressive symptoms increase. The marijuana use of course increases his depressive symptoms the next day. He has taken many different types of medication but none has ever fully eliminated his depressive symptoms for more than six months. Although he completed high school, he is currently unable to attend college full time because of the symptoms. His parents have taken him from doctor to doctor and from treatment program to treatment program in hopes of finding a cure for his depression. They continue looking for new treatments.

Although it is a positive action for families to continue to explore new treatment options, the intensity with which this family pursues these options interferes with their ability to deal with the disorders effectively. Theirs is an all-or-nothing approach, which tends to focus on one treatment method at a time. Intervention strategies for this stuck point need to help the family view the individual as still able to accomplish many things. Competency-based interventions (see Chapter 1) are very useful with this stuck point. The therapist can point out that their son in fact completed high school and may be successful in college if allowed to initially take only one or two courses at a time.

The therapist needs to emphasize the skills and abilities of the family member: that he has reduced his marijuana use and has been willing to experiment with many different types of medications; that many other young adults would refuse to do that. In addition, many of the disorders require the use of multiple treatments in order to ensure a maximum functioning level. The therapist can help the family view new treatments as an addition to existing treatments instead of a complete replacement and encourage the family to learn to evaluate if a new treatment is having a positive effect—looking for improvements, not the complete remission of symptoms.

### Doing Too Little or Too Much

This stuck point involves families doing too much for the individual and thus not allowing her to live up to her potential, or doing too little which leaves her floundering and repeatedly failing at everything she does. Anxiety, anger, and frustration usually drive these behaviors.

Myra, a thirty-five-year-old who has cocaine abuse disorder and co-occurring anorexia nervosa, lives in an apartment paid for by her family. She has been hospitalized several times because of exceedingly low body weight. She uses cocaine when she is concerned about her appetite or when she feels depressed. Her family shifts back and forth between checking on her every day and making her eat in front of them, to storming out of the apartment when she refuses to eat and staying away for weeks at a time.

Intervention strategies at this stuck point need to help the family identify the sources of their anxiety and anger. They need to be aimed at helping the family understand the origin of their feelings and how to manage them more effectively. Psychoeducation programs about these disorders can be very useful in helping the family gain a better understanding of what the individual is actually capable of doing or not doing and why their behaviors do not make sense at times. This understanding can reduce the family's reactivity to what previously had been viewed as defiant or irrational behaviors and thus allow them to respond in a more consistent manner. Participation in family support groups or family treatment can also help them gain a longer-term perspective of the recovery process, thus reducing their anxiety when change does not occur immediately. The key to these interventions is to help the family develop a greater sense of patience with their family member and reduce their reactivity when symptoms increase.

## Lack of Family Consensus

Families are often not in agreement about what course of action to take. This conflict is usually based on both real differences in family members' opinions concerning what to do and a family process that approaches conflict from a win/lose position instead of a compromise and consensus-building position.

> David, a thirty-one-year-old with schizophrenia and co-occurring alcohol dependence disorder, alternates between living with family members and being homeless. He is usually not medication compliant and drinks as often as he can afford it. Several family members believe that the best course of action is to let him hit bottom and not help him out at all, while several other family members are so concerned about his safety that they often let him live with them until his behaviors make it intolerable.

Intervention strategies at this point must focus on helping family members clearly identify their positions and the reasons for them. During this process there are many opportunities for a therapist to correct inaccurate or incomplete information that family members have about the disorder, which at times can change a family member's position. Acknowledge that each family member's position has merit. Also, win/lose communication patterns must be pointed out and solution-focused communication patterns implemented. Most important, when consensus cannot be achieved among family members, the therapist must verbalize that although each family member has the individual's best interest at heart, unless the family arrives at a unified approach, successful treatment will not be possible. The therapist must also point out that no family member can honestly support a position they are in disagreement with; however, it is possible for them to support the concept that a single course of action is needed. Then the family members must decide among themselves who is willing to temporarily back off from a position to see if another family member's position could be successful. Part of this compromise includes the agreement of family members that if that intervention does not work, then other family members' positions will be attempted. The key to these interventions is promoting a clear understanding of the disorder by all family members and ensuring they approach their disagreements from a compromise and consensus-building communication pattern.

## *Loss of Self to the Family*

Loss of self occurs when family members totally commit themselves to the care and needs of another family member, and thus do not attend to their own needs.

Barbara, age twenty-five, has been diagnosed with alcohol abuse and co-occurring post-traumatic stress disorder; she lives at home with her parents. The psychiatric disorder was the result of a tragic automobile accident when she was seventeen, in which four of her friends were killed. Though she completed high school, she has been very isolated from people her own age and her extended family since the accident. She still has very disturbing dreams and sometimes seems not to be listening when her parents are speaking to her. She uses alcohol at times to help her go to sleep or to make herself feel better. She has held only a few part-time jobs. Her parents make no demands on her and have centered all their life activities around her. They have not gone on vacation since the accident and have greatly reduced contact with their other grown children and relatives.

This stuck point is similar to a therapist doing too much for a client and the results are also similar. The message being communicated is that Barbara is unable to take care of herself. Thus intervention strategies need to focus on increasing the family's awareness of Barbara's ability to be more self-sufficient. Sometimes this behavior is the result of anxiety and fear from not knowing what will happen if the family does not do everything, and sometimes it is the result of a pervasive family pattern that has certain family members responsible for taking care of other family members. When the origin of this behavior is anxiety and fear, psychoeducation and family support interventions can be very successful. The therapist can also help the family reduce some of their feelings of responsibility by pointing out that certain things, such as checking on how well the individual is doing, will now be the responsibility of the therapist. When the behavior is the result of a long-term family behavioral pattern, it will be more difficult for a therapist to interrupt this behavior. Individual work focusing on helping such family members gain a greater sense of self and entitlement to meeting personal needs is usually necessary. Family work concerning this issue is usually more effective when it focuses on shifting some of this responsibility to other family members. In this instance it might be possible to convince the parents that it would be best for their daughter if she spent more time with her siblings or other family members. Such a framing of the issue does not challenge the rule that the family is responsible for her care, but does promote her interaction with other family members who may allow her to take more responsibility. The individual and family work on this issue should be done concurrently.

### *Not Grieving the Loss*

When a family does not allow itself to feel the full extent of the pain, sadness, and loss experienced concerning original hopes and ambitions for the family member with the psychiatric or substance use disorder, this stuck point is experienced. This stuck point often occurs in families who generally have difficulties expressing feelings.

Ben, age thirty, who has schizoaffective disorder and co-occurring cocaine dependence disorder, has been abstinent and psychiatrically stable for nearly a year. Ben and his family accept the need for continued abstinence and medication compliance. Ben first developed his psychiatric symptoms in his third year of college. His cocaine use began a year later. He completed college but has never held a professional job. Although the family accepts his limitations as he has not worked in two years, they still feel hurt and pain when they think about what might have been.

Therapists can help families move through this stuck point by creating an awareness that pain and sadness are common family experiences in dealing with these issues, pointing out how difficult it may be to acknowledge and express these feelings. Therapists can provide families opportunities in a safe environment to experiment with expressing their pain, and assure the family that doing so will not harm them or the family member. Psychoeducation, family support groups, and family therapy are all effective vehicles that can accomplish these goals, although a combination of all three is most effective.

## *CONCLUSION*

When substance abuse and mental health therapists work with families in which a member has substance use and mental disorders, they must remember that every family member is affected by the disorders and that the family has in some way organized itself in an attempt to cope effectively with the disorders. Some of these organizational strategies are helpful and some are not. Families need help in developing a balanced view about these disorders and optimism concerning the potential outcomes. Therefore, therapists need to emphasize that the disorders are treatable and that members of the family are not responsible for causing the disorder; rather, they are responsible for taking a position that treatment is necessary.

In addition to these activities, therapists must also emphasize the following six obligations that all family members must accept if the family is to successfully deal with these disorders:

1. Take time for themselves and do things they enjoy.
2. Learn about the disorders and their treatment.
3. Never tolerate inappropriate, abusive, or dangerous behavior.
4. Support the greatest level of independence that a family member with the disorder can achieve.
5. Insist that the family member with the disorder use all available community resources targeted toward treatment and monitor the quality of these services.
6. When a disagreement arises concerning a course of action to accomplish these goals, family members must compromise and develop some form of family consensus.

# Chapter 10

# Promoting Long-Term Stability: Relapse Prevention and Symptom Management

Many clients in multifarious caseloads have disorders whose symptoms persist because the medication never totally controls them. Thus clients need treatment intervention strategies—called relapse prevention or symptom management—to help them maintain abstinence from alcohol and other drugs or manage long-term psychiatric symptoms. Often therapists introduce these skills after clients have attained abstinence. Although the focus of treatment actively shifts to relapse prevention and symptom management at this point, interventions designed to promote the development of these skills really begin the first day of treatment. This chapter defines the nature of relapse prevention and symptom management activities; proposes a model that clusters these activities according to the client's level of recovery and treatment; and discusses how these activities may need to be modified with a multifarious caseload.

Although relapse prevention is most often associated with the substance abuse field and symptom management with the mental health field, they are really interchangeable terms. Models designed to address these issues have been proposed for substance-using clients (Daley, 1987; Gorski, 2000; Marlatt and Gordon; 1985), clients with long-term mental disorders (Hatfield and Lefley, 1993; Herz and Lamberti; 1995; Liberman et al., 1986), and clients with co-occurring disorders (Daley and Lis, 1995; Ortman, 2001). All of these models have the same goal: to provide the knowledge and skills necessary to effectively manage a disorder's ongoing or recurring symptoms. They also all use psychoeducation (see Chapter 6) and skill training to accomplish this goal. Although the specifics of what needs to be addressed differ from individual to individual and from disorder to disorder, the process of how and when it is addressed differs little. All these terms describe a single clinical process that is an integral part of treatment for clients with disorders that have long-term symptoms. To prevent confusion, for the remainder of this chapter, relapse prevention and symptom management activities will be referred to as recovery management.

The type of recovery management interventions used will differ depending on a client's level of recovery and treatment participation. Psychoeducation and skill-training activities for clients who are still using substances and denying their mental disorders are very different from those used with clients who accept their substance use and mental disorders and who are abstinent and medication compliant. It is helpful to group the various psychoeducation and skill-training recovery management interventions into three clusters that follow the normal process of recovery and treatment participation. These clusters are: interventions for prerecovery and antitreatment clients; interventions for early recovery and treatment-engaged clients; and interventions for later recovery and minimal or posttreatment clients. The interventions in each of these clusters address a particular worldview held by clients and provide them with the knowledge and skills necessary to either move toward acknowledging the need for recovery establishing a recovery lifestyle, or maintaining long-term recovery. The following sections describe the interventions used during each phase of recovery and treatment participation, their goals, and how to use them in a multifarious caseload.

## *CLUSTER OF INTERVENTIONS FOR PRERECOVERY AND ANTITREATMENT CLIENTS*

Clients who feel that treatment has been forced upon them, that they do not have a problem, and do not need to make any major life changes have usually been mandated into treatment by the courts, their families, or by some other organization with authority over them. For these clients, the goals of interventions for long-term stability are to promote acknowledgment of their substance use and mental disorders and develop enough motivation to engage with treatment. Thus the interventions during this phase lay the groundwork for establishing abstinence and/or psychiatric stability. These interventions are generally considered standard treatment practices and are not often considered recovery management activities, but without them traditional recovery management interventions would be ineffective.

A low-demand psychoeducation group that presents information about the nature, effects, and treatment requirements of substance use and mental disorders is the primary intervention tool used to help these clients begin to accept that they have a condition with which they need help. However, not every client possesses the cognitive skills necessary to make use of this information. Chapter 6 describes the common learning deficits that clients participating in these psychoeducation programs often have and presents methods that can be used to overcome these deficits. Clients must also have some specific skills to be able to effectively participate in a treatment program: accepting services; tolerating interacting with other human beings; giving and receiving feedback; and changing behaviors. Not every client brings these skills initially to treatment; those who started drug and alcohol use at an early age, for example, never developed these skills during the appropriate developmental stage. Therefore, for some clients, initial treatment is as much a habilitative process as it is a rehabilitative process. Participating in these psychoeducation programs helps such clients learn how to be in a room with other people; develop the discipline of showing up for services; receive and give information and feedback from others; and how to change behaviors, such as being quiet for a period of time, asking questions at appropriate times, and not saying inappropriate things to others.

Some of these skill deficits may be the direct result of the substance use or psychiatric symptoms, so some clients require detoxification, psychiatric hospitalization, or both before they can develop other skills. Some clients may be too psychiatrically unstable or too toxic from their substance use to learn new information or skills. For example, a client who has been drinking large amounts of alcohol daily for several years and who is psychotic as a result of not taking his medication for several months has only a slim chance of being able to retain and integrate new information or develop new behavior skills. However, once a client is detoxified and psychiatrically stabilized, he will be cognitively able to benefit from psychoeducation and skill-training activities.

How long an individual needs this cluster of interventions will vary greatly from client to client. Some clients quickly acknowledge their disorders and engage in treatment, while others continue to resist accepting this reality throughout an entire treatment episode. Although psychoeducation and skill-training interventions are normally presented in group settings during this phase of recovery and treatment engagement, clients who express misinformation or faulty beliefs about their disorders may need to work with a therapist individually and/or in family treatment. Also, the process of participating in these other modalities helps develop the skills necessary to successfully participate and engage in treatment. Thus when clients' behaviors are inappropriate, the therapist can coach clients regarding what is expected of them in a treatment setting. The more information clients have about their disorders and the more they understand the basic rules for participating in treatment, the more difficult it becomes for them to continue to deny their symptoms and behaviors that prevent them from successfully participating in treatment.

In addition to providing accurate information, psychoeducation interventions must also provide hope. The message of all psychoeducation interventions must be that these disorders are treatable and that treatment results in a better life. Psychoeducation interventions that only focus on the negative consequences of a disorder may push a client further into denial. Such one-sided information, instead of promoting acceptance of the disorder and motivation to engage in treatment, may paint such a negative picture of the disorder, that to accept it means accepting a life full of misery. Thus psychoeducation programs must balance the negative effects of a disorder with the positive effects of dealing with it effectively.

## CLUSTER OF INTERVENTIONS FOR EARLY RECOVERY AND TREATMENT-ENGAGED CLIENTS

The cluster of interventions targeted for clients in this phase of recovery and treatment participation is designed for individuals who are psychologically in treatment voluntarily even if they have a court order that requires their attendance. They have personally identified and acknowledged having a substance use or mental disorder or both. Their worldview, whether they are new to treatment or have been involved for some time, is that they have a disorder or at least a problem for which they need treatment. The goal of psychoeducation and skill-training interventions for this group is to promote the knowledge and skills necessary to manage their substance use and mental disorders effectively and begin a recovery lifestyle. This phase can take a long or short time depending on the impairments, the skills that clients already possess, and how hard the clients want to work on their issues. This is the phase that is most often associated with traditional relapse prevention and symptom management activities.

During this phase of recovery and treatment, interventions designed to enhance recovery focus on five primary areas: teaching common triggers, pressures, and stressors that can cause substance use or psychiatric relapse; early symptom identification; coping responses to triggers, pressures, stressors, or an increase in symptoms; preparing for unexpected events; and acknowledging and celebrating self-efficacy. Interventions to address these areas are often presented in specialized psychoeducation and skill-training groups; however, they are also introduced and reinforced in the other treatment modalities.

Psychoeducation is the most common format used to teach clients about triggers, pressures, and stressors that can lead to substance or psychiatric relapse. Many models can be used; Crewe (1974) proposed sixteen danger signs that increase the risk of returning to substance use; Gorski and Kelley (1996) proposed forty-six warning signs of impending use. In general, these precursors to substance or psychiatric relapse can be categorized as individual or relational. Marlatt and Gordon (1985) identified common individual issues, such as negative emotional states, positive emotional states, testing personal control, urges, and temptations. They identified common relational issues such as interpersonal conflict and social pressure.

Early identification of symptoms is also primarily a psychoeducation process that normally occurs in all treatment modalities. The primary principle behind this intervention strategy is that identifying when symptoms first return or increase makes it easier to prevent substance use or psychiatric relapse. Each client's disorder manifests itself its own way. Thus clients need to identify their earliest symptoms and their normal symptom levels. Exercises such as having clients identify all their symptoms and then sequence them in the order that they manifest themselves, can help clients identify their earliest symptoms. Other clients who experience some level of symptoms at all times can use exercises to monitor their normal range of symptoms and thus identify when an increased level of symptoms needs attention.

For example, a client with co-occurring bipolar disorder and alcohol abuse disorder noticed that his first symptom indicating a pending manic episode was a desire to smoke cigarettes. The course of the episode led to full-blown mania, significant alcohol use to help control the manic symptoms, and eventual hospitalization. Although it was very difficult to alter the course of this process in its later stages, it would have been very possible to prevent psychiatric and substance relapse when that first symptom manifested itself. In this case, the therapist and the doctor were able to prevent the return of mania by increasing the client's medication slightly for a short period and asking the client to carefully monitor this and other early symptoms; this strategy promoted recovery and maintained the client's stability.

Skill training is the primary intervention method used to promote effective coping responses. Some of the coping responses are designed specifically to prevent substance use or psychiatric relapse, while others target the skills needed to develop a satisfying recovery lifestyle. The goal of these interventions is to provide individuals with learning experiences that allow them to develop the behavioral and verbal skills necessary to deal with potential relapse situations or enhance life satisfaction. The most common skills taught during this period are practicing drug refusal, self-monitoring, dealing with unavoidable high-risk situations, taking responsibility for the management of the disorders, managing emotions, adhering to medication regimens, using professional resources appropriately, problem solving, managing conflict, and practicing social interaction skills. The Substance Abuse Management Model (SAMM) (Roberts, Shaner, and Eckman, 1999) is a model that focuses on the most common problems encountered in recovery for individuals with schizophrenia and alcohol disorders and offers detailed behavioral solutions for each. Linehan's (1993b) dialectic behavioral therapy for individuals with borderline personality disorder is an example of this. Participants learn mindfulness skills, interpersonal effectiveness skills, emotion regulation, and distress tolerance. Box 10.1 presents an example of a relapse prevention curriculum for more-impaired individuals with co-occurring disorders.

At times, clients will face a completely unexpected situation for which they have no planned response, such as after a fight with a friend, the client runs into another old friend who pulls out a marijuana cigarette and offers to smoke it with her. Such situations greatly

---

**BOX 10.1. A Relapse Prevention Curriculum**

Session 1      Mental Health and Substance Abuse Recovery Models

Session 2      Overview of Relapse Prevention Skills

Session 3      Warning Signs and Triggers

Session 4      Defense Mechanisms

Session 5      Cognitive Distortions and Self-Defeating Attitudes

Session 6      Emotional Management

Session 7      Anger Management

Session 8      Stress Management

Session 9      Planning and Problem Solving

Session 10     Communication and Assertiveness

Session 11     Relationships

Session 12     Nutrition and Health

---

increase the risk of substance use or psychiatric relapse. The purpose of recovery management interventions, used in all the treatment modalities that deal with surprise situations, is to help clients develop a plan for unplanned events. Such plans normally include an immediate action to take whenever any unforeseen event occurs that causes a rapid increase in urges or symptoms. A general plan for this situation could be a commitment ahead of time that twenty-four hours must pass before the client will use any drug she is offered. The key to any such plan is that clients are willing and committed to apply the plan when it is needed.

Interventions that acknowledge and celebrate self-efficacy follow the principles of competency-based interventions (see Chapter 1) and are used in all treatment modalities whenever a difficulty is successfully dealt with by a client. These interventions promote the client's belief that he is capable of successfully managing his mental health and/or substance use disorders. Without this sense of self-efficacy, long-term recovery is not possible. Thus each time clients successfully manage any of their symptoms, urges, pressures, or triggers, their competency in doing so is highlighted, thus helping build the clients' psychological view of themselves as capable and competent people who can achieve recovery.

## CLUSTER OF INTERVENTIONS FOR LATER RECOVERY AND MINIMAL OR POSTTREATMENT CLIENTS

Clients who receive this type of psychoeducation or skill-training interventions have been in recovery for at least a year but normally longer. If still in treatment, the treatment is very minimal, such as seeing a therapist once a month or the doctor every three months for a medication check. These individuals are also often active participants in self-help groups. Others will be returning to treatment to deal with a specific issue, and occasionally an individual who has made significant changes on their own or used a recovery self-help group (see Chapter 11) to effectively deal with a disorder, may be entering treatment for the first time. Regardless, these clients are sophisticated about recovery and should be treated as very informed partners in the treatment process. Their worldview is that they have a disorder that needs lifetime attention and on a day-to-day basis they are generally managing their symptoms effectively, but they need knowledge or skills to make this job easier. A crisis life event, such as the death of a family member, a divorce or separation, or loss of an important job, is usually the precipitating event that promotes this request for additional services. The crisis creates stress that has resulted in an increase of symptoms and puts the individual at greater risk for returning to substance use or psychiatric instability. The individual realizes that he does not possess the knowledge or skills necessary to deal with this situation effectively and asks for help. The goals of psychoeducation and skill-training interventions in this phase are to promote continued long-term stability by providing the knowledge and skills necessary to ensure that increased symptoms are managed effectively. These goals also give clients confidence that they can effectively handle similar events in the future, thus further strengthening their recovery. Because of the crisis nature of these situations and because of the knowledge and many skills that the recovering person can already call on, recovery management interventions during this phase are usually short-term.

## WHEN KNOWLEDGE AND SKILLS DO NOT WORK

Recovery management interventions focus on preventing substance use relapse and psychiatric instability; however, such relapses are common phenomena in the recovery process. Individuals with co-occurring mental health and substance use disorders are more prone to these relapses because they have more symptoms to manage. For a relapse to occur, an individual must first have established abstinence or psychiatric stability for a significant period of time (at least three or four months in a nonrestrictive environment). Intermittent but frequent substance use or psychiatric instability is not a relapse but rather a pattern of substance use and psychiatric behavior. Although such events can occur at any time in recovery, they are most common in the early recovery and treatment engagement phases.

Both the therapist and the client can view a relapse either as a failure or an opportunity. The most effective view is that relapses are possible and if they occur, they need to be interrupted immediately and then followed by a ruthless evaluation to assess why it happened. Such a response turns a relapse into a learning opportunity instead of a failure. Clients who return to substance use or psychiatric instability need to be asked, "What did you learn from this?" People learn much more from their failures and mistakes than their successes. Furthermore, the therapist can emphasize that we fail only when we stop trying. If this opportunity viewpoint is not emphasized, the client will be left with unresolved guilt or shame, which can only contribute to another relapse.

## CONCLUSION

Many clients that mental health and substance abuse therapists work with have disorders that require long-term and, in many instances, lifelong attention. Thus treatment plans must address the long-term management realities of these disorders and include recovery management interventions that promote long-term stability. The majority of this work is done in the early recovery and treatment-engaged phase; however, in some instances, important basic knowledge and skills must first be introduced before recovery can begin, and life crisis events may require additional recovery-management interventions after recovery is well established. Any return to substance use or psychiatric instability should be viewed as an opportunity to strengthen recovery skills rather than as a treatment failure. The next chapter focuses on recovery movements that often play an important role in the development and reinforcement of recovery-management interventions.

# Chapter 11

# Substance Abuse and Mental Health Recovery Movements

Recovery is the process of returning to health and well-being. It is a journey of personal growth, gaining strength, understanding, and wisdom as one returns to one's former condition prior to whatever misfortune was experienced. Various self-help programs of recovery now in place involve individuals in recovery helping one another. They are designed for both individuals with mental and substance use disorders and their families. Therapists with multifarious caseloads must be familiar with the concepts and operations of programs of recovery in order to help their clients effectively use these programs.

## *MENTAL HEALTH AND SUBSTANCE DEPENDENCY RECOVERY CONCEPTS*

The recovery concept is not as well established in the mental health treatment field as it is in the substance abuse treatment field. There is more conviction in the addictions' field that recovery is possible despite multiple relapses and repeated episodes of treatment. Mental health services, depending upon where they are offered, may still view people with serious mental illness as needing lifelong supportive services for a progressive, disabling disorder that has a negative prognosis. However, considerable in research and the consumer advocacy movements are redefining recovery and abandoning paternalistic, demeaning, protective, and pessimistic views.

Recovery, as a concept in mental health treatment, dates only from the 1980s. At the beginning of the twentieth century, Emil Kraepelin judged the outcome of schizophrenia to be so dismal that he called the disorder dementia praecox or premature dementia (U.S. Public Health

Service, 2001). Many professionals still believe that promoting limited expectations for treatment outcomes for major mental disorders is neither discriminatory nor unduly pessimistic. Low expectations, they say, can provide some protection for individuals who have unpredictable, disorganizing, and disabling disorders. Another concern is that the concept of recovery could be used to blame individuals who are not yet successful in their recovery, viewing them as being at fault or unmotivated. Mental health services also have been very reluctant to address spiritual issues, at least in the public sector, but incorporating spirituality into the recovery movements has been gaining ground.

A thirty-two-year longitudinal study of patients from a state psychiatric hospital (Harding et al., 1987) found significantly different courses of outcomes among the individuals. The study participants had been ill for an average of sixteen years, totally disabled for ten years, and hospitalized continuously for six years. They participated in a pioneering rehabilitation program and were released in a planned deinstitutionalization process with community supports in place. Thirty-two years later 34 percent of these individuals with a diagnosis of schizophrenia experienced full recovery in both psychiatric status and social functioning. Full recovery was defined as showing no current signs and symptoms of mental illness, taking no current medications, working, relating well to family and friends, integrating well into the community, and behaving in ways that gave no indication of mental illness. Another 34 percent of the individuals significantly improved. Ralph (2000) discussed an overview of twenty-seven World Health Organization studies on schizophrenia by de Girolamo who found that those assessed had a 6 to 66 percent recovery rate. Harding and Zahniser (1995) stated that schizophrenia does not have just one course and prognosis but an ever-widening heterogeneity of outcomes across time. These individuals can, and do, perform at every level of work and every level of work should be seen as a possibility. Thus there appears to be potential for a full or partial recovery from major mental disorders even after decades of illness. Deinstitutionalization, psychosocial rehabilitation, community-based treatment, consumer advocacy, and family advocacy have all joined to pave the way for the emerging concept of recovery from mental illness (U.S. Public Health Service, 2001).

The mental illness field has various definitions of recovery. The Missouri Department of Mental Health (1999) defines recovery as a process of healing physically and emotionally. Individuals in recovery adjust their attitudes, feelings, perceptions, beliefs, roles, and life goals. Recovery involves reclaiming independence, personal responsibility, belonging, power and mastery, meaning, and hope. Recovery does not change the reality that a catastrophic event has occurred but requires people to assume responsibility for having a satisfying, hopeful, and contributing life within the limitations of their disorder. Ralph (2000) defines mental health recovery as an ongoing process—a continuing, deeply personal, and individual effort. Recovery leads to growth and discovery and is accomplished one step at a time. Allott and Loganathan (2002) describe recovery as the reawakening of hope after despair; breaking through denial and seeking understanding and acceptance; moving from withdrawal to engagement; coping actively rather than adjusting passively; reclaiming a positive sense of self; and journeying from alienation to purpose. The Vermont Recovery Education Project (1999) defines recovery as finding hope, developing a personal understanding of the experience of mental illness, and developing the skills and knowledge to support wellness, and, in some cases, full recovery. Mead and Copeland (2000) state that the key facets of recovery are hope, responsibility for self, education about mental illness, self-advocacy, and peer support. Hope makes recovery possible and allows individuals with mental illness to change from looking to someone else to save them to working on their own healing.

The *Wellness Recovery Action Plan (WRAP),* developed by Copeland (2000), includes a daily maintenance plan that describes what feeling well is like and a list of things to do daily to maintain wellness. It includes identification of triggers, early warning signs, and worsening symptoms along with a planned response to these concerns. It identifies symptoms that indicate when individuals can no longer make decisions or take care of themselves and stay safe and offers a plan for supporters and health care professionals to institute until the individual can once again manage on his own.

The substance abuse field has long held the concept of recovery. Abstinence is the first step, but abstinence alone is not recovery. Recovery also includes the development of physical, psychological, social, and spiritual health (Gorski, 1989). One model by Goodwin (2000) divides recovery into three stages: physical, emotional, and spiritual. Another model by Hoskins (1989) uses three stages in recovery: treatment, Stage I recovery, and Stage II recovery. Treatment may involve medical care if physical withdrawal would place the individual at risk. Stage I recovery focuses on learning about addiction, achieving stable abstinence, and building minimal new social supports. Stage II recovery involves the issue of psychological development and building a lifestyle that promotes health and serenity. It is in this stage that recovering addicts can begin to enjoy life, which Hoskins believes is the only rational goal of recovery. Hoskins reports that most people who fail in recovery do so because they cannot come to terms with their spiritual needs. He defines spirituality as the individual's perception of self in relation to the universe and other beings in that universe.

These are but a few of the many recovery models described in the literature; however, most of the models agree that the recovery process involves movement from physical to psychological/emotional needs to social/interpersonal needs and finally to spiritual needs. Physical recovery may involve detoxification and recuperation from acute withdrawal. Cravings are intense and external support and encouragement are important to help deal with these physical discomforts. The psychological/emotional aspects of recovery involve dealing with such feelings as anger, fear, guilt, shame, remorse, hopelessness, and learning to take full responsibility for one's behaviors. The first part of the process is primarily an internal examination of oneself. Once abstinence becomes more comfortable and emotions and behaviors are better managed, the recovery process can begin to address relationship issues. Individuals must face the interpersonal consequences of their addiction. They must mend damaged relationships, make important new ones, and accept that some are irretrievably lost. The final focus of recovery is spiritual—learning to feel included in the universe and becoming connected with something else, be it God, a cause, or a group of people. It is the path that answers the questions: Who am I? Who are all these other people? What am I doing here? It allows one to seek a purpose in life that goes beyond personal pleasure or personal comfort.

Other important concepts of substance dependency recovery are powerlessness, release from compulsion, gratitude, humility, and forgiveness. Powerlessness is the inability to control the amount of a substance consumed once use begins. It does not refer to the decision to pick up that first drink or drug. Release from the compulsion to use, however, involves the ability to *choose* not to drink or use drugs rather than enforcing a prohibition on oneself against drinking and drugging. Gratitude involves focusing on what one has rather than what one does not have, while humility is accepting limitations and that it is all right to have limitations; forgiveness is both forgiving oneself for wrongs committed and letting go of resentments toward others. Each of these concepts help persons in recovery deal with many old bad habits and develop a positive view of life and the world around them.

## *SIMILARITIES AND DIFFERENCES BETWEEN SUBSTANCE DEPENDENCE AND MENTAL HEALTH RECOVERY CONCEPTS*

Mental health and substance dependence recovery concepts have many aspects in common but also a few notable differences. Understanding these similarities and differences is essential when working with a multifarious caseload.

### *Similarities*

*Both mental health and substance-dependent disorders are viewed as "no-fault" illnesses.* Although not always the case, the etiology of these disorders is now believed to be biopsychosocial and a great deal of research backs up this view. Individuals are born with biological vulnerabilities and personality traits, which promote early behaviors that increase the risk of developing these disorders. They also are impacted by social influences, which can promote behaviors that contribute to the development of the disorder or worsen the symptoms of the disorder. The fact that medication can reduce or eliminate the symptoms of many of these disorders supports this view. Families and individuals are no longer blamed for the individual having the disorder.

*The ultimate responsibility for ensuring recovery from mental health and substance-dependence disorders rests with the individual with the disorder.* In this case, individuals are "held harmless" for developing these disorders but not for avoiding treatment. All disorders now have treatments that can reduce and stabilize symptoms. Thus individuals with these disorders can manage both their recovery and their lives.

*The process of recovery from mental health and substance-dependence disorders requires hope.* Hope is the cornerstone of motivation, resilience, and determination. It is the medication for the fear "will I ever be normal again?" Hope is the step beyond the anger at having these disorders. Individuals with these disorders need to experience hope in order to accept the pain caused by their disorders and do the hard work necessary to achieve recovery. Those around them, especially service providers, can help promote hope by pointing out changes that they already have made or have the potential to make. However, individuals still have to be open to receiving this feedback and to interpreting it as hopeful. When there is hope, recovery is possible; when there is no hope, recovery is highly unlikely.

*Recovery in both mental health and substance-dependence disorders is defined as a process, not an event.* This process has physical, psychological/emotional, social, and spiritual elements. Most individuals begin with a physical focus and then move through the other elements. They are not striving for a point but an ongoing lifetime process. They need to continuously address their symptoms so they can develop greater proficiency in dealing with them over time—learning from their mistakes. They must learn the necessary skills to deal with life events so they do not destabilize changes they have already made. They must develop the resiliency to see that dealing effectively with such disorders makes other life events seem more manageable. Part of this process involves mending relationships and developing strong and stable new ones and finding one's place in the world. The process has transition points but it does not have an end point.

*Recovery from mental health and substance-dependence disorders requires diligence and daily involvement.* Recovery involves careful attention to daily activities, self-care behaviors, positive interpersonal interactions, participation in support activities, identification of triggers, and plans to manage cravings and/or psychiatric symptoms set off by triggers. Recovery emphasizes reaching out to others, reading literature, and seeking professional treatment when needed. Optimally, clients should stay involved in self-help support groups to receive and give support to others, write frequently in a journal, or participate in other activities that increase self-awareness, and take on life "one day at a time," as recommended by Alcoholics Anonymous.

*Recovery from mental health and substance dependence involves growing beyond the level of maturation achieved at the time of the onset of the disorder.* In the twelve-step community, the idea of becoming "weller than well" means examining one's life so that one may become more than one's expectations. By facing a disorder, clients can glean a sense of personal dignity and self-esteem and continue to grow in spite of the disorder. This view answers the question, "Achieve recovery, for what?"

### Differences

*Very little corresponds in mental health recovery with the impact of craving in substance-dependence recovery.* Craving is both a physical and psychological experience that plays a significant and much-feared role in relapse. The closest experience in mental health recovery is the longing individuals with a bipolar disorder may have for the energy and boundless optimism of a manic episode. For example, the individual hopes that the high of mania can be experienced without negative consequences just as individuals with drug dependency hope to be able to use without negative consequences. Most of the symptoms of a mental disorder are painful and people do not long to return to them.

*The term* enabling *has a very different meaning in mental health recovery than it does in substance-dependency recovery.* The enabling concept in mental health recovery means giving another person strength, resources, tools, conviction, and authority to achieve a desired purpose, such as increasing an individual's independent living skills. Enabling is giving hope. In substance-dependence recovery, however, this term is defined as shielding individuals with substance dependence from the consequences of their own behavior. Since motivation for change normally results from the negative consequences of substance use, enabling—such as making excuses for the alcohol-dependent spouse when he is hungover and does not go to work—prevents him from experiencing the full consequences of his behavior.

*The concept of maintenance is very different.* In substance-dependence recovery, maintenance describes an advanced state of recovery—individuals consolidate their gains and continue to improve upon them. Maintenance is viewed as lasting a lifetime. In the mental health recovery movement, maintenance implies limiting services to only medication and case management because of the need to ration services or limit access to more intense services. The concept has come to be defined as institutionalization in a community setting with little expectation of recovery or a meaningful life. When the term is used, individuals in the substance-use recovery community have a very different reaction than individuals in the mental health community.

## *RECOVERY CONCEPTS*
## *FOR CO-OCCURRING DISORDERS*

The concept of recovery from co-occurring disorders involves a focus on both mental and substance use disorders in a nonsequential manner. It involves concurrent attention to all disorders present in an integrated manner. Progress in one enhances the other and relapse in one decreases the stability of the other. The need for integration in the process of *recovery* is as important as integration in *treatment*. Daley and Thase (1994) propose key consumer activities for a successful recovery from co-occurring disorders. These include: having realistic expectations; participating actively; accepting responsibility for change; developing attitudes and behaviors that help with long-term recovery; being honest about problems, struggles, feelings, and thoughts; being patient and persistent; making a commitment to recovery; complying with treatment; being self-reflective; knowing when to ask for and being willing to accept help; learning new coping strategies to deal with problems; attending support groups; allowing room for mistakes and learning from them; developing inner resources; and focusing on identifying and building personal strengths. Not surprisingly, these incorporate most of the basic principles in the substance dependence and mental health recovery movements. The recovery movement for co-occurring disorders is not as well developed as the substance dependence and mental health movements; however, self-help groups specially designed for these individuals are now available in many communities in the United States.

## SELF-HELP GROUPS
## OF THE RECOVERY MOVEMENTS

Some individuals can manage to achieve sobriety, stabilization, and recovery with little external assistance. However, most find it necessary "not to do it alone," but instead use treatment and self-help groups for guidance, structure, assistance, and support so that they can deal effectively with the demands of recovery. Peer-run self-help groups are the primary vehicles that programs of recovery use to promote their message.

The most common types of self-help groups that individuals with substance-dependence disorders attend are Alcoholics Anonymous (AA) and Narcotics Anonymous (NA). The only requirement for participation in these groups is a desire to stop using alcohol and other drugs. Both of these self-help groups use the twelve steps and twelve traditions first developed by AA as the path to achieve recovery. The steps begin with acknowledging that one is powerless over a specific substance, taking a searching and fearless moral inventory, and making amends to people one has harmed. The steps end with carrying the message to others with the same disorder and living what has been learned in all aspects of one's life. The twelve traditions address such things as how groups are organized, run, and funded; anonymity; and relationships within and without the group. The publication, *Alcoholics Anonymous,* now in its fourth edition and referred to as "The Big Book," provides guidance and inspiration through stories of how individuals have achieved recovery (Alcoholics Anonymous, 2001). Numerous other self-help groups for a wide variety of conditions and issues also use these steps and traditions as a basis for their programs of recovery.

Many individuals can embrace and thrive on these twelve steps and traditions; however, others react strongly to the words "God" or "greater power," which are used in six of the twelve steps. For these individuals, AA and similar self-help groups appear to be religious organizations. Even though AA defines God as simply something that is greater then one's self, such as the group or as "Good Orderly Direction," the global concept makes it impossible for certain individuals to use such groups effectively. These individuals may work more effectively with Rational Recovery, now called Self-Management and Recovery Training (SMART), or other self-help groups that use more secular terms. Some individuals also have a problem with the concept of "powerlessness," which is directed toward the substance once its use has begun because it can reinforce other powerlessness concepts that women have been taught and experienced. Which self-help group individuals attend is much less important than the fact that they use all the resources available to them to achieve recovery.

Self-help groups for mental disorders are more recent in their development. One of the first was Emotions Anonymous (EA), which was founded in St. Paul, Minnesota in 1971. EA is designed for individuals with such issues as depression, abnormal fears, anger, or compulsive behavior. The program has adapted AA's twelve steps and twelve traditions to address these issues. The National Alliance for the Mentally Ill (NAMI), founded in 1979, and its affiliates run support groups for individuals with mental disorders and their families. Numerous other self-help groups or Web chat rooms for individuals with specific disorders, such as bipolar, depression, or borderline personality disorder, have also developed during recent years.

Between 1987 and 1992 the federal government's Center for Mental Health Services (CMHS) also funded fourteen demonstration projects of consumer-run self-help programs. The goals of these projects included increasing the number of self-help services available; demonstrating the feasibility and effectiveness of such programs; and fostering support for sustaining such programs. These demonstration projects ranged from walk-in centers to technical assistance and advocacy centers to establishing businesses run by recovering individuals. Many of these projects have continued and expanded and now serve as models for other self-help activities.

Self-help groups for individuals with co-occurring disorders have also developed in recent years. Many AA and NA meetings have been modified for individuals with co-occurring mental disorders. In addition, programs of recovery specifically for individuals with co-occurring disorders have sprung up. Dual Recovery Anonymous (DRA), which started in Kansas City in 1989, is based on many of the principles of AA. The two requirements for membership are a desire to stop using alcohol and other illicit drugs and a desire to manage emotional or psychiatric illness in a constructive way. The suggestions of DRA are: (1) Today, I will be free of alcohol and other intoxicating drugs; (2) Today, I will follow a health plan to manage my emotional or psychiatric disorders; (3) And today, I will practice the twelve steps of DRA. Another twelve-step recovery program specifically for individuals with co-occurring disorders is called Double Trouble.

## TREATMENT PROVIDERS
## AND THE RECOVERY MOVEMENTS

Substance abuse treatment professionals are inclined, via experience and training, to actively foster client involvement in a program of recovery. Mental health treatment professionals, on the other hand, are less inclined to advocate for such participation, partly because of their training and partly because the mental health recovery movement is much newer with far fewer meetings available. Mental health professionals tend to attempt to shelter their more vulnerable clients from what they may perceive as excessive expectations or potentially abusive community situations. Substance abuse professionals, on the other hand, tend to encourage their clients to participate fully in the community. Each position creates a potential risk when dealing with a multifarious caseload. The risk for mental health professionals is that by discouraging participation in such groups, their clients will not get the amount of support needed to successfully address their mental health and substance use disorders. The risk for substance abuse professionals is that they will push clients into community activities before they are ready or stable enough to participate effectively and thus precipitate a psychiatric crisis or treatment termination. This section discusses how mental health and substance abuse professionals can best interface with the recovery movements and their self-help groups.

Several models have been proposed concerning how treatment professionals can successfully work with these recovery movements. Mead and Copeland (2000) offer guidelines for treatment providers who want to have a recovery focus in their work with clients. They are advised to treat the client as a fully competent equal; focus on how the person feels and what they are experiencing rather than diagnosis or prognosis; share simple, safe, practical, noninvasive, inexpensive self-help skills and strategies; recognize strengths and progress; encourage participation in support groups; accept that each person's life path is up to them; and, ensure that planning and treatment are fully collaborative. A recovery focus is not merely the reframing of clinical work into trendier terms.

The Ohio Mental Health Consumer Outcomes Initiative from the Office of Consumer Services, Ohio Department of Mental Health (2001) developed twelve principles that formed the basis of their Mental Health Recovery Process Model, which provides guidance to clinicians concerning clinical attitudes, approaches, and behaviors. These principles are: the consumer directs the recovery process; the mental health system must be aware of its tendency to enable and encourage consumer dependency; consumers recover more quickly when they have hope, consider spirituality, and have their culture understood, their education needs identified, and their social needs addressed; individual differences are recognized and valued; recovery is most effective when a holistic approach is used; all interventions are merged including medical, psychological, social, and recovery; clinicians' emphasis on hope and their ability to foster trusting relationships influence recovery; clinicians must operate from a strengths/assets model; clinicians and consumers collaboratively develop a recovery management plan; family involvement enhances recovery; mental health services are most effective when based in the consumer's community; and community involvement is important to the recovery process.

O'Hagan (2000) wrote a paper for the Mental Health Commission of New Zealand on ten recovery-based competencies needed in the training of psychiatrists, comprehensive nurses, social workers, and mental health support workers. These competencies include: understanding recovery principles and experiences; recognizing and supporting the personal resourcefulness of people with mental illness; understanding and accommodating diverse views on mental illness, treatment, and recovery; having the self-awareness and skills to communicate respectfully and develop good relationships with consumers; understanding and actively protecting consumers' rights; understanding the impact of and working to reduce discrimination and social exclusion for consumers; acknowledging different cultures; having comprehensive knowledge of community services and resources and actively supporting consumers' use of these resources; understanding the consumer movement and the ability to support consumer participation in services; and having knowledge of family perspectives and the ability to support family participation in services. Each of these models has many overlapping principles, but the key factor in each is that treatment needs to be a true partnership between the treating professional and the client receiving the services.

One of the challenges of participating in a peer-run program of recovery is that the behaviors associated with some of the disorders have the potential to interfere with an individual's comfort with or acceptance at such meetings. Therapists need to know which programs and meetings in their area are more accepting of their more-impaired clients. Therapists also need to inform the clients about how these meetings work, their right to leave at any time, their right to share or not share, what is appropriate to share and what is not, and how best to use or ignore what others share with them. Having them team up with another client who is familiar with a particular meeting can make them more comfortable about attending. In addition, therapists can promote the development of specialized self-help groups either in the community or at the treatment agency, though this can be very labor intensive and requires identifying a stable leadership core to run the meeting.

Finally, although the mental health and substance dependence recovery movements have many more similarities than differences, therapists must take these differences into consideration when working with clients who have co-occurring disorders. These clients will often participate in the self-help groups of more than one recovery movement. Therapists working with multifarious caseloads need to learn as much as they can about each of these programs of recovery. They must be able to have an informed discussion with clients about what they are learning in these meetings and how it relates to their treatment goals. They must also be able to help clients understand why one program of recovery might recommend one particular course of action while another recommends another course of action. The therapist's ultimate purpose is to help some clients integrate various principles and concepts from the different recovery movements so they can develop a comprehensive personal program that addresses multiple disorders. It should never be forgotten that the treatment professionals and the recovery movements are on the same team.

## *CONCLUSION*

Each of the recovery movements can play an important part in the successful outcome for most clients on a multifarious caseload. For therapists to effectively promote their clients' participation in these programs, they must understand how they work and believe in their effectiveness. Currently, many mental health professionals know very little about the programs of recovery for substance dependence, and many substance abuse professionals know little about the programs of recovery for mental disorders. Many therapists from both professions know little about the programs of recovery for co-occurring disorders. Therapists working with multifarious caseloads must become very familiar with all of these programs of recovery if they are to support their clients' participation in them.

Chapter 12

# Supervising Staff
# with Multifarious Caseloads

Although a great deal of professional literature focuses on the supervision of staff treating either mental health or substance use disorders (Bernard and Goodyear, 1992; Borders and Leddick, 1987; Machell, 1987; McDaniel, Weber, and McKeever, 1983; Powell, 1993; Worthington, 1987), little focuses on supervising staff treating clients with co-occurring disorders (Hendrickson et al., 1999). This chapter presents twelve issues that frequently need supervisory attention for clinical staff working with clients who have multiple disorders and suggests supervisory strategies to address these issues. These issues fall into three broad categories: issues that deal with the needs of clients; issues regarding the needs of staff; and issues concerning the needs of treatment systems. The clinical aspects of addressing many of these issues are presented in detail in other sections of this book. This chapter focuses on how a supervisor can best help clinical staff effectively deal with these issues. As with other recommendations in this book, these proposed supervisory strategies should be viewed as additional or specialized techniques that can be added to the supervisor's toolbox, and should in no way be seen as replacing the many other sound and effective methods of supervision in use.

## ISSUES THAT DEAL WITH CLIENT NEEDS

### Dealing with Diverse Treatment Needs

As discussed in Chapter 1, therapists often have caseloads composed of clients with a wide range of mental health and substance use disorders. The substance use disorders may range from alcohol abuse to narcotics dependence and mental health disorders might range from generalized anxiety disorder to schizophrenia. Because individuals with co-occurring disorders present with such a wide variety of disorders and thus have a wide range of impairments, treatment intervention strategies must be tailored to the individual needs of each client. Some clients can easily achieve abstinence and can tolerate intensive confrontational therapy, while other clients lack the necessary skills to initially achieve abstinence and decompensate quickly if confrontation is too intense.

The role of supervision when encountering this issue is twofold. The first is to help clinicians learn how to develop individualized treatment plans that take into consideration the differences that their clients have in symptom level, level of impairment, and coping skills. The second is to familiarize them with subgroup models presented in Chapter 5 that help organize this population into more heterogeneous clusters that have similar treatment needs.

### Defining Treatment Goals for Diverse Caseloads

The multitude of problems that this population presents is often overwhelming and can create confusion concerning what issues to treat and when to treat them. For example, a client might present with a recent suicide attempt, delusions and hallucinations, sexual identity confusion, anger, mistrust, possible HIV and hepatitis C, alcohol dependence and cannabis, cocaine, and narcotic abuse. This can be a very intimidating picture even for an experienced treatment professional. When a clinician is unclear about the direction and focus of treatment, there is little chance for success.

The role of supervision in this instance is to help clinicians develop comprehensive treatment goals that clearly define the purpose of treatment. Table 1.2 in Chapter 1 presents treatment goals that are useful for clinicians working with caseloads that have multiple diagnoses. The treatment goals are based on the type of disorders that clients have. Using this model for the previous example, a therapist can develop a treatment plan that has the ultimate goals of psychiatric stability and abstinence. Although many treatment objectives must be met before these goals can be achieved, having clear goals for the ultimate purpose of treatment helps therapists identify the specific objectives and treatment interventions that need to be included in their treatment plan.

### *Identifying the Views of Family/Peer Networks Concerning Treatment*

Families and peers can have significant influence on the behavior of clients. They can promote and support or hinder and undermine new behaviors. A therapist, however, cannot always determine the full extent of this impact without actually interacting with these individuals.

A client with major depressive disorder and alcohol and cocaine dependence who had been abstinent and psychiatrically stable for four months suddenly begins missing a few scheduled appointments and not going as frequently to her self-help groups. The only thing she tells her therapist is that she is experiencing some family problems.

The therapist is unclear if she is using this as an excuse, or if there are real problems, what they are, and how they might impact her recovery.

The role of the supervisor here is to try to recruit the family and peer groups into the information-gathering process and treatment activities. Chapter 8 provides several recommendations on how to involve the family in the treatment process. In this instance, the supervisor works first to help the therapist understand how important it is to get detailed information about these stated family problems and then strategize how to obtain this information.

After some resistance, the client finally shares with the therapist that her family thinks she is spending too much of her time in treatment activities and is against the taking of antidepressant medication. The client also says that she had received some feedback at her self-help groups that taking medication for a long time might interfere with her recovery.

Once the issue of family problems has been clarified, the supervisor can work with the therapist on how to involve the family more positively in the treatment process and how to help the client deal with conflicting treatment recommendations.

## ISSUES THAT DEAL WITH STAFF NEEDS

### Identifying Staff Training Needs

Usually, clinicians who work with clients with multiple diagnoses have expertise in treating either substance use or mental health disorders, but not both. To ensure that these clients receive effective treatment, supervisors need to identify their clinical staff's knowledge and skill gaps in these areas and promote training opportunities to fill these gaps. Figure 1.1 and Table 1.1 in Chapter 1 present the philosophical, knowledge, and skills bases that clinicians working with this population most often need to add to their professional repertoire. Staff who develop these attitudes, knowledge, and skills can effectively treat clients with multiple disorders. Supervisors can use these tables to develop assessment tools to identify the particular training needs of their clinical staff.

Once supervisors identify these needs, they can lobby for or designate agency training money to send staff to specialized trainings or bring experts in these areas into the agency to conduct training. This method allows numerous staff members to attend the sessions concurrently and process their understanding of the new information with one another. This strategy also is especially cost effective and places limited demands on staff time. On the other hand, one-time trainings tend to increase knowledge more than skills and offer no reinforcement of newly acquired information; as a result, staff members often return to old practices.

A second method of increasing staff competencies is to have clinical staff with different expertise colead a group. Together, both clinicians can effectively address all the substance abuse and mental health issues that arise in the group, and through observations of how the other therapist handles certain situations and from the feedback they give each other, both begin to develop the expertise needed to treat multiple disorders. The strength of this method is that multi-need clients have their treatment needs met while the clinicians are still developing the necessary competencies to effectively treat them. It also allows staff to be both expert and student at the same time. On the other hand, this method requires two staff members to work collaboratively and to have the interest and motivation to learn new competencies. Such groups also usually require staff to have more than one supervisor, so a multiple supervisory arrangement needs to be worked out (see the System Blending section of this chapter). Simply having individuals with different expertise on a multidisciplinary team seldom increases the competencies of other team staff unless the other staff members are required to work with clients with multiple disorders and have the opportunity to observe integrated treatment skills in action.

The third method is to integrate mental health and substance abuse issues into all aspects of the supervisory process and to address all the mental health and substance use concerns regarding assessment, treatment plans, and intervention strategies in clinical discussions. This of course requires the supervisor to have expertise in both of these areas. When this is not the case, an expert can be consulted to both upgrade the supervisor's expertise and provide clinical guidance for the staff. Although any of these methods would be helpful in increasing staff competencies, if they all were used concurrently, staff would acquire new attitudes, knowledge, and skills much more quickly.

## *Helping Staff Manage Function and Role Shifts*

The multiple treatment and support needs of clients in a multifarious caseload often require clinicians to perform a wide variety of functions and roles. For example, a therapist with a client with alcohol dependence and schizoaffective disorders at times provides individual, group, or family therapy for this client; at other times he performs case management or advocacy functions. These shifts in roles and functions are often confusing for clinicians and may run counter to some of their professional training. It is not uncommon to hear a clinician say, "Am I a therapist, a case manager, or a community advocate?"

When clinicians are struggling with this issue, supervisors need to help them answer "yes, yes, yes" to these questions. Supervisors can help by connecting specific clinical tasks to treatment goals. The supervisor can point out that to achieve the goals of abstinence and psychiatric stability, the clinician must be a therapist who promotes acceptance of the disorders and a desire for abstinence and medication compliance when conducting a treatment group. However, the therapist must be a case manager when working with the client to complete all the necessary forms to ensure medication availability and a community advocate when promoting a client's acceptance into a supportive housing program. Should any of these tasks not be performed, the chance of treatment success is greatly reduced. In addition, one role or function is not more important than another in determining the ultimate success of treatment.

## Maintaining a Positive View Concerning the Potential for Change

Many clients with serious impairments have had many previous treatment and other failures in life. Therapists encountering such clients may develop a pessimistic viewpoint concerning their ability to offer successful treatment. In this case, supervisors need to focus on the problems and failures that reinforce this pessimistic point of view for both the therapist and the client.

A client enters treatment with a history of discontinuing medication that controls the symptoms of his bipolar disorder, then returns to alcohol use in order to reduce some of the emerging manic symptoms, and ends up being hospitalized. Soon after beginning treatment the client reports that he does not think his medication is helping. The therapist immediately assumes that the client has begun his same old pattern over again and tells his supervisor that he is not going to put much effort into the case because the client is on the way to the hospital again.

In such situations, the supervisor needs to promote competency-based interventions, which are described in Chapter 1. These interventions focus on clients' strengths and what is going right with therapy, and promote a sense of optimism that even more change is possible. In this case, the supervisor points out that the client is currently coming to therapy and taking his medication and asks the clinician why he thinks the client can be medication compliant and abstinent for periods of time. What skills or motivation does the client have to do this? How could these be used to either interrupt the relapse cycle or at least extend the period of time of stability? By asking such questions the view that change is possible greatly increases. Therapists often initially resist competency-based supervisory strategies because they feel too "Pollyannaish" or respond in some manner such as, "get real," so supervisors often have to persist in using this type of intervention. Supervisors can also help clinicians develop competency-based skills by having them incorporate client strengths into all treatment plans, especially for individuals about whom they are pessimistic. Supervisors can monitor the level of pessimism by asking clinicians to always include the client's prognosis in their clinical discussions. To ensure that the treatment plans reflect realistic and achievable goals for the client in the previous case, the supervisor may suggest that the initial goals be an increase in how long the client is medication compliant and abstinent and a decrease in the time spent in relapse and in the hospital. In doing so, success is defined as any change, and change can be built on to promote more change.

### Ensuring Integrated Treatment

Providing effective integrated treatment involves being aware of and addressing how multiple disorders interact with each other and how their interactions affect a client. Chapter 1 offers a detailed description of integrated treatment.

During a clinical supervision session with a therapist who has a client with social phobia and cannabis abuse disorders and occasional panic attacks, the therapist discusses how she has been working with the anxiety disorders, both with medication and behavior intervention. However, the client perceives little change in symptoms. The therapist does not discuss how she is addressing the marijuana use at all.

In such a case, the supervisor needs to address this.

To help clinicians become proficient in providing integrated treatment, supervisors can ensure that treatment plans for clients with multiple disorders include problem statements and treatment goals and objectives for each disorder. The supervisor can ask therapists during their clinical supervision to discuss how their treatment interventions address the treatment goals for each disorder. A third strategy is to occasionally ask the therapist what she thinks will happen to one disorder if the symptoms of the other disorder increase or decrease. In this example, the supervisor needs to ask about the status of the client's marijuana use, the treatment goals for that disorder, the intervention strategies the therapist is using to accomplish these goals, and how the marijuana use might be affecting the lack of decrease in symptoms. Such questions help bring into focus what is being done to address all the disorders and how these disorders might be affecting each other.

### *Dealing with Anxiety and Unhelpful Clinical Behavior*

Many clients with multiple disorders are unable or unwilling to initially work toward the treatment goals of abstinence or psychiatric or interpersonal stability. Sometimes, the level of client symptoms and/or impairments can lead to life-threatening situations. In fact, many clients with multiple disorders die prematurely, either by suicide or because of the consequences of their behavior. Blumenthal (1988) reports that 90 percent of adults who commit suicide have a mental disorder and up to 80 percent have a substance use disorder. Working with such clients can create a great deal of anxiety for therapists and cause either overfunctioning or expressions of hostility toward a client.

A client has schizoaffective, alcohol dependence, and opioid abuse disorders and is also HIV positive and has hepatitis C. This client is only partially compliant with his medications for both his mental health and physical disorders. He also has a history of getting paranoid and getting into fights in which he has been seriously injured.

At this point, the therapist has no leverage to use to promote abstinence or medication compliance. The client is willing only to regularly see the therapist individually on a weekly basis.

Supervisors can help clinicians deal more effectively with anxiety and inappropriate behavior by promoting clear and appropriate therapeutic boundaries and by helping them design interventions that match best treatment practices with client readiness. In this example, the therapist comes to supervision very anxious about this client. He rightly believes that the client's life is in jeopardy, if not immediately, certainly in the long run. He is also angry and frustrated with the client concerning his treatment noncompliance. What the therapist really wants from supervision is a magic intervention strategy that will enlighten and motivate the client to become treatment compliant. What the supervisor must do first is acknowledge the reality that the therapist is dealing with a client who might die, but the responsibility of that does not lie with the therapist alone. The supervisor, other professionals involved in the client's treatment, and the client also have responsibility concerning the outcome of treatment. By doing this, the total burden of the case is taken off the shoulders of the therapist. The next step for the supervisor is to point out that the client has found something helpful in seeing the therapist because he attends treatment once a week. Since no outside leverage is available, the supervisor then helps the therapist identify short-term achievable goals that can form the basis for eventually achieving the long-term goals. Examples of these are getting the client to attend a psychoeducation group about either his mental health or physical disorders or encouraging the client to take his medication more days than not. Such strategies begin to help the therapist see that something positive is already happening in therapy and that change is possible. The supervisor should also point out that the client has only marginally engaged with treatment and that other therapists would not be getting any different results at this stage of recovery. Finally, the supervisor can help the therapist establish appropriate boundaries concerning treatment outcome responsibility by having him evaluate his treatment interventions and results based on the principle that clinicians are responsible for input but not outcome, because clients have free will. Thus the therapist's knowledge, skills, and intervention strategies can be evaluated from a standard or best practices model instead of what the client chooses to do with the intervention. Such strategies help clinicians manage their anxiety and feelings of anger and frustration.

## ISSUES THAT DEAL WITH TREATMENT SYSTEM NEEDS

### How to Measure Change and Success

The long-term treatment goals for clients with multiple disorders take time to achieve, so it is important that agencies and clinicians use measures that help them identify the small steps that clients take toward these goals. Without these measures, clinicians cannot document or recognize important changes that clients are making and agencies cannot accurately measure their success rates. The lack of such information can lead to a sense of failure, burnout, or even funding reductions. Thus, supervisors need to expose clinicians to different models of change so they can clearly see and easily measure their clients' changes. Supervisors also need to take an active role in designing performance standards that meaningfully measure their agency's effectiveness. Chapter 13 presents several particularly useful measures for clients with co-occurring disorders that can be associated with performance standards.

### Ensuring That Interactions Are Collegial

Usually, numerous professionals provide services to the same clients, bringing different levels of training, experience, and perspective on the focus of treatment. These differences always create the potential for interdisciplinary conflicts during collaboration or treatment coordination. Common areas of conflict include: Should the focus of treatment be on the mental health problem, the substance use problem, or some other aspect of treatment; where should the client be treated; does the usage indicate a substance dependence or a substance abuse disorder; should abstinence be required or worked toward; are the observed psychiatric symptoms the result of a mental disorder or substance-induced disorder; should usage result in removal from a program; should medication be prescribed to someone still using alcohol or drugs; and what medications should be prescribed.

Since the answers to these questions often vary depending on the client and the clinicians on the case, the supervisor must create a work atmosphere that is open to viewpoints of others and open to examining one's own reactions to others. To provide effective treatment for individuals with co-occurring disorders, a great deal of knowledge and skills must be integrated from a variety of professional disciplines and treatment models. Thus the professional differences encountered when addressing some of these issues must be framed by the supervisor as an opportunity to expand one's own knowledge and skill base, instead of as a power struggle. The supervisor can do this by emphasizing that no single discipline or profession has all the knowledge or skills to effectively address all the needs of this population. Supervisors can also promote this atmosphere by helping staff see how another treatment approach might be different, but the goal of that treatment is still the same. Finding this common ground can help keep the discussion between professionals focused on treatment techniques instead of philosophical or personal differences, thus greatly increasing their ability to find additional common ground.

Supervisors also need to attend to underconfident clinicians ("I do not know enough to give my input into the treatment plan") and overconfident clinicians ("I am more capable of helping this individual than others"). Both positions interfere with the development of collegial treatment relationships and can limit the treatment options available to clients. Supervisors must take a stand that the viewpoints of all professionals involved in the treatment of a client are of equal importance to the successful outcome of treatment. The supervisor needs to help the underconfident therapist accept his expertise and find the voice to express it. For another therapist, the intervention involves lowering the therapist's defenses enough to see that considering the options of others can only increase his clinical effectiveness.

### Dealing with Ethical Concerns

Several ethical concerns often arise when clinicians work with individuals with co-occurring disorders. They involve personal sharing, physical contact, disclosure of information, and documentation of services. Some mental health professionals are trained to disclose virtually nothing about themselves, while many substance abuse professionals are themselves in recovery and are comfortable sharing that and other personal information. Likewise, when it comes to physical contact, most substance abuse professionals are used to being warm and familiar toward their clients; they consider it normal to touch a hand or shoulder or to close a session or group with a hug. In fact, substance abuse therapists, who themselves are in recovery, may encounter clients at self-help group meetings. Mental health professionals, on the other hand, are often trained not to touch, but rather to teach clients to use words rather than actions to express themselves. Supervisors must help clinicians develop appropriate boundaries concerning sharing and touching that are based on whether particular actions would be helpful or disruptive for a particular client. For some clients appropriate sharing or touching by a therapist can promote a sense of security, affiliation, and hope that is helpful to the treatment process. However, for other clients, such actions can create confusion about the therapeutic relationship. Because of the emotional or cognitive complications of their disorders, clients might interpret such behaviors as threatening, intrusive, or an invitation for a nonprofessional personal relationship. Thus depending on the training and professional orientation of a therapist and the clients in treatment, the supervisor may need to either promote appropriate sharing or touching or discourage such activities.

Difficulties concerning the disclosure of information usually occur because of misunderstandings of the different laws governing confidentiality and who is authorized to receive client information. Confidentiality regulations covering substance abuse treatment are some of the strictest in the nation. They are set by federal law (federal rules and regulations on the Confidentiality of Alcohol and Drug Abuse Patient Treatment Records, 42 CFR Part 2) and are uniformly applied to all professionals providing substance abuse treatment. Mental health confidentiality laws have recently been modified by the Health Insurance Portability and Accountability Act (HIPAA) that nationally standardizes the exchange of mental health information and replaces all state laws, except where they are more stringent. The substance abuse confidentiality guidelines apply to treatment activities, not types of agencies providing services. Thus if therapists are providing substance abuse treatment in a mental health clinic, they must abide by substance abuse confidentiality regulations. Supervisors need to clearly define for their staff what confidentiality rules they must abide by and to whom they can disclose information. Two publications by the federal government's Center for Substance Abuse Treatment (CSAT) offer excellent guidance in every day language on how to comply with regulations: *Technical Assistance Publication (TAP) Number 13, Confidentiality of Patient Records for Alcohol and Other Drug Treatment,* and *TAP 24, Welfare Reform and Substance Abuse Treatment Confidentiality: General Guidance for Reconciling Need to Know and Privacy.*

Another ethical consideration that may challenge the therapist is the frequent and ongoing work with other agencies. If there is collaboration and cooperation, all is well. However, many therapists run into barriers that limit the client's access to services at other agencies or the ability to succeed at using those services. The therapist, in an attempt to advocate for the client, may fall into a demanding and angry mode of interaction with the other service providers. At such times, therapists may overanalyze another professional (such as stating that she is doing this because of issues she has with her own children) or question the quality of that program. At worst, when such interactions are not clearly documented, the therapist could be charged with slander or at least disrupt the relations between the two agencies in such a manner that future client referrals become even more difficult. Supervisors must be very proactive when their staff is having difficulties with referral agencies. They must help their staff clarify their issues in a non-personal way, express what they need from the other agency and why they think the other agency can provide it. Supervisors need to emphasize to staff that they should not confront the other agency until they have clear answers to those three questions. Of course, staff will need to vent about the individuals and rules with which they are frustrated; however, that should be kept only within the context of supervision. In many cases, the supervisor will need to address the problems and take the lead in discussing them with the supervisor of the other agency. The key is to keep the discussion between the staff of both agencies at the professional level and the focus on treatment, not personal issues.

Finally, some clinicians find that treatment documentation is an ethical concern. However, documentation is often the only means by which clinicians can demonstrate that they are using best practices to treat a client. It also documents that the treatment needs of each disorder are addressed and that clinicians have followed all local, state, and federal requirements concerning such issues as duty to warn, reporting suspected child or elder abuse, and maintaining client confidentiality. However, clinicians often fail to effectively fulfill this essential clinical responsibility. Supervisors must set very clear guidelines for staff concerning what and when clinical information must be documented and then monitor that it is being done.

### System Blending

Many treatment services for co-occurring disorders are collaborative efforts between substance abuse and mental health programs. Such collaborative efforts can result in a variety of supervisory configurations. Supervisors may find themselves supervising some staff for certain activities and other staff for other activities. Also, staff may receive additional supervision from other supervisors. Such supervisory situations have the potential to create confusion and conflicts over who is responsible for what and what clinical intervention is best for a specific situation.

For example, a substance abuse therapist is lent for ten hours a week to a mental health program to conduct substance abuse assessments and to colead two groups with a mental health therapist for clients with co-occurring disorders. The substance abuse therapist finds himself in a dual supervision situation. The supervision of his treatment activities at the substance abuse treatment program is unchanged, but a mental health supervisor now supervises his activities at the mental health program. During a substance abuse assessment at the mental health program, a client who has bipolar and alcohol dependence disorders and a history of misusing her medication refuses to sign a release that would allow the substance abuse therapist to talk with her private doctor. The substance abuse therapist, who is used to denying services to clients who refuse to sign such releases, brings the situation to the attention of his mental health supervisor. Instead of receiving support for his position, he is advised to work on building more trust in the therapeutic relationship so that the client will be willing to sign the release. When he tells his substance abuse supervisor about this, the supervisor states that such a suggestion prevents the doctor from knowing about her alcohol dependence disorder and enables her to continue misusing her medication. Thus the clinician ends up receiving conflicting supervisory advice and begins to believe that his substance abuse work at the mental health program will fail because its standard practices may be less than helpful.

Supervisors involved in collaborative treatment activities must work closely together and develop clear guidelines concerning supervisory responsibility. In addition, each supervisor must become familiar with the treatment philosophies, policies and procedures, standard treatment practices, and the politics that create the work environments of clinical staff. Such knowledge and awareness will help supervisors reduce potentially confusing or contradicting treatment recommendations; better understand why a therapist from another agency might choose a particular treatment approach; and help staff going into a new clinical setting understand why things may be handled in a different manner. In this example, had the supervisors spent time together prior to the implementation of this collaborative effort, they could have developed guidelines concerning supervisory responsibilities and increased their understanding of each other's treatment system. They would have probably also developed a process for resolving clinical differences. The mental health supervisor would also have had a better understanding of the importance of setting limits concerning potential drug use; the substance abuse therapist and supervisor would have had a better understanding of the importance of keeping an individual with a major mental disorder in treatment. Thus instead of the development of warring camps, the supervision could have focused on how to gain contact with the doctor and still keep the client in treatment.

## *CONCLUSION*

The art of supervision will always be part intuition and part technique. The amount and type of supervision staff members need vary depending on knowledge and skill level, experience, and individual temperament. However, when a supervisor is aware that certain situations may need supervisory attention and has options available for addressing them, his supervision will be more effective. Thus applying the previous supervisory strategies flexibly can improve the treatment environment and increase the clinical expertise that staff members need to be effective with individuals with multiple disorders.

Chapter 13

# Measuring Change: Reasonable Outcome and Performance Standards

This chapter provides mental health and substance abuse therapists with guidance in helping them measure client change and comparing their change rates with national averages. Mental health and substance abuse therapists must be aware of these measures if they are to develop a sense of competency in working with multifarious caseloads. This chapter first reviews the benefits of treatment, presents methods that therapists with multifarious caseloads can use to measure change, describes important variables that are associated with treatment success, provides national averages concerning treatment outcomes, and finally, proposes benchmarks that can be used to compare their success rates with national averages.

## BENEFITS OF TREATMENT

Although years of research concerning substance abuse and mental health treatment show that "treatment works," therapists must sincerely believe this in their hearts if they are to be effective. This section reviews the major findings concerning the benefits of this treatment.

The federal government has sponsored five major national studies concerning the effectiveness of substance abuse treatment in public programs (Gerstein et al., 1994; Hubbard et al., 1989; Hubbard et al., 1997; Substance Abuse and Mental Health Services Administration, 1994; Simpson and Sells, 1982). Another major study looked at the effectiveness of private substance abuse treatment programs (Hoffman and Miller, 1992) and twenty-four states have conducted major studies on the effectiveness of their substance abuse treatment services (Gerstein et al., 1994; National Association of State Alcohol and Drug Abuse Directors, 2002). The United Kingdom also has conducted a major study of the effectiveness of that nation's substance abuse treatment programs (Gossop et al., 1997). What each study found was that substance abuse treatment provides many benefits to both the individual and society. Box 13.1 summarizes these findings.

The scope of mental health issues that receive treatment attention (from major mental disorders, such as schizophrenia, to personal growth) and the many variations in treatment approaches make it impossible to conduct large national studies of multiple treatment programs, as has been done in the substance abuse field. Whereas substance abuse programs deal with either abuse or dependence disorders and generally have treatment goals of either abstinence or nonproblematic substance use, mental health treatment programs address multiple conditions that have many differing treatment goals. Mental health outcome research focuses on specific conditions that have specific treatment goals. Studies find that medication, behavioral, and talk therapies are all effective in improving both the daily functioning and the quality of life for individuals with these disorders (Mental Health: A Report of the Surgeon General, 2001). This is particularly true when they are used in combination.

Outcome studies of individuals receiving treatment for co-occurring disorders have not been as extensive as for individuals who have received traditional mental health and substance abuse treatment services, yet the results have been similar. Outcome studies concerning

---

**BOX 13.1. Benefits of Substance Abuse Treatment**

- Reduced drug use
- Reduced criminal activities
- Reduced health costs
- Reduced homelessness
- Reduced suicide attempts
- Reduced food stamp needs
- Reduced child welfare cases
- Increased employment and earnings

this population have examined outpatient services (Bond et al., 1991; Drake, McHugo, and Noordsy, 1993; Hellerstein, Rosenthal, and Miner, 1995), intensive or assertive community treatment services (Drake et al., 1998; Durell et al., 1993; Meisler et al., 1997), and residential treatment services (Bartels and Drake, 1996; Mierlak et al., 1998). These studies find that treatment, when modified to meet the special needs of individuals with co-occurring disorders, also provides many benefits for these clients and society. Box 13.2 summarizes these findings.

## MEASURING CLIENT CHANGE

Many methods are effective in measuring client change during treatment. Three of the most helpful ones for working with a multifarious caseload are client readiness for change (Prochaska, DiClemente, and Norcoss, 1992); substance abuse treatment scale (Mueser et al., 1995); and tracking changes toward abstinence and recovery (Hendrickson, Stith, and Schmal, 1995). The latter two were developed specifically for individuals with co-occurring disorders. Each measures different aspects of client change and only requires a minimum amount of time and resources to document. A description of each and the client changes they identify follow.

### Client Readiness for Change

This five-stage model measures clients' readiness for treatment and behavior change. These stages are labeled precontemplation,

---

**BOX 13.2. Benefits of Treating Co-Occurring Disorders**

- Reduced substance use
- Reduced psychiatric symptoms
- Reduced hospitalizations
- Increased use of appropriate treatment services
- Increased stable housing
- Improved quality of life

contemplation, preparation, action, and maintenance. *Precontemplation* indicates that the client has neither interest in treatment nor any intention to change behavior. In the *contemplation* stage, the client is aware of a problem and thinks he might want to overcome it in the future. *Preparation* is the stage in which the client intends to take action and begins to plan how to do that. In the *action* stage, the client is in treatment and modifying behavior. *Maintenance* is the stage during which the client works to prevent relapse and consolidate gains. Clients' readiness for change can be easily measured through the publicly available thirty-two-item questionnaire, University of Rhode Island Change Assessment (URICA) which can be administered and scored in a short period of time. This measure allows mental health and substance abuse therapists to track changes in clients' acceptance of a problem and their willingness to make or maintain behavioral changes.

### Substance Abuse Treatment Scale

This eight-stage model, based on a four-stage model originally proposed by Osher and Kofoed (1989), measures clients' levels of participation in treatment and decreases in substance use. This model divides each of Osher and Kofoed's four stages of engagement, persuasion, active treatment, and relapse prevention into early or late stages. During the *preengagement stage,* the potential client has no contact with a treatment professional. During the *engagement stage,* the client has irregular contact with a treatment professional. In the *early persuasion stage,* the client has regular contact with a treatment professional but has not changed his substance use. The *late persuasion stage* involves regular contact with a treatment professional and clients discussing their substance use and reducing use somewhat. The *early active treatment stage* involves, in addition to the activities noted in the late persuasion stage, a stated goal of working toward abstinence. The *late active treatment stage* occurs when the client has achieved abstinence for less than six months. In the *relapse prevention stage,* abstinence has been achieved for six months. Occasional lapses are allowed in this stage but not days of relapse or problematic use. The final stage, *remission or recovery,* is achieved when the client has had no substance use problems for over a year and is no longer in treatment for the substance use disorder. This model allows therapists to measure changes in both treatment participation and substance use behavior.

### Tracking Changes Toward Abstinence and Recovery

This model measures observable changes in clients' behavior and verbal expressions of attitudes and motivation concerning substance use. Each of its stages has a specific substance use behavior, attitude, and motivation toward substance use. In the *first stage,* substance use behaviors continue with no acknowledgement that substance use is a problem and the client has no motivation to abstain. In the *second stage,* a client abstains as a result of outside pressure (such as the court or family), but does not acknowledge that use is a problem and has no motivation to abstain if the outside pressure were discontinued. In the *third stage,* a client acknowledges that use is a problem but the use continues and there is no motivation expressed for abstinence. In the *fourth stage,* the substance use continues but the client acknowledges that use is a problem and expresses a desire to achieve abstinence. The *fifth and final stage* is reached when the client achieves abstinence, acknowledges that use is a problem, and expresses a desire to continue abstinence. This model allows therapists to track changes in clients during the normal course of treatment from observable behaviors and verbalizations.

Each of these models provides therapists and treatment agencies with methods to measure change during a specific treatment event and to provide a basis for differentiating positive treatment outcomes from negative treatment outcomes. Treatment agencies or professionals must determine how to classify a treatment success. Is any positive movement from one stage to another during treatment considered a successful treatment event, or must a specific amount of positive change take place before treatment is considered successful? One treatment professional or agency might decide that only abstinence should be considered a treatment success; another might see the reduction of substance use or moving from denial to accepting that substance use is a problem as success; still others might see moving from refusing treatment to accepting treatment services as a treatment success. Of course, these are philosophical questions, but they need to be answered before treatment outcomes can be measured. Obviously, the higher the standards, the lower the success rates will be, which is an important factor for individual therapists and agencies to consider when establishing performance standards.

## PREDICTING TREATMENT OUTCOME

As discussed earlier in this chapter, treatment for substance use and mental disorders has been found to be overwhelmingly more effective than no treatment. Various factors contribute to positive treatment outcomes. Research finds seven variables linked to positive treatment outcomes for substance abuse treatment: longer treatment stays, being older, being employed, being married, family involvement in treatment, participation in self-help groups, and, for narcotic addicts, having the proper methadone dosage (Ball and Ross, 1991; Hartel et al., 1995; Hoffman, Harrison, and Belille, 1983; Hubbard et al., 1989; Mammo and Weinbaum, 1993; McCrady et al., 1986; O'Farrel, 1989; Ornstein and Cherepon, 1985; Simpson and Sells, 1982;Vallant, 1983; Westermeyer, 1989). Similar factors have been found to contribute to positive treatment outcomes for individuals with co-occurring mental disorders (Bond et al., 1991; Hendrickson, Stith, and Schmal, 1995; Maisto et al., 1999). Factors that are associated with positive mental health outcomes vary from disorder to disorder. However, medication compliance is a critical factor for many disorders.

Of these variables, the key predicting variable for individuals with a substance use disorder appears to be *retention in treatment,* both for individuals with and without co-occurring mental disorders. In general, the longer an individual stays in treatment the better he does. Several large substance abuse treatment outcome studies (Hubbard et al., 1989; Hubbard et al., 1997; Simpson and Sells, 1982), find that ninety-day retention in treatment is the critical threshold that predicts long-term substance abuse changes—both for outpatient treatment and residential treatment. The critical threshold for methadone maintenance was one-year retention. A study by Hendrickson and Schmal (2000) also finds that ninety-day retention is the critical threshold for predicting positive treatment outcome for individuals with co-occurring serious mental illness and substance use disorders. These studies also find that as retention extends beyond ninety days, success rates continue to increase. Fortunately, individual therapists and treatment programs can easily measure treatment retention or completion rates with few if any changes in the current way they keep information about their clients. The next sections review national averages and make recommendations concerning the performance standards that individuals or agencies can use to measure their treatment effectiveness.

## *RETENTION RATES*

The major national substance abuse studies (Hubbard et al., 1989; Hubbard et al., 1997; Simpson and Sells, 1982) find that 36 to 57 percent of individuals in outpatient treatment stay in treatment ninety days or more; 42 to 53 percent of individuals in long-term residential treatment stay in treatment ninety days or more; and 34 to 50 percent of individuals stay in methadone maintenance for one year or more.

Client retention rates in treatment programs for individuals with co-occurring disorders were similar. The range for ninety-day retention in outpatient treatment was 34 to 47 percent (Bennett, Bellack, and Gearon, 2001; Case, 1991; Drake, McHugo, and Noordsy, 1993; Hanson, Kramer, and Gross, 1990; Hendrickson and Schmal, 2000; Kofoed et al., 1986); the retention in residential treatment, though only reported at six months, ranged from 34 to 37 percent (Bartels and Drake, 1996; Mierlak et al., 1998). Thus we can speculate that ninety-day rates would be similar because most residential treatment drop outs occur within the first thirty days. Information concerning retention on methadone maintenance by individuals with co-occurring disorders has not been reported.

## *READMISSION RATES*

Although readmission rates are often viewed as a negative treatment outcome, several substance abuse studies (Hubbard et al., 1989; Simpson and Sells, 1982) find that accumulative treatment time can be as effective as a single treatment episode. Thus readmission can ultimately contribute to a positive treatment outcome. So what might individual therapists and treatment programs expect concerning the readmission rates of their clients?

All but the initial national substance abuse studies found that 54 to 59 percent of clients entering substance abuse treatment had been in some form of substance abuse treatment prior to that admission. Because the Drug Abuse Reporting Program (DARP) study covered the period (1969-1973) when treatment programs for substance abuse were just developing and when most users of drugs other than alcohol had recently begun their use, it can be assumed that its lower readmission figure (40 percent) was more the result of the lack of long-term drug use and the scarcity of treatment resources. Treatment Episode Data (TED) (Substance Abuse and Mental Health Services Administration, 1998b), which maintains information on substance abuse treatment programs receiving federal funding, reports that the more intensive the treatment service, the more likely that it is not the client's first admission. Thirty percent of clients admitted to outpatient programs had prior substance abuse treatment services, while 50 percent of clients admitted to residential programs and 70 percent of individuals admitted to methadone programs had prior treatment admissions.

Readmission rates for individuals with co-occurring disorders are not well studied. A study by Hendrickson and Schmal (2000), which looked at readmission rates of this population to outpatient treatment groups over an eighteen-year period, reports that the average length of time between the first and second group treatment admission was approximately thirty-two months and 95 percent of the second admissions occurred within 7.5 years. Using that 7.5-year time frame as a benchmark, they estimate the readmission rate to these groups to be 41 percent. This of course did not include admissions to other treatment programs. Thus the true readmission rate for this population is higher and possibly similar to the readmission rates for general substance abuse treatment programs. Client change, retention, and readmission studies offer important benchmarks that can help treatment professionals and programs determine if they are performing as well as other professionals and programs across the nation.


## REASONABLE PERFORMANCE STANDARDS

Performance standards allow therapists or treatment programs to compare what they desire to achieve with their actual performance. Performance standards should always be based on research concerning national averages, the nature of the treatment population, and the resources available to the agency or therapist. Programs that have lower client/staff ratios, a fully funded continuum of care, and a client population that is generally willing to be compliant with treatment would be expected to set higher performance standards than the national average, while programs with limited resources and a very resistant and noncompliant treatment population might establish lower performance standards than the national average. The three most important performance standards that all therapists and programs working with multifarious caseloads can easily measure are the rates of retention, readmission, and client change during treatment.

## *CONCLUSION*

Therapists and treatment agencies need to know that they are effective. To do so, they must be able to document their effectiveness. However, few agencies or therapists have the resources to conduct complex research studies concerning their treatment effectiveness. To help overcome this dilemma this chapter provided three models for measuring client change during treatment that require little time or resources. It also presented national averages concerning the important outcome factors of retention and readmission that can help therapists and programs develop reasonable performance standards. Armed with this information, therapists and agencies can implement methods to measure their success and thus not only be accountable, but also gain confidence in their ability to promote change.

# References

Alcoholics Anonymous (2001). *The Story of How Many Thousands of Men and Women Have Recovered from Alcoholism.* New York: Alcoholics Anonymous World Services, Inc.

Allott, P. and Loganathan, L. (2002). "Discovering Hope for Recovery from a British Perspective, A Review of a Sample of Recovery Literature, Implications for Practice and Systems Change." Retrieved May 2002 from <http://critpsynet. freeuk.com/LITERATUREREVIEWFinal.htm>.

American Psychiatric Association (1980). *Diagnostic and Statistical Manual of Mental Disorders,* Third Edition. Washington, DC: Author.

American Psychiatric Association (1987). *Diagnostic and Statistical Manual of Mental Disorders,* Third Edition Revised. Washington, DC: Author.

American Psychiatric Association (2000). *Diagnostic and Statistical Manual of Mental Disorders,* Fourth Edition, Text Revision. Washington, DC: Author.

American Society of Addiction Medicine (2001). *Patient Placement Criteria for the Treatment of Substance-Related Disorders,* Second Edition Revised. Chevy Chase, MD: American Society of Addiction Medicine.

Ananth, J. (1989). Missed diagnosis of substance abuse in psychiatric patients. *Hospital and Community Psychiatry,* 40 (3), 297-299.

Appleby, L., Dyson, J.D.V., Altman, E., and Luchins, D.J. (1997). Assessing substance use in multiproblem patients: Reliability and validity of the addiction severity index in a mental hospital population. *The Journal of Nervous and Mental Disease,* 185 (3), 159-165.

Atkinson, R.M., Tolson, R.L., and Turner, J.A. (1993). Factors affecting outpatient treatment compliance of older male problem drinkers. *Journal of Studies on Alcohol,* 54, 102-106.

Balancio, E. F. (1994). Clinical Case Management. In Robert W. Surber (Ed.), *Clinical Case Management, A Guide to Comprehensive Treatment of Serious Mental Illness* (pp. 3-20). Thousand Oaks, CA: Sage Publications, Inc.

Ball, J.C. and Ross, A. (Eds.) (1991). *The Effectiveness of Methadone Maintenance Treatment: Patients, Programs, Services and Outcome.* New York: Springer-Verlag.

Bartels, S.J. and Drake, R.L. (1996). Residential treatment for dual diagnosis. *Journal of Nervous and Mental Disease,* 184, 379-381.

Bean-Bayog, M. (1988). Alcoholism as a cause of psychopathology. *Hospital and Community Psychiatry,* 39 (4), 352-354.

Beck, A. T. and Freeman, A. (1990). *Cognitive Therapy of Personality Disorders.* New York: The Guilford Press.

Beck, A. T., Wright, F. D., Newman, C. F., and Liese, B. S. (1993). *Cognitive Therapy of Substance Abuse.* New York: The Guilford Press.

Bellack, A.S. and Mueser, K.T. (1993). Psychosocial treatment for schizophrenia. *Schizophrenia Bulletin,* 19 (2), 317-336.

Benjamin, L. S. (1993). *Interpersonal Diagnosis and Treatment of Personality Disorders.* New York: The Guilford Press.

Bennett, M.E., Bellack, A.S., Gearon, J.S. (2001). Treating substance abuse in schizophrenia: An initial report. *Journal of Substance Abuse Treatment,* 20, 163-175.

Bernard, J.M. and Goodyear, R.K. (1992). *Fundamentals of Clinical Supervision.* Boston, MA: Allyn & Bacon.

Black, D. W. and Larson, C.L. (1999). *Bad Boys, Bad Men, Confronting Antisocial Personality Disorder.* New York: Oxford University Press.

Blackwell, J., Beresford, J., and Lambert, S. (1988). Patterns of alcohol use and psychiatric inpatient admissions. *Journal of Substance Abuse Treatment,* 5, 27-31.

Blume, A.W., Davis, J.V., and Schmaling J.B. (1999). Neurocognitive dysfunction in dually-diagnosed patients: A potential roadblock to motivation behavior change. *Journal of Psychoactive Drugs,* 31 (2), 111-115.

Blumenthal, S.J. (1988). A guide to risk factors, assessment, and treatment of suicidal patients. *Medical Clinics of North America,* 72 (4), 937-971.

Bond, G.R., McDonel, E.C., Miller, L.D., and Pensec, M. (1991). Assertive community treatment and reference groups: An evaluation of their effectiveness for young adults with serious mental illness and substance abuse problems. *Psychosocial Rehabilitation Journal,* 15 (2), 31-43.

Borders, L. and Leddick, G. (1987). *Handbook of Clinical Supervision.* Alexandria, VA: American Association of Counseling and Development.

Brown, N.W. (1998). *Psychoeducational Groups.* Philadelphia: Accelerated Development.

Bulik, C.M. (1987). Drug and alcohol abuse by bulimic women and their families. *American Journal of Psychiatry,* 144 (12), 1604-1606.

Burns, D.D. (1999). *The Feeling Good Handbook,* Revised Edition. New York: Plume.

Carroll, K.M. and Rounsaville, B.J. (1993). History and significance of childhood attention deficit disorder in treatment-seeking cocaine abusers. *Comprehensive Psychiatry,* 34, 75-82.

Case, N. (1991). The dual-diagnosis patient in a psychiatric day treatment program: A treatment failure. *Journal of Substance Abuse Treatment,* 8, 69-73.

Castellani, B., Wootton, E., Rugle, L., Wedgeworth, R., Prabucki, K., and Olson, R. (1996). Homelessness, negative affect, and coping among veterans with gambling problems who misused substances. *Psychiatric Services,* 47 (3), 298-299.

Caton, C.L.M., Gralnick, A., Bender, S., and Simon, R. (1989). Young chronic patients and substance abuse. *Hospital and Community Psychiatry,* 40 (10), 1037-1040.

Center for Mental Health Services (1998). *Managed Care Initiative Panel on Co-occurring Disorders: Co-Occurring Psychiatric and Substance Disorders in Managed Care Systems: Standards of Care, Practice Guidelines, Workforce Competencies, and Training Curricula.* Rockville, MD: SAMHSA.

Center for Substance Abuse Treatment (1994a). *Assessment and Treatment of Patients with Coexisting Mental Illness and Alcohol and Other Drug Abuse: Treatment Improvement Protocol (TIP) Series # 9.* Washington, DC: DHHS Publication No. (SMA) 94-2078.

Clark, R.E. and Drake, R.E. (1994). Expenditures of time and money by families of people with severe mental illness and substance use disorders. *Community Mental Health Journal,* 30 (2), 145-163.

Cleary, J. and Paone, D. (2000). "Case Management: Methods and Issues," Technical Assistance Paper of The Robert Wood Johnson Foundation, Medicare/Medicaid Integration Program, University of Maryland Center on Aging, National Chronic Care Consortium. Retrieved March 2002 from <http://www.nccconline.org/pdf/Case Management.pdf>.

Cloninger, C.R. (1987). Neurogenic adaptive mechanisms in alcoholism. *Science,* 236, 410-416.

Commission for Case Manager Certification (CCMC, 2000). "Code of Professional Conduct for Case Managers with Disciplinary Rules, Procedures, and Penalties." Rolling Meadows, Illinois. Retrieved April 2000 from <http://www.ccmcertification.org>.

Copeland, M. E. (2000). *Wellness Recovery Action Plan.* West Dummerston, VT: Peach Press.

Crewe, C.W. (1974). *A Look at Relapse.* Center City, MN: Hazelden.

Daley D.C. (1987). Relapse prevention with substance abusers: Clinical issues and myths. *Social Work,* 45 (2), 8-42.

Daley, D.C. and Lis, J.A. (1995). Relapse prevention: Intervention strategies for mental health clients with comorbid disorders. In A.M. Wasshto (Ed.), *Psychotherapy and Substance Abuse: A Practitioner's Handbook* (pp. 243-263). New York: The Guilford Press.

Daley, D.C. and Thase, M.E. (1994). *Dual Disorders Recovery Counseling: A Biopsychosocial Treatment Model for Addiction and Psychiatric Illness.* Missouri: Herald House/Independence Press.

Daley, D.C. and Zuckoff, A. (1999). *Improving Treatment Compliance: Counseling and System Strategies for Substance Abuse and Dual Disorders.* Center City, MN: Hazelden.

Damron, S. and Simpson, W. (1985). Substance Abuse and Schizophrenia: A Health Maintenance Perspective. Presentation at the 93rd Annual Meeting of the American Psychological Association, September.

Drake, R.E., McHugo, G.J., and Noordsy, D.L. (1993). Treatment of alcoholism among schizophrenic outpatients: 4-year outcomes. *American Journal of Psychiatry,* 150 (2), 328-329.

Drake, R.E., Osher, F.C., Noordsy, D.L., Hurbut, S.C., Teague, G.B., and Beaudett, M.S. (1990). Diagnosis of alcohol use disorders in schizophrenia. *Schizophrenic Bulletin,* 16, 57-67.

Drake, R.E., Osher, F., and Wallach, M. (1991). Homelessness and dual diagnosis. *American Psychologist,* 46, 1149-1158.

Drake, R.E. and Wallach, M.A. (1989). Substance abuse among the chronic mentally ill. *Hospital and Community Psychiatry,* 40 (10), 1041-1045.

Drake, R.E. and Wallach, M.A. (1993). Moderate drinking among people with severe mental illness. *Hospital and Community Psychiatry,* 44 (8), 780-782.

Drake, R.W., McHugo, G.J., Clark, R.E., Teague, G.B., Xie, H., Miles, K., and Ackerson, T.H. (1998). Assertive community treatment for patients with co-occurring severe mental illness and substance use disorder. *American Journal of Orthopsychiatry,* 68 (2), 201-215.

Dunn, G.E., Ryan, J.J., Paolo, A.M., and Van Fleet, J.N. (1995). Comorbidity of dissociative disorders among patients with substance use disorders. *Psychiatric Services,* 46 (2), 153-156.

Durell, J., Lechtenberg, B., Corse, S., and Frances, R.J. (1993). Intensive case management of persons with chronic mental illness who abuse substances. *Hospital and Community Psychiatry,* 44, 415-416.

Eland-Goossensen, A., Van De Goor, I., Garretsen, H., and Schudel, J. (1997). Screening for psychopathology in the clinical practice. *Journal of Substance Abuse Treatment,* 14 (6), 585-591.

Ellis, A. (1988). *Rational Emotive Therapy with Alcoholics and Substance Abusers.* New York: Pergamon.

Erinoff, L. (1993). *National Institute on Drug Abuse Research Monograph Series: Assessing Neurotoxicity of Drug of Abuse, # 136.* Washington, DC: NIH Publication No. 93-3644.

Fischer, P.J. (1991). *Alcohol, Drug Abuse, and Mental Health Problems Among Homeless Persons: A Review of the Literature.* Rockville, MD: National Institute of Mental Health.

Frances, A., First, M.B., and Pincus, H.A. (1995). *DSM-IV Guidebook.* Washington, DC: American Psychiatric Press, Inc.

Gazda, G.M., Ginter, E.J., and Horne, A.M. (2001). *Group Counseling and Group Psychotherapy: Theory and Application.* Boston: Allyn & Bacon.

Gerstein, D.R., Johnson, R.A., Harwood, H.J., Suter, N., and Malloy, K. (1994). *Evaluating Recovery Services: The California Drug and Alcohol Treatment Assessment (CALDATA).* Sacramento: California Department of Alcohol and Drug Programs.

Gerstley, L.J., Alterman, A.I., McLellan, A.T., and Woody, G.E. (1990). Antisocial personality disorder in patients with substance abuse disorders: A problematic diagnosis? *American Journal of Psychiatry,* 147 (2), 173-178.

Gladding, S. (1995). *Group Work: A Counseling Specialty,* Second Edition. Englewood Cliffs, NJ: Prentice-Hall.

Goodwin, D. W. (2000). *Alcoholism, The Facts,* Third Edition. Oxford, England: Oxford University Press.

Gorski, T. T. (1989). *Passages Through Recovery, An Action Plan for Prevention Relapse.* Center City, MN: Hazelden.

Gorski, T.T. (2000). The CENAPS model of relapse prevention therapy (CMPT). In J.J. Boren, L.S. Onken, and K.M. Carroll (Eds.), *Approaches to Drug Abuse Counseling* (pp. 23-38). NIH Publication no. 00-4151. Bethesda, MD: National Institute on Drug Abuse.

Gorski, T.T. and Kelley, J.M. (1996). *Counselor's Manual for Relapse Prevention with Chemically Dependent Criminal Offenders, TAP 19.* DHHS Publication No. (SMA) 99-3340. Rockville, MD: Substance Abuse and Mental Health Services Administration.

Gossop, M., Marsden, J., Stewart, D., Edwards, C., Lehmann, P., Wilson, A., and Segar, G. (1997). The national treatment outcome research study in the United Kingdom: Six-month follow-up outcomes. *Psychology of Addictive Behaviors,* 11 (4), 324-337.

Gunderson, J. G. and Gabbard, G. O. (Eds.) (2000). *Psychotherapy for Personality Disorders.* Washington, DC: American Psychiatric Press, Inc.

Gunderson, J. G. and Links, P. (1996). Borderline personality disorder. In G.O. Gabbard and S.D. Atkinson (Eds.) *Synopsis of Treatments of Psychiatric Disorders, Second Edition* (pp. 967-978). Washington, DC: American Psychiatric Press, Inc.

Hanson, M., Kramer, T.H., and Gross, W. (1990). Outpatient treatment of adults with coexisting substance use and mental disorders. *Journal of Substance Abuse Treatment,* 7, 109-116.

Harding, C., Brooks, G.W., Asolaga, T.S.J.S., and Breier, A. (1987). The Vermont Longitudinal Study of Persons with Severe Mental Illness. *American Journal of Psychiatry,* 144, 718-726.

Harding, C. and Zahniser, J. (1995). "Reasons for Optimism on Schizophrenia." *Acta Psychiatrica Scandinavice,* 90 (Supple. 384), 140-146. Retrieved from the Schizophrenia Home page May 14, 2002 at <http://www.schizophrenia.com/news/optim.html>.

Hartel, D.M., Schoenbaum, E.E., Selwyn, P.A., Kline, J., Davenny, K., Klein, R.S., and Friedland, G.H. (1995). Heroin use during methadone maintenance treatment: The importance of methadone dose and cocaine use. *American Journal of Public Health,* 85, 83-88.

Hasin, D.S., Tsai, W.Y., Endicott, J., Mueller, T.I., Coryell, W., and Keller, M. (1993). The effects of major depression on alcoholism: Five year course. *American Journal of Addictions,* 75-81.

Hatfield, A.B. and Lefley, H.P. (1993). *Surviving Mental Illness: Stress, Coping and Adaptation.* New York: The Guilford Press.

Hellerstein, D.J., Rosenthal, R.N., and Miner, C.R. (1995). A prospective study of integrated outpatient treatment for substance-abusing schizophrenic patients. *The American Journal of Addictions,* 4, (1), 33-42.

Hendrickson, E.L. (1988). Treating the dually diagnosed (mental disorder/substance abuse) client. *TIE-Lines*, 5, 1-4.

Hendrickson, E.L. (1989). Taking a look at psychoeducation and: A group for dual-disorder clients. *TIE-Lines*, 6, 3-5.

Hendrickson, E. and Schmal, M. (2000). Dual Diagnosis Treatment: An 18-Year Perspective. Paper presented at MISA Conference sponsored by MCP-Hahnemann University, Philadelphia, PA, October.

Hendrickson, E.L, Schmal, M.S., Albert, N., and Massaro, J. (1994). Dual disorder treatment: Perspectives on the state of the art. *TIE-Lines*, 11, 1-15.

Hendrickson, E.L., Schmal, M.S., Ekleberry, S., and Bullock, J. (1999). Supervising staff treating the dually diagnosed. *The Counselor*, March/April, 18-22.

Hendrickson, E. L., Stith, S.M, and Schmal, M.S. (1995). Predicting treatment outcome for seriously mentally ill substance abusers in an outpatient dual diagnosis group. *Continuum: Developments in Ambulatory Mental Health Care*, 2 (4), 271-289.

Herman, M., Galanter, M., and Lifshultz, H. (1991). Combined substance abuse and psychiatric disorders in homeless and domiciled patients. *American Journal of Drug and Alcohol Abuse*, 17, 415-422.

Herz, M.I. and Lamberti, J.S. (1995). Prodromal symptoms and relapse prevention in schizophrenia. *Schizophrenia Bulletin*, 21, 541-551.

Herzog, D.B., Nussbaum, K.M., and Marmor, A.K. (1996). Comorbidity and outcome in eating disorders. *The Psychiatric Clinics of North America*, 19 (4), 843-859.

Hesselbrock, M., Meyer, R., and Keener, J. (1985). Psychopathology in hospitalized alcoholics. *Archives of General Psychiatry*, 42, 1050-1055.

Hien, D., Zimberg, S., Weisman, S., First, M., and Ackerman, S. (1997). Dual diagnosis subtypes in urban substance abuse and mental health clinics. *Psychiatric Services*, 48 (8), 1058-1063.

Hoffman, N.G., Harrison, P.A., and Belille, C.A. (1983). Alcoholic anonymous after treatment: Attendance and abstinence. *International Journal of Addictions*, 18, 311-318.

Hoffman, N.G. and Miller, N.S. (1992). Treatment outcomes for abstinence-based programs. *Psychiatric Annals*, 22 (8), 402-408.

Holderness, C.C., Brooks-Gunn, J., and Warren, M.P. (1994). Co-morbidity of eating disorders and substance abuse: Review of the literature. *International Journal of Eating Disorders*, 16, 1-34.

Hoskins, R. (1989). *Rational Madness, the Paradox of Addiction*. Blue Ridge Summit, PA: Tab Books, Inc.

Hubbard, R.L., Craddock, S.G., Flynn, P.M., Anderson, J., and Etherridge, R.M. (1997). Overview of 1-year follow-up outcomes in the drug abuse treatment outcome study (DATOS). *Psychology of Addictive Behaviors*, 11 (4), 261-278.

Hubbard, R.L., Marsden, M.E., Rachal, J.V., Harwood, H.J., Cavanaugh, E.R., and Ginsburg, H.M. (1989). *Drug Abuse Treatment: A National Study of Effectiveness*. Chapel Hill: University of North Carolina Press.

Hussain, A. (2000). "A Discussion on the Role of Case Management within Community Mental Health, Community Mental Health and Social Work," Retrieved April 2002 from <http://www.crescentlife.com/psychissues/role_of_case-management.htm>.

Hutzell, R., Eggert, M. (1990). Multiple personality in an alcohol treatment population. *VA Practitioner,* 7 (1), 109-113.

Inspector General, Health and Human Services (1995). *Services to Persons with Co-occurring Mental Health and Substance Abuse Disorders: Provider Perspectives.* Washington, DC: U.S. Department of Health and Human Services.

Jonas, J.M., Gold, M.S., Sweeny, D., and Pottash, A.L.C. (1987). Eating disorder and cocaine abuse: A survey of 259 cocaine abusers. *Journal of Clinical Psychology,* 48, 2.

Kahn, A. J. (1998). "Themes for a History: The First Hundred Years of the Columbia University School of Social Work," Paper prepared for presentation at Plenary Session I, Centennial Celebration, June 12, 1998. Retrieved April 2002 from <http://www.columbia.edu/cu/ssw/welcome/ajkahn/>.

Kantor, M. (1992). *Diagnosis and Treatment of the Personality Disorders.* St. Louis, Tokyo: Ishiyaku EuroAmerica, Inc.

Kessler, R.C., Nelson, C.B., McGonagle, K.A., Edlund, M.J., Frank, R. G., and Leaf, P.J. (1994). The epidemiology of co-occurring addictive and mental disorders: Implications for prevention and service utilization. *American Journal of Orthopsychiatry,* 66 (1), 17-31.

Khantzian, E. (1985). The self-medication hypothesis of addictive disorders: Focus on heroin and cocaine dependence. *American Journal of Psychiatry,* 142 (11), 1259-1264.

Khantzian, E. and Treece, C. (1985). DSM III psychiatric diagnosis of narcotic addicts. *Archives of General Psychiatry,* 42, 1067-1071.

Kofoed, L., Kania, J., Walsh, T., and Atkinson, R.M. (1986). Outpatient treatment of patients with substance abuse and coexisting psychiatric disorders. *American Journal of Psychiatry,* 143, 867-872.

Lambert, M.T., Griffith, J.M., and Hendrickse, W. (1996). Characteristics of patients with substance abuse diagnoses on a general psychiatry unit in a VA medical center. *Psychiatric Services,* 47 (10), 1104-1107.

Leff, J and Vaughn, C. (1985). *Expressed Emotion in Families.* New York: The Guilford Press.

Lehman, A.F. (1996). Heterogeneity of person and place: Assessing co-occurring addictive and mental disorders. *American Journal of Orthopsychiatry,* 66, 32-41.

Lehman, A.F., Myers, C.P., Dixson, L.B., and Johnson, J.L. (1996). Detection of substance use disorders among psychiatric inpatients. *The Journal of Nervous and Mental Disease,* 184 (4), 228-233.

Liberman, R.P., Cardin, V., McGill, W., Falloon, I.R.H., and Evans, C.D. (1987). Behavior family management of schizophrenia: Clinical outcome and costs. *Psychiatric Annals,* 17 (9), 610-619.

Liberman, R.P., Jacobs, H. E., Boone, S. W., Foy, D.W., and Mueser, K.T. (1986). Skills Training for the Community Adaptation of Schizophrenics. In B.W. Brenner (Ed.), *Treatment of Schizophrenia* (pp. 230-248). Toronto: Hans Huber.

Linehan, M.M. (1993a). *Cognitive-Behavioral Treatment of Borderline Personality Disorder.* New York: The Guilford Press.

Linehan, M.M. (1993b). *Skills Training Manual for Treating Borderline Personality Disorder.* New York: The Guilford Press.

Ling, C. (2002). "Why and What You Should Know About Case Management," University of Phoenix, Center for Professional Education: San Jose, CA. Retrieved March 2002 from <wysiwyg://84/http://www.nurseweek.com/ce/ce2506a.html>.

Machell, D.F. (1987). Obligations of a clinical supervisor. *Alcoholism Treatment Quarterly,* 8 (1), 69-86.

MacMillan, J., Gold, A., Crow, T., Johnson, A., and Johnstone, E. (1986). Expressed emotion and relapse. *British Journal of Psychiatry,* 148, 133-143.

Maisto, S.A., Carey, K.B., Carey, M.P., Purnine, D.M., and Barnes, K.L. (1999). Methods of changing patterns of substance use among individuals with co-occurring schizophrenia and substance use disorder. *Journal of Substance Abuse Treatment,* 17 (3), 221-227.

Majewska, M.D. (Ed.) (1996). *National Institute on Drug Abuse Research Monograph Series: Neurotoxicity and Neuropathology Associated with Cocaine Abuse, # 163.* Washington, DC: NIH Publication No. 96-4019.

Mammo, A. and Weinbaum, D.F. (1993). Some factors that influence dropping out from outpatient alcoholism treatment facilities. *Journal of Studies of Alcohol,* 45, 359-362.

Marlatt, G.A. and Gordon, J.R. (Eds.) (1985). *Relapse Prevention: Maintenance Strategies in the Treatment of Addictive Behaviors.* New York: The Guilford Press.

Matano, R.A. and Locke, K.D. (1995). Personality disorder scales as predictors of interpersonal problems of alcoholics, *Journal of Personality Disorders,* 9(1), 62-67.

Mayfield, D., McCleod, G., and Hall, P. (1974). The CAGE Questionnaire: Validation of a new alcoholism screening instrument. *American Journal of Psychiatry,* 131, 1121-1123.

McCann, J.T. (1995). The MCM-III and treatment of the self. In P.D. Retzlaff (Ed.), *Tactical Psychotherapy of the Personality Disorders: An MCMI-III–Based Approach* (pp. 137-137). Boston: Allyn & Bacon.

McCrady, B.S., Noel, N.E., Abrams, D.B., Stout, R.L., Nelson, H.F., and Hay, W.M. (1986). Comparative effectiveness of three types of spouse involvement in outpatient behavioral alcoholism treatment. *Journal of Studies on Alcohol*, 47, 459-467.

McDaniel, S., Weber, T., and McKeever, J. (1983). Multiple theoretical approaches to supervision: Choices in family therapy training. *Family Process*, 22, 491-500.

McGovern, M.P. and Morrison, D.H. (1992). The chemical use, abuse, and dependence scale (CUAD): Rationale, reliability, and validity. *Journal of Substance Abuse Treatment*, 9, 27-38.

McGovern, T.F. (1994). Therapy with the dually diagnosed person. In N.S. Miller (Ed.), *Treating Coexisting Psychiatric and Addictive Disorders* (pp. 161-176). Center City, MN: Hazelden.

McLellan, A.T., Luborsky, L., Woody, G.E, and O'Brien, C.P. (1980). An improved diagnostic evaluation instrument for substance abuse patients: The Addiction Severity Index. *Journal of Mental and Nervous Disease*, 168, 26-33.

McLellan, A.T., Luborsky, L., Woody, G.E, O'Brien, C.P., and Druley, K.A. (1983). Predicting response to alcohol and drug abuse treatment. *Archives of General Psychiatry*, 40, 620-625.

McWilliams, N. (1994). *Psychoanalytic Diagnosis, Understanding Personality Structure in the Clinical Process*. New York: The Guilford Press.

Mead, S. and Copeland, M. E. (2000). "What Recovery Means to Us." Retrieved February 10, 2002 from <http://www.mentalhealthrecovery.com/read13.html>.

Mee-Lee, D. (1994). Managed care and dual diagnosis. In N.S. Miller (Ed.), *Treating Coexisting Psychiatric and Addictive Disorders* (pp. 257-269). Center City, MN: Hazelden.

Meisler, N., Blankertz, L., Santos, A.B., and McKay, C. (1997). Impact of assertive community treatment on homeless persons with co-occurring severe psychiatric and substance use disorders. *Community Mental Health Journal*, 33 (2), 113-122.

Meissner, W. W. (1994). *Psychotherapy and the Paranoid Process*. Northvale, NJ: Jason Aronson Inc.

Meloy, J. (1996). Antisocial personality disorder. In G.O. Gabbard and S.D. Atkinson (Eds.), *Synopsis of Treatments of Psychiatric Disorders*, Second Edition (pp. 959-968). Washington, DC: American Psychiatric Press, Inc.

Mercer, D.E. and Woody, G.E. (1999). *An Individual Drug Counseling Approach to Treat Cocaine Addiction: The Collaborative Cocaine Treatment Study Model*. National Institute on Drug Abuse Therapy Manuals for Drug Addiction, Manual 3, NIH Publication 99-4380. Rockville, MD: National Institute on Drug Abuse.

Metropolitan Washington Council of Governments (1995). *The Treatment of Dual Diagnosis: A Policy Report for the Washington Metropolitan Region*. Washington, DC: Author.

Mierlak, D., Galanter, M., Spivack, N., Dermatis, H., Jurewica, E., and De Leon, G. (1998). Modified therapeutic community treatment for homeless dually diagnosed men. *Journal of Substance Abuse Treatment*, 15 (2), 117-121.

Millon, T. (1981). *Disorders of Personality, DSM III: Axis II.* New York: John Wiley and Sons, Inc.

Millon, T. (1996). *Personality and Psychopathology: Building a Clinical Science. Selected Papers of Theodore Millon.* New York: John Wiley and Sons, Inc.

Millon, T. and Davis, R. (1996). An evolutionary theory of personality disorders. In J.F. Clarkin and M.F. Lenzenweger (Eds.), *Major Theories of Personality Disorder* (pp. 221-346). New York: The Guilford Press.

Minkoff, K. (1989). An integrated treatment model for dual diagnosis of psychosis and addiction. *Hospital and Community Psychiatry,* 40, 1031-1036.

Minkoff, K. (1991). Program components of a comprehensive integrated care system for seriously mentally ill patients with substance disorders. In K. Minkoff and R.E. Drake (Eds.), *New Directions for Mental Health Services, No. 50: Dual Diagnosis of Major Mental Illness and Substance Disorder* (pp. 13-27). San Francisco: Jossey-Bass.

Minkoff, K. (2001). Developing standards of care for individuals with co-occurring psychiatric and substance use disorders. *Psychiatric Services,* 52 (5), 597-599.

Missouri Department of Mental Health (1999). "Implementing Missouri's Show Me System Redesign." A Public Discussion Paper, Missouri Department of Mental Health. Retrieved May 2000 from <http://www.modmh.state.mo.us/publications/pdp/discussion.htm#DMH'sPhilosophyofRecovery>.

Montague, D.L. (Ed.) (2000). "Comprehensive Case Management." *Addiction Messenger,* Volume 3, ATTC Northwest Frontier, Salem, Oregon. Retrieved April 2002 from <http://www.open.org/nfatc/nfatc@open.org>.

Morse, G. (1998). "A Review of Case Management for People Who are Homeless: Implications for Practice, Policy, and Research." Retrieved March 16, 2002 from <http://aspe.hhs.gov/progsys/homeless/symposium/7-Casemgmt.htm>.

Mueser, K.T., Drake, R.E., Clark, R.E., McHugo, G.J., Mercer-McFadden, C., and Ackerson, T.H. (1995). *Toolkit for Evaluating Substance Abuse in Persons with Severe Mental Illness.* Concord, NH: New Hampshire-Dartmouth Psychiatric Research Center.

Nace, E.P. (1989). Substance use disorders and personality disorders: Comorbidity. *The Psychiatric Hospital,* 20 (2), 65-69.

Nace, E.P. (1990). Substance abuse and personality disorder. In D.F. O'Connell (Ed.), *Managing the Dually Diagnosed Patient, Current Issues and Clinical Approaches* (pp. 183-198). Binghamton, NY: The Haworth Press.

National Association of Social Workers (1992). "NASW Standards for Social Work Case Management, Washington, D.C." Retrieved March 2002 from <http://www.naswdc.org/pubs/standards/casemgmt.htm>.

National Association of State Alcohol and Drug Abuse Directors (2002). *Alcohol and Other Drug Treatment Effectiveness: A Review of State Outcome Studies.* Washington, DC: Author.

Noordsy, D.L. and Fox, L. (1991). Group intervention techniques for people with dual disorder. *Journal of Psychosocial Rehabilitation,* 51, 67-78.

O'Farrell, T.J. (1989). Marital and family therapy in alcoholism treatment. *Journal of Substance Abuse Treatment,* 6, 23-29.

O'Farrell, T.J., Cutter, H.S.G., Choquette, K.A., Floyd, F.J., and Bayog, R.D. (1992). Behavioral marital therapy for male alcoholics: Marital and drinking adjustment during the two years after treatment. *Behavior Therapy,* 23 (4), 529-549.

O'Hagan, M. (2000). "Realizing Recovery Through the Education of Mental Health Workers, Recovery-based Competencies and Resources for New Zealand." Retrieved May 2002 from <http://www.mhc.govt.nz/Publications/Publications/Recovery_Competencies.pdf>.

Ohio Office of Consumer Services Recovery Process (2001). "Model and Emerging Best Practices Overview." Retrieved August 2001 from <http://www.mh.state.oh.us/initiatives/outcomes/resrecovover.html> and <http://www.mh.state.oh.us/initiatives/outcomes/rerecovprinc.html>.

Olevitch, B.A. and Ellis, A. (1999). *Using Cognitive Approaches with the Seriously Mentally Ill.* Westport, CT: Praeger Publishers.

O'Malley, S.S., Kosten, T.R., and Renner, J.A. Jr. (1990). Dual diagnoses: Substance abuse and personality disorder. In D.A. Adler (Ed.), *Treating Personality Disorders* (pp. 135-153). San Francisco: Jossey-Bass.

Onken, L.S., Blaine, J., Genser, S., and Horton, A.M. (Eds.) (1997). *Treatment of Drug-Dependent Individuals with Comorbid Mental Disorders.* NIDA Research Monograph 172, NIH Publication No. 97-4172. Rockville, MD: National Institute on Drug Abuse.

Ornstein, P. and Cherepon, J.A. (1985). Demographic variables as predictors of alcoholism treatment outcome. *Journal of Studies on Alcohol,* 46, 425-432.

Ortman, D. (2001). *The Dual Diagnosis Recovery Sourcebook.* Chicago: Contemporary Books.

Osher, F.C. and Kofoed, L.L. (1989). Treatment of patients with psychiatric and psychoactive substance abuse disorders. *Hospital and Community Psychiatry,* 40, 1025-1030.

Parsons, L.A., Butters, N., and Nathan, P.E. (1987). *Neuropsychology of Alcoholism: Implications for Diagnosis and Treatment.* New York: The Guilford Press.

Peele, S. (1985). *The Meaning of Addiction, Compulsive Experience and Its Interpretation.* Lexington, MA: Lexington Books, D.C. Heath and Company.

Pepper, B. (1995). A community-client protection system (CCPS) for the 21st century. *TIE-Lines,* 13, 7-9.

Pepper, B., Kirshner, M.C., and Ryglewicz, H. (1981). The young adult chronic patient: Overview of population. *Hospital and Community Psychiatry,* 32, 463-469.

Pepper, B. and Massaro, J. (1992). Trans-institutionalization: Substance abuse and mental illness in the criminal justice system. *TIE-Lines,* 9 (2), 1-4.

Pepper, B. and Ryglewicz, H. (1984). The young adult chronic patient: A new focus. In J. Talbott, (Ed.), *The Chronic Mental Patient: Five Years Later* (pp. 154-168). New York: Grune and Stratton.

Powell, B.J., Penick, E.C., Othmer, E., Bingham, S.F., and Rice, A.S. (1982). Prevalence of additional psychiatric syndromes among male alcoholics. *Journal of Clinical Psychiatry,* 43 (10), 404-407.

Powell, D.J. (1993). *Clinical Supervision in Alcohol and Drug Abuse Counseling.* New York: Lexington Books.

Prochaska, J.O., DiClemente, C.C., and Norcross, J.C. (1992). In search of how people change: Applications to addictive behaviors. *American Psychologist,* 47, 1102-1114.

Ralph, R.O. (2000). "Review of Recovery Literature, A Synthesis of a Sample of Recovery Literature 2000." Prepared for the National Technical Assistance Center for State Mental Health Planning (NTAC) and the National Association for State Mental Health Program Directors (NASMHPD). Retrieved May 2002 from <http://www.nasmhpd.org/ntac/reports/ralphrecovweb.pdf>.

Regier, D.A., Farmer, M.E., Raem, D.S., Locke, B.Z., Keith, S.J., Judd, L.L., and Goodwin, F.K. (1990). Comorbidity of mental disorders with alcohol and other drug abuse. *Journal of American Medical Association,* 246 (19), 2511-2518.

Richards, H. J. (1993). *Therapy of the Substance Abuse Syndromes.* Northvale, NJ: Jason Aronson Inc.

Ridgely, M.S., Goldman, H.H., and Talbott, J.A. (1986). *Chronic Mentally Ill Young Adults with Substance Abuse Problems: A Review of Relevant Literature and Creation Of A Research Agenda.* Baltimore: University of Maryland School of Medicine.

Ridgely, M.S., Osher, F.C., and Talbott, J.A. (1987). *Chronic Mentally Ill Young Adults with Substance Abuse Problems: Treatment and Training Issues.* Baltimore: University of Maryland School of Medicine.

Ries, R.K. (1993). The dually diagnosed patient with psychotic symptoms. *Journal of Addictive Diseases,* 12 (3), 103-122.

Ries, R. K. (1994). *Assessment and Treatment of Patients with Coexisting Mental Illness and Alcohol and Other Drug Abuse, Treatment Improvement Protocol (TIP) Services, #9.* Washington, DC: Center for Substance Abuse Treatment, U.S. Department of Health and Human Services, Public Health Service.

Roberts, L.J., Shaner, A., and Eckman, T.A. (1999). *Overcoming Addictions: Skills Training for People with Schizophrenia.* New York: W. W. Norton and Co.

Rodin, G. and Izenberg, S. (1997). Treating the narcissistic personality disorder. In M. Rosenbluth and I.D. Yalom (Eds.), *Treating Difficult Personality Disorders* (pp. 107-122). San Francisco: Jossey-Bass.

Rosenberg, S.D., Drake, R.E., Wolford, G.L., Mueser, K.T., Oxman, T.E., Vidaver, R.M., Carrieri, K.L., and Luckoor, R. (1998). Dartmouth assessment of lifestyle instrument (DALI): A substance use disorder screen for people with severe mental illness. *American Journal of Psychiatry,* 155 (2), 232-238.

Ross, C.A., Kronson, J., and Koensgen, S. (1992). Dissociative comorbidity in 100 chemically dependent patients. *Hospital and Community Psychiatry,* 43, 840-842.

Ross, H., Glaser, F., and Germanson, T. (1988). The prevalence of psychiatric disorders in patients with alcohol and other drug problems. *Archives of General Psychiatry,* 45, 1023-1031.

Rounsaville, B.J., Eyre, S., Weissman, M., and Kleber, H. (1983). The antisocial opiate addict. In B. Stimmel (Ed.), *Alcoholism and Substance Abuse* (pp. 154-168). Binghamton, NY: The Haworth Press.

Rounsaville, B.J., Weissman, M.M., Kleber, H., and Wilber, C. (1982) Heterogeneity of psychiatric diagnosis in treated opiate addicts. *American Journal of Psychiatry,* 39, 161-166.

Rupcich, N., Frisch, G.R., and Govoni, R. (1997). Comorbidity of pathological gambling in addiction treatment facilities. *Journal of Substance Abuse Treatment,* 14 (6), 573-574.

Ryglewicz, H. (1991). Psychoeducation for clients and families: A way in, out, and through in working with people with dual disorders. *Psychosocial Rehabilitation Journal,* 15, 79-89.

Ryglewicz, H. and Pepper, B. (1996). *Lives at Risk: Understanding and Treating Young People with Dual Disorders.* New York: The Free Press.

Sandberg, C., Greenberg, W.M., and Birkmann, J.C. (1991). Drug-free treatment selection for chemical abusers: A diagnostic-based model. *American Journal of Orthopsychiatry,* 61 (3), 358-371.

Schuckit, M.A. (1983). Alcoholic patients with secondary depression. *American Journal of Psychiatry,* 140 (6), 711-714.

Schuckit, M.A. (1985). The clinical implications of primary diagnostic groups among alcoholics. *Archives of General Psychiatry,* 42, 1043-1049.

Sciacca, K. (1991). An integrated treatment approach for severely mentally ill individuals with substance disorders. In K. Minkoff and R.E. Drake (Eds.), *Dual Diagnosis of Major Mental Illness and Substance Disorder* (pp. 13-27). New Directions for Mental Health Services, No. 50. San Francisco: Jossey-Bass.

Selzer, M.L. (1971). The Michigan Alcoholism Screening Test: The quest for a new diagnostic instrument. *American Journal of Psychiatry,* 127, 89-94.

Siegal, H.A., Consensus Panel Chair (1998). *Comprehensive Case Management for Substance Abuse Treatment.* Treatment Improvement Protocol (TIP) Series, #27, Washington, DC: Center for Substance Abuse Treatment, Substance Abuse and Mental Health Services Administration.

Simpson, D.D. and Sells, S.B. (1982). Effectiveness of treatment for drug abuse: An overview of the DARO research program. *Advances in Alcohol and Substance Abuse,* 2, 7-29.

Sperry, L. (1995). *Handbook of Diagnosis and Treatment of the DSM-IV Personality Disorders.* New York: Brunner/Mazel.

Sperry, L. and Carlson, J. (1993) *Psychopathology and Psychotherapy, From Diagnosis to Treatment.* Muncie, IN: Accelerated Development, Inc.

Substance Abuse and Mental Health Services Administration (1994). *The National Treatment Improvement Study (NTIES).* Rockville, MD: Author.

Substance Abuse and Mental Health Services Administration (1998a). *Improving Services for Individuals at Risk of, or with, Co-Occurring Substance-Related and Mental Health Disorders.* Rockville, MD: Author.

Substance Abuse and Mental Health Services Administration (1998b). *Treatment Episode Data (TED): National Admissions to Substance Abuse Treatment Services.* Rockville, MD: Author.

Surber, R.W. (1994). An approach to care. In R.W. Surber (Ed.), *Clinical Case Management, A Guide to Comprehensive Treatment of Serious Mental Illness* (pp. 3-20). Thousand Oaks, CA: Sage Publications, Inc.

Tessler, R. and Dennis, D. (1989*). A Synthesis of NIMH-funded Research Concerning Persons Who Are Homeless and Mentally Ill.* Rockville, MD: National Institute of Mental Health.

Toland, A.M. and Moss, H.B. (1989). Identification of the alcoholic schizophrenic: Use of clinical laboratory tests and the MAST. *Journal on Studies of Alcohol,* 50, 49-53.

Turkat, I. D. (1990). *The Personality Disorders, A Psychological Approach to Clinical Management.* New York: Pergamon.

Tyrer, P., Casey, P., and Ferguson, B. (1988). *Personality Disorder and Mental Illness, Personality Disorders: Diagnosis, Management and Course.* London: Wright, Butterworth Scientific.

U.S. Public Health Service (2001). Mental Health: A Report of the Surgeon General. Washington, DC: Author.

Vallant, G.E. (1983). *The Natural History of Alcoholism: Causes, Patterns, and Paths to Recovery.* Cambridge, MA: Harvard University Press.

Vermont Psychiatric Survivors, Inc. and the Vermont Department of Developmental and Mental Health Services (1999). "Vermont Recovery Education Project." Retrieved February 2002 from <http://www.MentalHealthRecovery.com/vtrecovery.html>.

Walant, K.B. (1995). *Creating the Capacity for Attachment: Treating Addictions and the Alienated Self.* Northvale, NJ: Jason Aronson Inc.

Walker, D.R. (2000). *Task Force on Dual Diagnosis: Final Report and Recommendations.* Salem, OR: Oregon Department of Human Services.

Wallace, J. (1986). The other problems of alcoholics. *Journal of Substance Abuse Treatment,* 3, 163-171.

Wallen, M.C. (1994). Treating the dually diagnosed in addiction settings. In N.S. Miller (Ed.), *Treating Coexisting Psychiatric and Addictive Disorders* (pp. 69-81). Center City, MN: Hazelden.

Walsh, J. (2000). *Clinical Case Management with Persons Having Mental Illness: A Relationship-Based Perspective.* Belmont, CA: Wadsworth/Thomason Learning.

Weiss, K.J. and Rosenburg, D. (1985). Prevalence of anxiety disorder among alcoholics. *Journal of Clinical Psychiatry,* 46, 3-5.

Weiss, R.D., Najavits, L.M., and Greenfield, S.F. (1999). A relapse prevention group for patients with bipolar and substance use disorders. *Journal of Substance Abuse Treatment,* 16 (1), 47-54.

Wenzel, K., Bernstein, D.P., Handelsman, L., Rinaldi, P., Ruggiero, J., and Higgins, B. (1996). Levels of dissociation in detoxified substance abusers and their relationship to chronicity of alcohol and drug use. *The Journal of Nervous and Mental Disease,* 184 (4), 220-227.

Westerman, M.M., Myers, J.K., and Harding, P.S. (1980). Prevalence and psychiatric heterogeneity of alcoholism in a United States urban community. *Journal of Alcohol Studies,* 42 (7), 672-681.

Westermeyer, J. (1989). Nontreatment factors affecting treatment outcome in substance abuse. *American Journal of Drug and Alcohol Abuse,* 15 (10) 13-29.

Wilens, T.E., Biederman, J., Spencer, T.J., and Frances, R.J. (1994). Comorbidity of attention-deficit hyperactivity and psychoactive substance use disorders. *Hospital and Community Psychiatry,* 45 (5), 421-424.

Woody, G., McLellan, A.T., Luborsky, L., and O'Brien, C. (1985). Sociopathy and psychotherapy outcome. *Archives of General Psychiatry,* 42, 1081-1086.

World Health Organization. (1994) *Pocket Guide to the ICD-10 Classification of Mental and Behavioral Disorders.* Washington, DC: American Psychiatric Press, Inc.

Worthington, E.L. (1987) Changes in supervision as counselors and supervisors gain experience: A review. *Professional Psychology,* 18, 189-208.

# Index

Page numbers followed by the letter "i" indicate illustrations.